AF600280

GHOSTLY LANDSCAPES

Film, Photography, and the Aesthetics of Haunting in Contemporary Spanish Culture

Ghostly Landscapes

Film, Photography, and the Aesthetics of Haunting in Contemporary Spanish Culture

PATRICIA M. KELLER

UNIVERSITY OF TORONTO PRESS
Toronto Buffalo London

Toronto Buffalo London
www.utppublishing.com

ISBN 978-1-4426-4888-3

Library and Archives Canada Cataloguing in Publication

Keller, Patricia M., 1977–, author
Ghostly landscapes : film, photography, and the aesthetics of haunting in contemporary Spanish culture / Patricia M. Keller.

(Toronto Iberic)
Includes bibliographical references.
ISBN 978-1-4426-4888-3 (bound)

1. Photography – Spain – History – 20th century. 2. Landscape photography – Spain – History – 20th century. 3. Historiography and photography – Spain. 4. Art and history – Spain. 5. Loss (Psychology) in art. 6. Spain – History – Civil War, 1936–1939 – Art and the war. I. Title. II. Series: Toronto Iberic

TR87.K45 2015 770.946 C2015-905934-8

This book has been published with the assistance of the Hull Memorial Publication Fund of Cornell University.

University of Toronto Press acknowledges the financial assistance to its publishing program of the Canada Council for the Arts and the Ontario Arts Council, an agency of the Government of Ontario.

Canada Council for the Arts Conseil des Arts du Canada

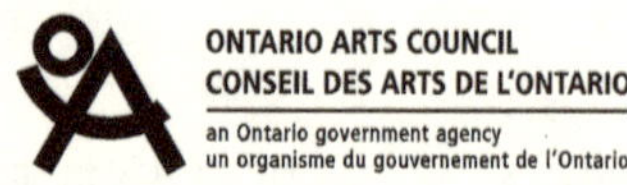

Funded by the Government of Canada | Financé par le gouvernement du Canada | Canada

Dedicated to Cristina Moreiras Menor
with love and gratitude

Contents

Illustrations

Acknowledgments

There are many people I would like to thank for their love, friendship, and unconditional support throughout my time working on this project. My parents, Fred and Judy Keller, and my brother, Paul. My dear friends Rhiannon Welch, Michael Kicey, Jon Snyder, Cristina Moreiras, Juli Highfill, David Caron, Alex Herrero, Gareth Williams, Tracy McNulty, Cary Howie, Ross Chambers, Marcel Muller, Jonathan Culler, Mitchell Greenberg, Marie Claire Vallois, Justin Crumbaugh, Steve Marsh, Tatjana Gajic, Nate Horrell, Becky Givan, Jason Frank, Anna Watkins Fisher, Antoine Traisnel, Brían Hanrahan, Alex Livingston, Merike Andre-Barrett, Vivian Choi, Cristina Dopico Rey, Mariola Dopico Rey, Silvia Bouzas, Miguel Martínez Amoraga, Dani González Diaz, Mercedes Pereiro Numer, Tomás Bevia, Tamar Carroll, Lars Schumann, Colette Walls, Diane Brown, Edward Curran, Julian Daniel Gutierréz Albilla, Luis Martín Cabrera, Susana Draper, Steven Valloney, Robert Wells, Kelly Novitski, Sion Harrington, Victoria Farris, Calvin and Michelle Welch, Mark Tandall, Chantel Paul, Scott Davis, Amanda Jo Goldstein, Tom McEnaney, Ingrid Duran, Andrew Utterson, J.P. Sniadecki, Josh Bonnetta, Michael Ashkin, Leslie Brack, Bernie Yenelouis, Amy Villarejo, Nick Salvato, Sabine Haenni, Mary Fessenden, Renate Ferro, Brad Zukovic, Cecelia Lawless, and Pierre Sassone. To all of my students at Michigan and Cornell. And to my friends and colleagues in the Department of Romance Studies at Cornell. I especially thank Tim Murray and the Society for the Humanities for their amazing support network over the years and, in particular, for providing me an intellectual home during the 2012–13 academic year. I would like to thank the Hull Fund at Cornell University for their generous subvention of this book. Also, I thank *Filmoteca Española* in Madrid for granting permission to reproduce film stills from the newsreels, and especially Trinidad de Rio for her wonderful assistance during my research at the film archive. An extra special thanks to the three photographers I discuss in this book – Manuel Sendón, María Bleda, and José María Rosa – who so generously shared their work with me. Their photography has been an enormous source of fascination and inspiration over the years. Finally, I wish to extend my deepest gratitude to Siobhan McMenemy and Robert Davidson at University of Toronto Press for all of their encouragement, patience, and enthusiasm for this project, and to Frances Mundy and Matthew Kudelka for their tremendous support and keen editorial eye.

This book is written in loving memory of Bob Spires and is dedicated to Cristina Moreiras, two extraordinary mentors and friends.

GHOSTLY LANDSCAPES

Film, Photography, and the Aesthetics of Haunting in Contemporary Spanish Culture

Introduction: Ghostly Landscapes

What is a specter? What is its history and what is its time? The specter, as its name indicates, is the *frequency* of a certain visibility. But the visibility of the invisible. And visibility, by its essence, is not seen, which is why it remains *epekeina tes ousias*, beyond the phenomenon or beyond being.

Specters of Marx (Derrida 1994, 100–1)

Even ghosts require media.

Victorian Hauntings (Wolfreys 2002, 22)

On Ghosts (After Images, Before Time)

To speak of ghosts is to always speak of a loss that returns. This loss – signalled by an untimely departure, an absence, a death, something unfinished or something unclaimed – is often what provokes a ghost's reappearance, its conjured or unconjured coming back to and unsettling of a time other than its own. This book, which is about the losses created by but also returned to us through images, be they moving or still, begins with the notion that loss can tell us something not only about the distant past but also how we live in the present and imagine the future. To that end, this book explores what loss and return – the twin signs of the ghost – reveal about both the *time* and the *image* of history – its loops and cycles, its perforations and folds, its stages and monuments, its theatres of concealment and its spectral apparitions, its uncanny afterlife and its persistent afterimage.

In a powerful passage from his essay in *Compelling Visuality*, Georges Didi-Huberman articulates this intimate link between time and image when he writes:

> Whenever we are before the image, we are before time. Like the poor illiterate in Kafka's story, we are before the image as before the law: as before an open doorway. It hides nothing from us, all we need to do is enter, its light almost blinds us, holds us in submission. Its very opening ... holds us back: to look at it is to desire, to wait, to be before time. But what kind of time? What plasticities and fractures, what rhythms and jolts of time, can be at stake in this opening of the image? (2003, 31)

I too am interested in this question of time – the question of what temporal plasticities, fractures, rhythms and jolts the image makes possible. In what threads or glimpses of time the image screens for us, the ones it paradoxically may illuminate *and* conceal. For Didi-Huberman, the image opens – which is to say, it *wounds* – time.[1] Thus the image turns time not against itself but into a ghostly other. Insofar as this ghostliness – this rupture in time's continuum – is opened by the image, we could say that this also produces a certain anxiety or uncanny affect of time. In generating the alterity of time's passage, the image makes an otherwise straightforward understanding of time appear abstruse, or feel dense and laden. But how do we *see* this time, weighted and burdened as it now is? How might it be visualized for us? This problem of grasping time through sight, indeed through the act of seeing – an act that, according to John Berger and David Levi Strauss, is always both an interrogative practice (the eye is the "organ of asking," they beautifully remind us [Berger, in Strauss 2005, vii]) and a conscious political choice – is in many ways also the central problem of ghostly affect or the spectral – the "frequency of certain visibility," as Jacques Derrida affirms (1994, 101). For ghosts exist as shadows cast upon the known world, as dark empirical forces seen and unseen that create and participate in what is commonly called haunting. In the pages that follow, I will offer a more detailed and nuanced account of this phenomenon in an effort to give full weight to the many meanings the term "haunting" evokes, culturally and politically, and in particular to parse out what import that term bears for the visual and aesthetic realms. For now, I simply note that haunting occurs at a disjuncture in time or, as Derrida drawing on Shakespeare's Hamlet invokes, a "time out of joint."[2]

The "time out of joint" aphorism, in essence, abbreviates the primary thrust of ghostliness, or spectrality, two key terms I rely on throughout my readings. That is, time can be (and can be *made* to be) out of sync with itself. Within a network of time, moreover, multiple temporalities may be mutually constitutive and at the same time mutually contradictory. But temporal disjointedness, as another key sign of the ghost, can indicate other paradoxes as well: time splintered and detached yet proximate and accessible, or even time's complicity and self-alienation, the way it is deeply entangled with – though simultaneously estranged from – itself. These temporal aporias interestingly underscore one of the main points Derrida outlines in his theory of hauntology: that ghosts exemplify not only a non-presence (the presence of an absence) but also the condition of non-contemporaneity, a term he uses to describe the notion that the present is unhinged from itself. Under this rubric, the present is never constituted by being "in" the moment but rather by being *undone* by the moment, being *outside* of itself. The present, as it were, is never "now" but always "now" and "not now," or "now" and "other." Hence, the present becomes the condition of untimeliness, always carrying with it a peculiar double-force: a strange pre-emptive beforeness and a latent afterness. Like the image, then, that injures time, ghosts invoke and perform this non-contemporaneity; they persist as an untimely time that destabilizes the order of things. It is worth nothing here that Derrida's ontological concept of haunting as demonstrated through the figure of the ghost – that which is paradoxically present and absent, already departed and imagined to arrive at some future time, that which has *already been* and is still *yet to come* – importantly parallels his political conception of mourning. For Derrida, politics is only possible through a structural relationship with the "time and space of mourning," a relationship that arises from reflection on the intractable reality of loss as something both profoundly outside us and at the same time profoundly rooted "in us" (1993, 62). For loss, understood as that which is signified by disappearance, is separate from our being. But loss always also is defined by what remains or what reappears. This reappearance in the wake of such departure is the image left to us and "in us," that which, at the limits of the visible, is tethered to and often inseparable from our being-in-the-world (Derrida 2001, 159). Loss is thus never only a static other that we gaze at; it always suggests a sameness, a unity with ourselves, a kind of internal sight. Thus, to recognize loss – to mourn it – means, for Derrida, to visualize it as outside but also constitutive of ourselves. It means to keep our eyes open to loss, to "hold" it in a hospitable gesture, just as its figure, the ghost, "holds us" (2001, 19).[3]

Ghosts mark temporal limits but also temporal exceptions. Indeed, as entities unbound to time – that is, entities that exceed time because they override the linear sequencing of past–present–future – ghosts are truly exceptional in every sense of the word. In their states of exception, they can bring back the past – even if only briefly through appearance or affect rather than with materiality and substance – as much as they can, in Fredric Jameson's words, "make the present waver" (1999, 38). To contemplate the ghost then means to take an active interest in the multiple threads of time – indeed, in time's exceptionality – that we encounter when we look at images and, more importantly, when we *read* images. It means to embrace the kaleidoscopic nature of time, history, and image and to give credit to the temporal ruptures and discontinuities in an otherwise symmetrical, linear, and progressive understanding of the world. But the present study proposes that to contemplate and perhaps more importantly to *engage* with ghosts is also and by equal measure a task of thinking about the intimate, indeed entangled ties between the spectral world and the visual one. This task, moreover, involves thinking through the ways in which ghostly iterations are situated delicately, in the threshold between the visible and the invisible, at the limit between presence and absence, on the edge of illumination and darkness, light and shadow. It is important to remember, though, that as frequencies "beyond being" and therefore beyond seeing and being seen, ghosts not only sit on the cusp of the visible world but also challenge the very visibility of the world from a place of marginality.[4] At the same time and as the term "frequency" suggests, ghostly transmission requires a medium through which it can direct its energy, a space of manoeuvrability through which it can channel and be channelled, through which it can come to light in its passing through. This book, by positioning ghosts as liminal figures at the intersection of temporality and visuality, addresses the time and image of distinct media that channel the non-contemporaneous, the uncanny, and the untimely.

Lastly, while ghosts are often associated with the spirit world, imagined as unnatural, disembodied entities, this book concentrates on other aspects of their composition and approaches them as invisible yet radically affective structures situated between non-presence and presence, between loss and re-emergence. As liminal yet cyclical figures, ghosts complicate and undermine modern narratives of continuous, linear historical progress; they defer presence and they un-ground our sense of time, stripping it of the illusion of stable progression and foreseeable culmination, by signalling not merely the return in the present of something formerly lost but also the pre-emptive consignment of the present itself to the category of loss.[5] By enacting an uncanny restoration of the past coupled with a pre-emptive loss of the present, ghosts indicate at once a deep unity as well as a deep wound within time – an object or feeling pertaining to one time now disturbingly appears in and injures another time, making it non-contemporaneous with itself.

The Aesthetics of Haunting

Ghosts appear and unsettle; they disquiet and disturb. Ghosts haunt. And haunting is both the expression and the measure of spectrality. Haunting, in other words, is the phenomenon by which an unsettled, asymmetrical relation manifests itself and becomes known even if it remains invisible. If, as I stated earlier, ghosts render the otherwise easy distinction between the visible and non-visible or the invisible something of a paradox (in the best scenarios) or something of an impossibility (in the worst scenarios), then haunting in many ways *uncomplicates* this rendering. Haunting testifies to the fact that ghosts – elusive and abstract but affective structures – return to the world, that they exert a force on us, and that they too are, drawing on Avery Gordon's elegant description, "the shape of force and lost hands" (1997, 6). This book too is an inquiry into that shape, and specifically into the visual forms and aesthetic dimensions of such shaping.

In her poetic and provocative account of the sociological implications of ghostliness, or what she refers to as "ghostly matters," Gordon describes haunting as the actuality of "seething absences and muted presences" (1997, 21). According to her account, what ghosts do is furnish evidence, even if immaterial and fleeting, of the dynamic charge of the place of the present as framed by the past but looking towards the future. Another way of articulating this would be to say that the ghostly lays bare the fact that the present is always indebted to other temporalities – ones that both anticipate and survive it. But these shifting temporalities are, for Gordon, always concerned with the social. Indeed, haunting, in her estimation, is always a form of social mediation, a way of exhibiting the "inarticulate experiences, symptoms and screen memories, spiraling affects … and the traffic in domains of experience that are anything but transparent and referential" (1997, 25). Similarly, for political theorist Wendy Brown, haunting denotes the past "hovering" over the present but importantly also indicates the desire to "stake a claim" on the present (2001, 153). Spectral return, for Brown, obliges us to make the past an outrage to the present, to bring a former injustice into a potential space of continued suffering and, it follows, a potential space of redemption and justice. In short, if something continues to exhibit wounds, then it maintains the potential for being seen as wounded. For Brown, like Gordon, this lingering quality – the fact that ghosts return, that they hover and haunt – suggests the need or the desire to communicate work that is yet to be done. Significantly, for these theorists, this need or desire for articulation has a strong social component that ideally can shift from individual to broader institutional forms of responsibility.

Haunting, then, is not only about feeling the past in the present, or about the ways in which the present is indebted to the past (the way the contemporary is structured in relation to its debt to history and historical narrative); it also becomes a question of futurity – a question of how to act in the present in a way that regards history not as something lodged in the past but as something that lives, infiltrates, and sustains present and future time. Similarly, in thinking about futurity, critic Gerhard Richter analyses hauntedness as something that relates to the "experience and thinking of afterness," which for him is linked explicitly to notions of legacy and inheritance (2011, 15). In this logic of afterness, according to Richter, to be haunted is a concern not only of how we come into contact with something formerly lost that returns to us, but also of how we *choose* to carry it and perhaps even how we choose to embrace it (or not). This choice to affirm that the ghost matters and to live consciously and respectfully with those ghostly matters is, for many critics and theorists, a form of politics – a politics of living with spectres. This politics – which is a way of correcting our loss of historical perspective and consequently our static and deadened relationship with the past – is fundamental to mourning the wounds of modernity and creating a better, more hopeful future, as Gordon, drawing on Adorno and Horkheimer's "Theory of Ghosts," explains (2002, 19–20). Undoing our "disturbed relationship to the dead – forgotten and embalmed," as we in the modern world have made them, means to a certain degree *investing* in spectrality – not only witnessing ghosts as they return but also capitalizing on that return as a critical decisive moment that can change the stakes of our being in the modern world (Adorno and Horkheimer 2002, 216). This, incidentally, is not so much about eliminating the destructive forces of modernity that create the conditions for ghostliness to arise; rather, it is redirected at a deep awareness, a mindfulness, of such destruction and violence – at a willingness to *see* it. This line of argumentation is fundamental to the present study because it suggests that seeing and looking at the origins of spectres – at the violence and loss that usher them, almost always urgently, into the world of the living – is the locus for politics. Put differently, a principal claim of this book is that there can be no value in memory, no charge of forgetting, no proper way to mourn the past or to understand history and time, without a radical notion (and, as I argue throughout, a radical embrace) of loss. Such a claim participates in a broader discussion about the "counterintuitive understanding of loss" as a condition of being, whether "general, abstract, and even metaphysical," as David Eng and David Kazanjian articulate in their introduction to *Loss: The Politics of Mourning* (2003, ix–x, 1-5).[6] In advocating for both a theorization and an embrace of loss, the present study insists that a reconceptualization of loss through a deeper inquiry into its aesthetic dimensions, its image and time, can bring absence, shadows, ghostly affect, invisibility, and haunting into a space of productivity. Rather than placing loss on the terrain of the negative or the pathological, and rather than consigning it to the realm of psychology or the psychoanalytical, the readings offered in *Ghostly Landscapes* aim to examine the cultural and political ways in which loss affectively disrupts and conditions being. That is to say, this book, in taking a cue from other meditations on the importance of loss and the process of mourning, seeks not to identify specific objects of loss but rather to bring the concept of loss into a space of interpretation, one of creative and political potentiality. Thus, I turn to images whose aesthetic qualities not only encompass loss, deliberately integrating it poetically and politically into their frames, but also invite and challenge our seeing of this integration. That the aesthetics of haunting in these works should both call us to see and obscure our sight is precisely a common point that binds together the disparate texts studied throughout this book. These are works – images – that pay attention to traces, whether through a formal practice of erasure or through a creative style of framing and a grammar of illuminating the barely visible. These are images that look after seeing.

The trace is in fact a – perhaps *the* – key element of any aesthetics of haunting and is especially important for this study, which follows closely the traces created and made visible through the media of film and photography as well as the traces that emerge from archival and representational practices. In a very short but extraordinary essay titled "On Visibility," John Berger likens traces to ghosts when he situates them both outside visibility and between temporalities, between the "has been" of the past and the "will become" of the future: "it is very possible that visibility *is* truth and that what lies outside visibility are only the 'traces' of what has been seen or will become visible (1993, 219). For Derrida, traces are fundamental to the ghostly ontology underlying haunting and its effect – we might say the aftershock (though not his word) – of the spectral or "becoming body," an effect that he likens to the "phenomenal flickering of the trace of the other" (1994, 64). There is always a question not only of communication, mediation, and articulation but also of legibility in that ghosts not only leave traces but also are themselves traces – things that live on in their passing, things that take on a kind of afterlife in their deaths.[7]

When we set out to interpret this trace, we embark on what David Punter aptly calls "spectral criticism" – a form of interpretation that "thrives inevitably not on the originary voice but on the *echo*" (2002, 273). In contrast to critical modes of reading rooted in a "materialistic" approach to textuality, spectral criticism, according to Punter, emanates from emptied substances, erasures, vacancies, and absences. In focusing on the very immateriality of the text as well as its temporal fluctuations, this form of reading "sees texts as paradoxical in their relation to the past, fundamentally unparented and 'unhouseled, disappointed, unaneled,' to quote from *Hamlet*; they speak to us indeed all the time of the past, but the voice they use is not authoritative, it is instead monitory, omenistic, it warns of dooms past and to come and above all it reiterates our own complaint of *being not at home in the world*, of being adrift" (261; my emphasis). I place *Ghostly Landscapes* square in the centre of this kind of criticism, not only for its acute attention to the spectral as it emerges in and through the image, but also for its particular mode of interpretation, which engages in an awareness of what we do not see, of what is not shown, of what is lost or missing. In Punter's words, this exemplifies nothing but a "deeply uncertain humility in the face of the text, a necessary opposition to the vaunted possibilities of accurate historical exhumation, a realization of the partiality of all our efforts" (271). But it is important to remember as well that this kind of reading carries with it a deep desire to theorize the invisible, not because it is entirely unknown, but on the contrary and in a fundamentally paradoxical way because it has made itself all too known, all too present. In privileging loss as a principal object of inquiry, this book participates to a certain degree in a "reinvocation of a terrorizing but desired communion with the dead" (260). To the extent that, as Punter following Derrida notes, "history is a series of accounts of the dead, but also a series of accounts *by* the dead," then to engage with spectres and to engage critically through a spectral lens means to grapple with the uneven weight of history; it means to encounter history as an accumulation of losses, and it means to listen to "the voices [that] spectralize the possibility of knowledge" (262).

Thus, haunting relates inextricably to a set of problematics: the visible/invisible divide, the fine line between presence and absence, testimony, affect, the trace, justice, debt, desire, inheritance, "afterness." To combine these understandings of haunting with questions of aesthetics shifts us onto slightly different, though related, territory. Aesthetics, a realm that is invested principally in questions of perception, highlights a crucial aspect of haunting. For haunting is the affective component of spectrality that allows its otherwise imperceptible qualities to become felt and known – that is, to be perceived. Haunting, in this regard, could be thought of as the moment when actual blind spots can be transformed into potential sources of illumination, frames of affect and referentiality. In line with the previous discussion of ghosts, images, and time, I employ the term "aesthetics of haunting" to refer to an index of visibility, or a perceptible indexing of the trace. Such an aesthetics offers a visual indexicality that seeks to gauge both the invisible (the vanishing point or point of disappearance) and the trace (the point, even if only faint, of reappearance and potential legibility).

So far, I have discussed some of the ways in which ghosts are tethered to a network of entangled temporalities and a certain logic of the image, arguing that ghostly affect has to do with asynchronicities but also with traces and latencies or afterimages in the visual sphere. But it is often said that ghosts haunt particular *places* by frequenting them. In their haunting – that is, in their persistent affective return to certain places (in literature, this is quite often though not exclusively a return to a house), ghosts render those places eerie, uncanny, and at times even uninhabitable. This haunting is thus not merely the consequence of a temporal rupture; it also has to do with *location*, both in the sense of geographical place and in the sense of social, cultural, and visual space. Haunting, in other words, has to do with landscape.

Landscape, a Way of Seeing

If ghosts *unsettle* time, then landscape *measures* time. Landscape is a record of time – it holds history and "remembers" it materially. But landscape can also be understood, much like the ghost, as an image – as something that screens and projects, something that evinces visibility and precludes sight.

In his beautiful and exquisitely dense essay "Uncanny Landscape," Jean-Luc Nancy contends that "the landscape begins with a notion, however vague and confused, of distancing and of a loss of sight" (2005, 53). This is a remarkable statement, if at first glance a strange one. What Nancy means is not that the landscape inaugurates a failure of sight but rather that there is a kind of losing of oneself – a kind of merging that occurs – when we fully experience the landscape through observation. Landscape, as a concept, becomes possible when we understand it as an opening and as an occasion or "presentation" of sense rather than simply as a view of the land. In other words, landscape for Nancy is never (or at least never *only*) a window onto a place; it is never only a frame through which we look at a place. Likewise, landscape is never only the place itself but rather always suggests that something *is taking place*. It is an event and thus an experience of seeing and feeling. In this reconceptualization, landscape is situated between a place of representation and a space – or "spacing," as Nancy says, or a "staging," as I will argue – of presentation and hence of presence. Nancy writes:

> A landscape contains no presence: it is itself the entire presence. But that is also why it is not a view of nature distinguished from culture but is presented together with culture in a given relationship (of work or rest, of opposition or transformation, etc). It is a representation of the land *as the possibility of a taking place of sense*, a localization or *a locality of sense*, which makes sense only by being occupied with itself, making itself "itself" as this corner, this angle opened onto an area opposite or onto a spectacle already laid out; but it is an angle opened onto itself, creating an opening and thus a view, not as the perspective of a gaze upon an object (or as vision) but as a springing up or a surging forth, *the opening and presentation of a sense that refers to nothing but this presentation*. (58 my emphasis)

The "locality" and "opening and presentation of a sense" to which Nancy alludes is precisely what "springs up" or "surges forth" from the landscape – it is not merely a viewing, but a total experience of a self-contained, self-seeing practice, and it makes sense "only by being occupied with itself." The view, often thought to be the defining characteristic of landscape, is in Nancy's calculation not about perspective or gaze but interestingly – and here, recalling Didi-Huberman's account of the image, it is about an *opening* – about a wound. This opening is an invitation not so much to look at a particular place as to see the particularities of the view as such – not to *view* or "survey" the land but to begin to see the land itself *as a view*, as something that denotes a way of seeing, "a visual contemplation of an externalized scene" rather than a mere depiction of the visible world (Wylie 2009, 277). Echoing this idea, cultural geographer John Wylie tells us that "landscape is both the phenomenon itself *and* our perception of it" (2007, 7).[8] As something that "takes shape within the realms of human perception and imagination … landscapes are not just about *what* we see but about *how we look*" (7).

For Nancy and Wylie, landscape has a particular ontological dimension. It is not something that shows presence; it is *itself* presence. This relationship between landscape and presence is intriguing. For unlike ghosts, which always denote a *non*-presence or the presence of an absence, landscape, on the contrary, brings into balance an affirmation of being, a movement towards or gesture of presence. In the fullest phenomenological sense, landscape is concerned with a certain "bringing-to-presence," aptly described by Wylie as "bringing to light things previously hidden or lost, unearthing memory, making invisible visible" (2009, 279). The idea that landscape as a mirror or screen reveals otherwise unknown because invisible truths likewise is foregrounded in Denis Cosgrove's seminal study *Social Formation and Symbolic Landscape*, in which he argues that landscape is not only a container that stores information outside the field of vision but also a canvas on which the otherwise hidden truths of the world unfold. This canvas/curtain dialectic suggests that landscape has the potential to illuminate *and* darken, that it gestures towards veiling the world from us *and* unconcealing it before our eyes – a dialectic that gets played out in what, for Cosgrove, is one of the principle tensions in landscape: its pull towards an always imagined space and its groundedness in the real, that is, in the materiality of place. In sum, insofar as landscape is tied to a way of seeing, it can also be aligned with un-seeing, with obscurities, lack of vision, and even blind spots.

That landscape should suggest something beyond place, scenery, and viewing – in other words, that it should suggest a way of seeing, experiencing, and relating to place (and for Nancy and Wylie, a "presencing," a way of being-in-the-world and relating to one's self in the world) – is crucial for understanding how it connects to distance, loss, and spectrality. In a stunning essay titled "Landscape, Absence, and the Geographies of Love," Wylie calls into question the co-presence of self and world traditionally aligned with landscape representation and, more broadly, with vision. While Wylie understands landscape as a complex matrix of temporalities, images, and encounters, as "a milieu of engagement, involvement, immersion, connection – a living tapestry of practices, imaginations, emergences, and erasures," he also sees it as a potential source of separation and loss (2009, 282). This loss has to do with the act of looking itself. Wylie writes that "looking at landscape is always looking-with-landscape. But looking-with landscape will always also, or so it seems, convoke a certain distancing in which a 'subject' and a 'world' are separately articulated" (282). Every landscape presents this paradox: looking *at* versus looking *with*. Landscape always and necessarily assumes being *within* a particular place at a particular time but also an inevitable departure from place enacted through a looking out with one's own eyes onto a place. It is both an image and a way of seeing that image, and as such, it assumes both a "presencing with" and a "distancing from."

Throughout my analysis I turn continually to visual materials across different media that specifically engage with this tension between ways of seeing and ways of un-seeing, between ways of bringing into sight and ways of undoing our vision or disrupting our sight. While I am concerned with the temporality and constructedness of actual, physical landscapes in some cases (as will become obvious), in a more general sense I employ landscape for its conceptual and theoretical underpinnings, which refer explicitly to regimes of visibility and systems of sight rather than exclusively to depictions of imaginary scenes or real places in the world. That said, not all of the texts analysed in this study explicitly depict landscapes, when understood as artistic or documentary representations of place. However, when we extend the notion of landscape to encompass the creation and/or revelation of specific viewing practices and tendencies, then it is correct to say that all of the texts examined in these pages intersect with this problematic. I consider landscape less as a territory to visit or traverse than as a *field of possibility*, as a conceptual plane wherein thought arises. In a concrete sense, this study links landscape, understood as a complex set of relations between the visible and the invisible world, between being and seeing, to the image and to the ghostly. As a potential space of affect and perception, as well as a potential reconfiguration of seeing and knowing, the triangulation landscape–image–spectrality guides these readings, though not without certain challenges.

Ghostly Landscapes: The Paradox

If landscapes denote a visible place, a way of seeing and a way of being in the world, and if ghosts, on the contrary, demarcate an invisible presence, an unseen but nonetheless affective trace, a way of *non*-being in the world, then "ghostly landscapes," the main title of this study, rests on a fundamental paradox. Indeed, whereas landscapes in their immediacy, presence, and materiality impart a stable set of images that allow us to see actualities ordered through an aesthetic of permanence, ghosts, with their evasiveness, non-presence, and immateriality, bear a distinct ephemerality that signals just the opposite – an unstable fluctuation of temporalities. My aim in joining these two seemingly oppositional concepts together in one framework is to capture the broader objectives of the project: to consider how, from within a series of actualities, possibilities arise; to contemplate how, from within a network of seeing, we gain insight into indeterminacies, impossibilities, and affective though invisible worlds.

That the project should hinge on a paradox is perhaps its best if not its most logical (or inevitable) aspect, since conceptually each term – "ghostly" and "landscape" – on its own harbours the paradoxical within it: the commingling of visible invisibilities, or emergent materializations of the immaterial. These definitions, by definition, defy logic. Weaving these concepts together is thus a way of thinking not only about their inherent relationship to each other (how the invisible inevitability leads to the visible, or how the material world can obscure and to some extent create the immaterial one) but also about how, in their combined meaning, as mutually reciprocal terms, they reproduce and reinforce the logic of the image. Through the wound, fracture, divide, or in this case paradox, an opening is created, a productive space of contemplation and critical engagement.

Landscapes that are ghostly, that are infused with a spectral quality, are also places *and*, we should remember, *ways of seeing* that bring something to presence *through* an absence. Accordingly, it is not this presence (the land or the act of seeing) that makes loss (the ghost) visible or available to us so much as the other way around. This book makes the claim that ghostliness both affects the visible world and constitutes a way of seeing. The ghostly, the absence or sign of loss itself, the non-seeing, returns to provoke a certain coming into being and therefore a coming into sight. By instigating a "certain frequency of visibility," the ghostly paradoxically illuminates a "presencing" in and of the world.

Contemporary Spain

Ghosts are everywhere in contemporary Spain and hold a pervasive and profoundly palpable place in the country's cultural landscape. Even a cursory review of modern Spanish history shows that their principle qualities – haunting, loss, uncanny return, disappearance, re-emergence, latency, anachrony, untimeliness – manifest themselves as a dominant force in Spanish culture, politics, and media. One can trace this force from remnants of colonialism that linger decades after the erosion of Spain's imperial power that inaugurated the turn of the twentieth century through to today's economic climate of unprecedented austerity and debt.

While ghosts are not unique to any one culture, this book departs from the idea that twentieth-century Spain offers fertile ground for theorizing their materialization.[9] Indeed, the violence, terror, and profound loss experienced during the Spanish Civil War (1936–39), coupled with the injustices that plunged the country into a systematic pattern of denial and burial during one of the most repressive dictatorships in modern history (1939–75), are what have given rise to the calls for justice and memory that ghosts have come to signify. It is thus a principal contention of this book that ghostly return in Spain reveals a powerful form of untimeliness and promise that manifests itself in order to make a traumatic past relevant to the present. Jo Labanyi, capitalizing on the Derridean notion of spectres in her introduction to *Constructing Identity in Contemporary Spain,* affirms that ghosts "are not psychological projections" but constitute a *real* presence – the "return of the repressed of history," which manifests itself as "the mark of an all-too-real historical trauma which has been erased from conscious memory but which makes its presence felt through its ghostly traces" (2002, 6). Because ghosts are not conjectures but rather are grounded in reality, they act as a counterbalance to forms of denial that were deeply embedded in Spain's cultural and political fabric under the dictatorship's "time of silence" and for many years afterwards during the post-dictatorship "transition."

Perhaps the most emotional and politically controversial example of confronting ghosts in recent history has been the surge in exhumations of Civil War mass graves. By unearthing the bodily remains of victims of the war and thus the material evidence of the violence, horror, and suffering that had been buried but not forgotten, exhumations stage, in a sense, the problem of loss intrinsic to spectrality. The problem of afterness and inheritance undoubtedly arises with the exhuming of the dead, not only because of the memories that the survivors of the war and its aftermath carry with them, but also, in a much more material sense, because the remnants recovered from the graves are then given back to the living. The victims of the war had been only shadows, disappeared bodies, or pale memories; the process of exhuming them has effectively turned their ghostly status into a material reality – one that no longer hinges on the trace but now on the disquieting force of death's facticity and actuality. The excavations themselves, which bring together disparate groups spanning the fields of anthropology, history, government, activism, forensics, law, human rights, media and communications, journalism, ethnography, literature, documentary film, and photography, are arguably the most potent examples of the literalized intersection between the landscape and the spectres that haunt that landscape.

One could argue, as several scholars have, that the ghost of Franco and the legacy of Francoism are two sides of the same coin, one that looms large in Spanish politics and culture today.[10] The unresolved and still notably (if not overwhelmingly) contentious debates over how to address collectively Francoism's phenomenally undying legacy are proof that the dictatorship haunts Spanish culture in ways that are *still* as undetermined as they are unfathomable, even now, nearly forty years after the dictator's death. In fact, there is little disagreement that this legacy – nominally, but also materially, spatially, and architecturally – remains visibly secure within the larger social order. The only disagreement – and it is a monstrous one – is over what should be done with this visible presence, and how and when.[11] If I have only alluded to the ongoing discussion of Francoism's legacy, it is simply because that legacy – itself a monstrosity – is vast, disparate, and at times quite difficult to track in its increasing proliferation and polyvalent forms, which stretch across various disciplines and fields. *Ghostly Landscapes* seeks to add to this discussion, not by exploring the materiality of this legacy – or what could be called somewhat paradoxically the materiality of Spain's "wound culture," as Cristina Moreiras Menor (2002) evocatively calls it – but rather through an exploration of the visual forms that tend to mediate and substantiate that materiality.

The rise in disparate political forms of memory mobilized around the core – and increasingly divisive – issue of "historical memory" in Spain is perhaps where a study of spectrality, situated at the coordinates of culture and aesthetics, visuality, temporality, and history, can make the greatest impact. At the heart of *Ghostly Landscapes*, then, is an intervention into the larger framework of memory studies and into what have now become extremely polarized perspectives within what Jo Labanyi has termed the "memory debates," which all too often consign "memory" and "forgetting" to oppositional sides of the same playing field, or all too quickly condense the work of memory into broader, ill-defined notions of history and "the historical" (2008, 119). Without wishing to dismiss the very important work being done right now around this issue of historical memory, I turn my focus towards a theoretical understanding of the ghost as a problematic or set of relations and inquiries not about the past per se, as something distant and removed from the present, but about the present and the experience of the contemporary as inextricably tethered to and unsettled by other times – past and future. Ghostliness poses questions not only about a past occurrence that re-emerges in the present, but also about a time yet to come and about how to act on that reoccurrence in the future.

By decidedly *not* giving attention to what ghosts specifically claim or reclaim, I do not mean to deny their potential to call up justice. My starting point is the problem of the ghost rather than the solution to spectrality. Put somewhat differently, I am less interested in (and in fact, the readings here are deliberately cautious about) attaching or ascribing a "positive gain" to ghosts that would merely reproduce in some form or another the very discursive problem of the polarized memory debates – aligning remembrance with a good positivistic achievement, and forgetting the bad, immoral, and corrupt. Instead, I focus on the necessarily complicated grey zones that ghosts evoke precisely because of their liminal status – that is, as a result of their being situated in between.

Hence, one of the main aims of this book is to draw on the liminality of the ghost as well as the conceptual language of ghostly landscapes as a way to intervene in such oppositional thinking. I situate my readings of visual culture – not limited to the study of images but, drawing on Nicholas Mirzoeff's work, encompassing the event of visuality – in this threshold in order to think dialectically with and through the image as opposed to against or around it.[12] This is precisely why the main focus and inspiration for *Ghostly Landscapes* is itself a paradox that threads together the ostensibly contrary structures of visibility and invisibility, presence and absence, permanence and ephemerality. Ultimately, my study considers the place of ghosts a fundamentally crucial one not so much for resolving cultural debates about the work of memory or the nature of history, as for presenting an *image* from which to think about the inevitably tangled relationship between the ghost and the landscape it haunts.

The Anatomy of Ghostly Landscapes

Ghostly Landscapes charts the cultural production of ghostliness at the intersection of contemporary visual culture and an aesthetics of haunting that arises in and through the image. Rather than offer a linear or historically chronological trajectory of that production, this book examines it through a constellation of visual media. Specifically, I look at three distinct yet interrelated media stretched across three pivotal moments in recent Spanish history: documentary newsreels from the immediate postwar period and the first phase of the Franco dictatorship; art films from the age of New Spanish Cinema during the *apertura;* and photographs from the post-transition period at the end of the century and beginning of the new millennium.

Because of the book's theoretical emphasis on ways of seeing, its analysis of these diverse texts and time frames is organized into the following visual paradigm: Optics, Apertures, and Interventions. Reflecting three functions of sight, the optics–apertures–interventions structure strategically positions these readings in relation to emergent questions unique to each medium. I offer a brief overview here, and in the paragraphs that follow a more detailed synopsis of each section. In the "optics" section of the book, this entails linking (and unlinking) documentary newsreels to notions of truth and objectivity that result from a totalitarian and archival science of seeing. The readings in this first chapter unpack how, under the impossible totalitarian project of capturing and archiving the entire world, the regime's film industry unwittingly constructed a self-reflexive portrait of its own politics of censorship and erasure. Still working within the medium of film but transitioning from the document to art, and from the archival to the experimental, the second chapter on "apertures" undertakes the mechanics of seeing to rethink not the blind association but rather the explicit tension between the camera and truth, revealed through the subjective and temporally imbricated underpinnings of cinematic images of landscape. In this chapter, the book shifts into the territory of New Spanish Cinema developed during a time of intense economic and cultural aperture and examines films produced in the 1950s and 1960s as an artistic response to political and ideological forms of erasure. The films analysed here creatively contest the totalizing, spectral gaze of Francoist cinema in favour of a more aesthetically experimental and overtly fragmentary approach. Through fragmentation these works visualize collective loss, ghostly return, and the place and time of cultural memory. In the third chapter on "interventions," these readings unfold through a meditation on seeing and reading the static image as a "process" and as "action." In this third and final chapter, the book's attention turns specifically to the notion of intervention in relation to the medium of photography. My readings examine how the photographs of three artists working in Spain today, Manuel Sendón and Bleda y Rosa, mediate vision by reconfiguring the image as a kind of spectral evidence – a material place where the immateriality of time surfaces and complicates rigidly dialectical notions of past and present, history and event, knowledge and perception. Here the book concludes that photography offers not the capture and arrest of time but rather a space of plurality and temporal suspension that allows time's ghostly exposure to intervene in our sight.

"Documentary Optics: NO-DOs' Archival Gaze and the Totalized Landscape" – the title of chapter 1 – examines state-sponsored newsreels and documentaries (NO-DO: *Noticiarios y documentales*) in relation to the logic of a totalitarian optics predicated on a system of accumulation and suture. Looking at early newsreels from the 1940s and 1950s, the readings here theorize the historical, political, and cultural effects of such optics and the disciplinary gaze that arises in fascist propaganda through the medium of documentary film. Analysing "meta-newsreels," or newsreels that carefully depict the making of the newsreels, this chapter claims that the visual rhetoric of these documents suggests an uncanny inversion of propagandistic logic that simultaneously exposes and obscures the mechanics of their own production, pairing self-reflexivity with the purported "objective writing" of history. Linking the meta-newsreels to commemorative newsreels from the 1960s, which recorded mass-scale performances commissioned by the Franco regime to underscore its own authority, the analysis then shifts to consider how the NO-DOs elicit broader questions concerning the links between spectacle, spectatorship, and spectral vision. These readings conclude by considering how fascist spectacles under Francoism – whether public events or optical illusions created by the camera – converted real, traumatized landscapes into illusory mass ornaments, thus enabling the past not to recede into the present but rather disappear from it altogether. The main inquiry of this chapter is twofold: to explore the role (and limits) of the archive in the construction of social memory, and to understand, through the newsreels, how visual propaganda created a particular kind of spectator. My readings shift from the imaginary landscapes fabricated in the editing room to real historical and national landscapes captured on film as they were being constructed and performed through spectacles to explore questions about the kind of knowledge produced through a totalitarian optical structure of seeing.

Adding to the analysis of newsreels, chapter 2 – "Cinematic Apertures: Carlos Saura's Untimely Landscapes" – discusses the politics of aperture in the context of New Spanish Cinema, focusing in particular on the visual poetics of two key art films produced in the 1950s and 1960s by the renowned auteurs Juan Antonio Bardem and Carlos Saura: *Death of a Cyclist* (*Muerte de un ciclista,* 1955) and *The Hunt* (*La caza,* 1965). If new wave cinema in Spain constituted a widening of the film industry's artistic lens, as I claim it does, then Saura, drawing on Bardem, embraced the new age of cinematic possibilities to depict Spanish landscapes not as illusory spectacles but as sites evincing real symptoms – ones formerly masked by the spectacles of the NO-DOs. By combining experimentation with neo-realism, these films revisualize the social reality of life under dictatorship by reinserting formerly omitted narratives of trauma and loss back into cinematic representations of Spain. Moreover, illustrative of an overt staging of history, Saura's film counters the newsreels' ostensibly "objective" documentary approach by portraying history as a subjective and incomplete narrative. Ultimately, *Ghostly Landscapes* locates Saura's productions at the centre of a cinematic critique against not only Francoist ideology but also Francoist optics, which, as highlighted in the first chapter, favoured totalizing, unified structures. In aesthetic terms, Saura's contributions to the new wave thus underscored another striking shift in Spanish cinema – as it moved away from objectivizing structures of totality and history, it turned towards a subjective aesthetics of fragmentation, emptiness, and loss. Whereas the first chapter delved into questions of knowledge and sight, production and mechanics, this second chapter turns to questions of temporality, of cinematic time and untimely landscapes. Through a reading of spectral cycles of time, I attempt to think about the ways in which Saura's work, with its play between stillness and movement, duration and death, the photographic and the cinematic, both contemplates and transforms time. I conclude by suggesting that Saura's cinema visually contests the logic of totalitarian optics by offering a space of possibility for witnessing the symptomatic expression of spectrality.

The third and final chapter of *Ghostly Landscapes* – "Photographic Interventions: Two Meditations on Landscape and Loss" – is devoted entirely to Spanish photography from the 1990s to the present. In linking photography back to cinema and documentary newsreels, this chapter examines recent tendencies in the medium that champion not the camera's ability to capture and document a static image of time or historical event, but rather its capacity to interrupt and transform conventional conceptions of history, image, and event. Drawing on photography as a form of intervention, the readings here focus on select works of two contemporary Spanish artists: the Galician-based Manuel Sendón and his project *Ailing Houses* (*Casas doentes*, 2007), and the Valencian photographic team Bleda y Rosa and their series *Memorials* and *Battlefields* (*Memoriales*, 2005–2010, and *Campos de batalla*, 1999). If fascist optics implemented an aesthetics of totality that resulted in spectacular erasure, and if Spanish art cinema's apertures exhibited symptoms of that erasure through an aesthetics of fragmentation and loss, then contemporary Spanish photography bridges the divide between erasure and re-emergence, and between absence and presence, through a kind of spectral aesthetic. Various photographs by these artists capture landscape in order to doubly reconfigure it as both a place of inscription and a site of loss; a place of writing and one of erasure. Overtly exposing the photographic image's capacity to quote from and transform reality, the works of Sendón and Bleda y Rosa ultimately problematize larger concerns outside the frame regarding mediation and the medium's claim to veracity, transparency, and technological objectivity. By reinforcing the camera's ability to subtly intervene in the reality it represents, these artists also invite viewers to contemplate how photographs intercept and ultimately reshape the way we see and read images and thus how they alter our perception of time and relation to history.

Throughout *Ghostly Landscapes*, I argue that the aesthetic nature and media specificity of film and photography give way to spectrality – fleeting images that materialize, crystallize, and then vanish before our eyes. But it is with photography, perhaps, that one can identify and measure best the force of this ghostly affect, which is precisely why I end my study there. By definition, photographs are nothing if not ghosts – the texture of time and light transformed into meaning, the invisible visualized. Walter Benjamin, who perceived photography's radical and indeed revolutionary potential, understood well its underlying spectral quality. For him, photography offered a dialectics at a standstill that could interrupt historical time by creating what Eduardo Cadava has poignantly described as the "spacing of time and the temporalizing of space" (1997, 61). With photography, time is translated not as arrest, not as death, but as the possibility of this spacing, of movement, action, presence, of a life after death. As such, what the photograph makes possible, which is to say what it visualizes, is the logic of spectrality: time's becoming and disappearing, time's materiality and impalpability.

Visualizing Loss

At the intersection of temporality and visuality, *Ghostly Landscapes* traces the historical and cultural as well as the aesthetic and affective weight of ghostliness, entering into different spaces to do so: the archive and the editing room, the battlefield and the garden, the stadium and the open road, the house and the gravesite. While this study is intended neither as a prescriptive investigation nor as an exhaustive genealogy of ghostliness in contemporary Spain, it does work to develop a new critical language for the problematic of visualizing loss that has transpired in this cultural context from the postwar period to the present. As such, the readings are meant to offer a selective but detailed analysis of the relationship between ghosts and landscapes in visual media and aims to reconsider both as key concepts that structure our engagement with the temporality *and* image of history. Instead of focusing solely on the social construction of vision, *Ghostly Landscapes* embraces the figure of the ghost and its entanglements with the concepts of landscape and image, with the textual and the visual, in a strategic effort to contemplate the visual construction of the social, cultural, and historical.[13] At the heart of this study is an attempt to articulate how the visualization of loss originates *in between* poetics and politics, in the synthesis – not the opposition – of place and seeing, of haunting and aesthetics.

The driving question in this study – How do we see what is lost? – might be complemented (and complicated) by another set of questions: Why is it important to visualize loss? Why is it crucial to *see* loss in the first place? And what do we gain from doing so? In the age of the world picture, the age of overexposure, instantaneity, and immediacy, of presence, hyperpresence, and the extenuation of reality, or reality's thinness in the ever-increasing and chaotic thickness of the global age, these questions, if nothing else, serve as reminders that seeing is always an inquiry into the world but never limited to the visible world. To limit the world to what the eye sees and thinks it knows only gives us half the picture. The task – and it is not necessarily an easy one – is to redirect our sight, to open it to the experience and possibility of spectral light and ghostly encounters, to allow it to wander through new landscapes.

Chapter One

Documentary Optics: NO-DOs' Archival Gaze and the Totalized Landscape

There is no archive without a place of consignation, without a technique of repetition, and without a certain exteriority. No archive without outside.

Archive Fever (Derrida 1996, 11)

The question of the archive is not, we repeat, a question of the past. It is not a question of a concept of dealing with the past that might *already* be at our disposal or not at our disposal, *an archivable concept of the archive*. It is a question of the future, the question of the future itself, the question of a response, of a promise and of a responsibility for tomorrow ... A spectral messianicity is at work in the concept of the archive and ties it, like religion, like history, like science itself, to a very singular experience of the promise.

Archive Fever (Derrida 1996, 36)

Fascism is a *technologically equipped primitivism*. Its factitious mythological rehashes are presented in spectacular context of the most modern means of conditioning and illusion.

Society of the Spectacle (Debord 2005, 61)

Documenting Spain (Looking Out, Looking In)

On 4 January 1943, the very first edition of Spain's national newsreels, properly known as the *Noticiario Cinematográfico Español*, made its official premiere in theatres. Among other things, audiences were shown highlights from the recent Christmas festivities in Spain, international sporting events such as a mass-scale athletic demonstration in Berlin, the latest women's hairstyles from Paris, and other news from around the world, including war news (advances by German forces, and the latest report from the Eastern Front) and an account of Ukraine's cotton industry. With its bizarre but impressively wide-ranging collage of news fragments, this first newsreel established the approach that would be taken by all newsreels to come. These newsreels set out to balance international and national news, the worldly and the local – a balance that would be maintained for the entire lifespan of the *Noticiario Español,* from its launching in 1943 to its "death" in 1981, the newsreel industry's final year of filming and production, nearly six years after Franco's death and the official end of the dictatorship.

As the primary instrument of the regime's propaganda machine, the *Noticiarios y Documentales Cinematográficos* (hereafter *noticiarios* or NO-DOs) were created not only to contribute to the popular education of Spaniards but also to reflect everyday life in Franco's Spain by arriving "al último rincón de nuestra Patria en el plazo de tiempo más breve" (at the farthest corner of our Nation in the shortest amount of time) (Tranche and Sánchez-Biosca 2005, 52).[1] Each *noticiario* was to showcase in the shortest time possible the noblest aspects of the nation, the prestige as well as the spiritual and cultural opulence of living under Franco's rule. According to Spain's Vice Secretary of Education at the time, Joaquín Soriano, the *noticiarios* were to be "instructivo, variado, y técnicamente perfecto" (instructive, diverse, and technically perfect); they were to place Spain at the centre of current world events and to place the world in the palm of every Spaniard's hand (52). According to Soriano, each *noticiario* was meant to "informar, instruir, y recrear" (inform, instruct, and entertain), all while constructing and reconstructing an idyllic, powerful image of Spain, in order to bring to the national screen the most memorable aspects of a life of peace and progress under the dictatorship (52).

In the context of NO-DO's objectives, what is perhaps most striking if not most remarkable about the 1943 first-edition newsreel is how it purports to be "worldly," or at least to be completely connected, contemporaneous, and "up to date" with world events – ironically, at a time when Spanish autarky had brought the country to a precariously isolated state, politically, economically, and culturally speaking.[2] In this first instalment, national news is not highlighted and takes somewhat of a backseat to global affairs. It seems that the visual and narrative strategy employed is to "inform, instruct, and entertain" through a kind of looking outward. This newsreel reflects a calculated and prioritized observation of world news, offering something that can appeal to every spectator, whether it be traditions or sports or fashion or the economy or, finally, the war.

As if to deliberately counter this "outward gaze," in 1945, NO-DO presented Spanish audiences for the first time with an in-depth, detailed, and introspective account of its own means of production. The Ministry of Propaganda and Cinematography created a meta-newsreel – referred to explicitly as a "newsreel biography" – that capitalized on a new tactic of looking inwardly to illustrate the newsreels' mode of production from behind the scenes: its filming process, its editing and montage techniques, its cataloguing and archiving procedures, and its strategies for dissemination to the masses. In offering spectators this unique insider's view, NO-DO documented the construction of its own archive, entering into the locus of regime propaganda, the very centre of manufacturing Francoist ideology as individual film canisters, each assembled and packaged for public consumption.[3] Over the course of its near-forty-year lifespan, NO-DO became an institution, an undoubtedly prominent one that generated an immense corpus of newsreels, documentaries, and still images.[4] Curiously, however, NO-DO made the newsreel biographies on only four occasions. Offering a rare but intriguing inquiry into national news production, the self-reflexive document from 1945 not only looks at the writing and archiving of Spanish history but also demonstrates a notable shift away from the worldly view of the first newsreel, which had been shown only two years earlier, in 1943. In effect, the 1945 meta-newsreel accomplishes a twofold manoeuvre: it simultaneously constructs the archive and enters into it. Put somewhat differently, it carefully, proudly, and rather informatively displays the mechanics of its propaganda machine while ostensibly and dramatically analysing itself in a critical, educational way.

The 1945 meta-newsreel enters and observes the archive. I suggest that this tactic incites the experience of an uncanny moment.[5] I use the word "uncanny" (*unheimlich*) here in the sense that Freud defined it via Schelling, as a term that "applies to everything that was intended to remain secret, hidden away, and has come into the open" (1955, 224). In what appears to be a reversal of conventional propagandistic logic, the meta-newsreel does the unthinkable – it penetrates the secret, otherwise concealed interior of its information depository in order to expose itself (its methods, its quality control, its agents) for Spanish audiences to witness and even to gain familiarity. Moreover, between educating, disciplining, and entertaining – recall the NO-DO slogan "informar, instruir, y recrear" (inform, instruct, and entertain) – this text also examines itself, thus making the archive visible and seen while simultaneously detailing how the archive sees, captures, and produces.[6] In other words, it provides an introspective or "inside seeing," a kind of autopsy, and uncovers for the viewer and/or student what would otherwise be impossible to see – the architecture of the archive, how it is structured, made, and maintained. On entering the archive, then, the meta-newsreel attempts to make visible, to *unconceal*, as it were, what we are otherwise blind to – namely, the invisible order and logic of the archive, its contents now allegedly fully exposed and projected. It is perhaps all too uncanny that the newsreel narrates how the archive embodies knowledge, how it organizes by selecting, how it contains without showing. The questions we are left to contemplate, of course, are: Why does it do this? And how, exactly? With what purpose or end goal does this visual text undertake a public self-examination? Perhaps more importantly, how does the meta-newsreel's relation to the archive both illuminate and obscure the production of history? How does the meta-newsreel simultaneously conceal and reveal the machinery of its propaganda techniques through a strange weaving of intertextuality and self-referentiality? How does it create what I will refer to as a system of totalitarian optics that operates on the masses? In what follows, I offer a close reading of the discursive and visual elements of the newsreel biography to explore the ways in which it draws on the archive both as a disciplinary mechanism and as an uncanny omnipresent structure of seeing, knowledge, and power. To be sure, this is not an exhaustive historical analysis of the *noticiario* or of NO-DO as a state institution, but rather an inquiry into the unsettling visual and temporal disjunctures produced (and reproduced) through the state's intimate portrait of the newsreel life cycle. I argue here that the visualization of the archive through such an inward gaze paradoxically falls within the parameters of conventional propagandistic logic even while working to completely reverse that logic.

Entering the Archive, an Uncanny Site

As a text that examines both its totality and its assemblage, its "all-seeing" objective eye and its subjective technique, the newsreel biography reproduces the uncanny in the form of a double-uneasiness. This is directly related to the paradox that defines the archive – namely, that everything the archive contains ultimately calls into question everything it does not, everything it *cannot* possibly contain. Even while highlighting its archival "achievement" and plenitude, the newsreel underscores the archive's limit. In short, what becomes visible is the archive's impossibility. This fact – that the archive cannot possess everything – prompts the viewer (and the researcher as well) to question what the archive *does* contain. Where does it end? And, similarly, where does it begin?[7] For the true paradox is this: that the totality of the archive inevitably raises the matter of its limit; that what is inside the archive calls attention to what lies outside. Derrida reminds us that this paradox reveals an important point about what and how the archive remembers, about what and how memory is inscribed in history. In his now landmark lecture *Mal d'Archive: Une Impression Freudienne,* translated into English as *Archive Fever,* Derrida posits that the archive's memory is as much a recovery of something left out, something outside, forgotten, or missing, as it is a creation, a making of history:

> This is another way of saying that the archive, as printing, writing, prosthesis, or hypomnesic technique in general is not only a place for stocking and for conserving an archivable content *of the past* which would exist in any case, such as, without the archive, one still believes it was or will have been. No, the technical structure of the *archiving* archive also determines the structure of the *archivable* content even in its very coming into existence and in its relationship to the future. The archivization produces as much as it records the event. (1996, 16–17)

This passage is revealing. According to Derrida, the archive's insistent desire to order, catalogue, classify, and accumulate beyond any reasonable capacity, along with its compulsion to identify origins, to structure, repeat, and remember, inevitably calls into question its "opposite." Everything the archive remembers thus inevitably points towards everything it forgets. What it leaves outside – that is, what it *cannot* structure or remember, or conversely what is there on the shelves but gets omitted nonetheless or remains unseen, unnoticed – starkly contrasts with the logic of archival space as one of memory, conservation, and inscription. This, I believe, is what Derrida means when he writes that "the archive always works, and *a priori,* against itself" (12). This aspect of the archive – its "working against itself" – is, ironically, the same one that might lead to the search for meaning in what is *not* found within the archive's structure. As a point of departure, I turn from thinking about this fundamental paradox that underwrites the archive, to a close reading of the first meta-newsreel, NO-DO 105A (1945). In looking at the document's content and form, I propose a reading that treats this newsreel as both historical document and literary narrative, in order to examine the intersection between visual record and fictional text, between the cinematic and the historical. Likewise, this close reading will examine how the meta-newsreel's narrative discourse – both textual and visual – reflects the logic of the archive as a place that produces *and* records, consigns *and* eradicates. By studying these twin features – production and visibility, filming and recording – my analysis seeks to uncover new corners of the archive that reveal otherwise unseen encounters with ghostly matters and that call into question the production of history, illuminating its cinematic, literary, and spectral qualities. After looking at the 1945 *noticiario,* I will offer another close reading of images and narrative from two additional newsreels from 1968 in an effort to examine the finer discursive elements and visual aesthetics of haunting underlying some of the regime's most prominent yet subtle propagandistic tactics. Finally, I explore NO-DO as an ideological tool and fascist spectacle in terms of the politics of spectrality.

Binocular Vision: The Mechanics of Propaganda

In line with Derrida's argument about memory and forgetting, I begin here with a specific focus on the newsreel's depiction of production – in particular, the production of vision – as related to the archive as a totalizing system of knowledge. This prompts us to ask, among many other questions, what makes the archive visible and what makes it invisible. More interesting still, how does the archive see *itself*? A question not easily answered but whose mystery can be examined in the first meta-newsreel, "NO-DO por dentro: Biografía de un Noticiario" (Inside the NO-DO: Biography of a Newsreel) (105A) The title itself promises an intimate look at the production of newsreels – a biography of how each is "born." After the standard NO-DO signature appears on the screen, followed by the synchronization of the title with the victorious sound of trumpets, the narrator begins his introduction as follows:

> Hace dos años nuestro estado creó NO-DO para suministrar una información cinematográfica verdaderamente objetiva e imparcial de todos los acontecimientos importantes y para cumplir al mismo tiempo una finalidad instructiva y divulgadora.

> Two years ago our state created the NO-DO to supply truly objective and impartial cinematographic information of all-important events and, at the same time, to fulfil an instructive and informative end.

From the outset, the narration emphasizes the work of not only the camera but also the cameramen, echoed in the repeated use of "las noticias" (the news) with "los noticiarios" (the newsreels) and "los operadores" (the operators, or the technicians). The perspective is "truly objective and impartial," educational and enlightening, and all of these suggested aspects coincide with a fantastic array of images that capture the danger and risk involved in filming the news. More striking than the narration, though, are the images collaged together in spectacular, rhythmic montage form – a series of pictures, each swiftly flowing into the next, is coupled with images that are superimposed on top of one another. As one image fades into the background, a new one emerges, establishing a sense of harmony and unity – rather than conflict and friction – among the disparate scenes and subjects framed. And paired with the words "objective," "impartial," and "true" is the imaging of a double-movement. First, the screen takes the shape of a pair of binoculars, symmetrically aligned not only to span the entire width of the screen but also to give the viewer the impression, or illusion, that he too is observing "objectively" through the double-lens. In this way, the binoculars both give the viewer perspective (i.e., we observe the way the camera does) and establish the newsreel's primary framing mechanism (i.e., it perfectly aligns viewer perspective with the perspective of an apparatus). Second, stretching the optics metaphor further, each eyepiece of the binoculars separately yet simultaneously focuses on different yet parallel – that is, asymmetrical yet synchronized – images of two cameramen in the act of filming. With their respective cameras in hand, each operator rotates 180 degrees towards the viewer, eventually pointing his lens directly at the spectator, now implicating us in their objective "capturing" of the world. Each cameraman is framed neatly within each separate lens of the binoculars that frame the screen; both face the viewer and then continue to turn, still filming, in opposite directions, now giving the optical illusion – as if in a kind of mirroring effect – that they see and capture each other. The viewer becomes witness to this mutual seeing and capturing within the span of only a few seconds.

It seems that almost before the newsreel has even begun, we the viewers are being presented with the overarching structure of what the

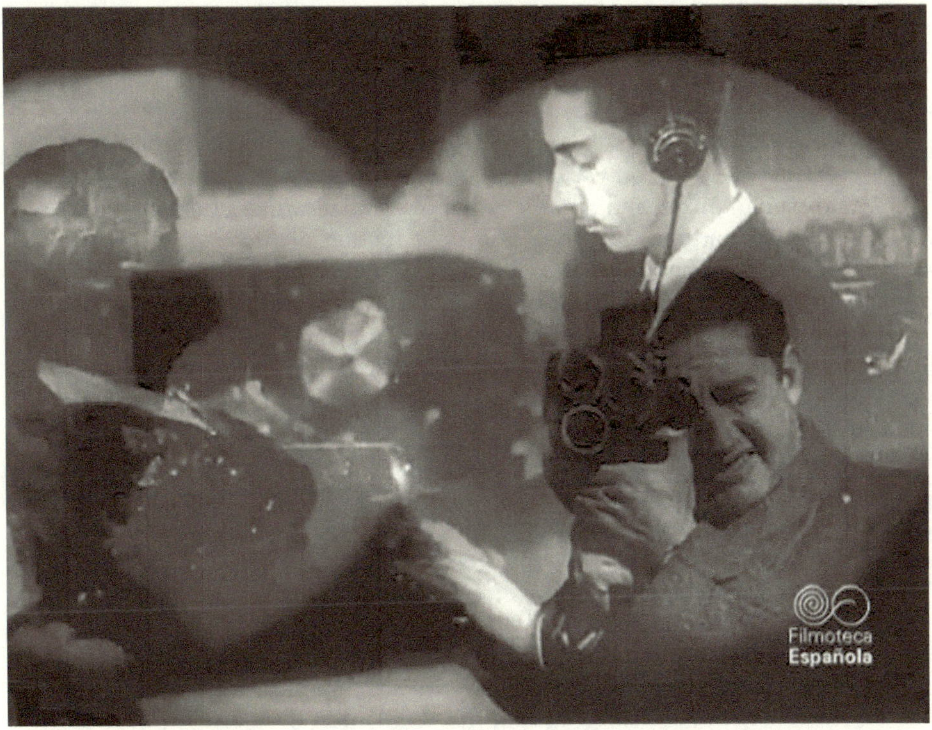

1.1 Binocular vision. The cameraman films us. (No. 105A, 1945) Copyright *Filmoteca nacional.*

NO-DO seeks to document. Indeed, the opening binoculars sequence constructs a *mise en abyme* for the entire newsreel by not only framing but also bringing into focus and thus sharpening an otherwise blurry vision of how "all important events" are captured and made. News that would remain distant from our everyday experience in the absence of the camera, the newsreel, and by extension the archive itself, now is brought into our view through a double-underscoring of the camera's function and position – one optical apparatus viewing other optical apparatuses at work. The message could not be clearer: *everything is and can be captured.* And the double-seeing and double-filming that the viewer involuntarily partakes in echoes yet another implicit message: we film what you see; you see us filming. As such, this opening sequence stages a synopsis of the entire biography, albeit an extremely brief and fleeting one. We all are observers, and by the same logic, we all are observed. In one swift move, the NO-DO's achievement is twofold: on the one hand, it conflates technology with experience, and on the other, it calls attention to the practice of state vigilance and control. Of course, what is crucial is the all-encompassing totality of the news, presented here not only as information and cinema but also as truth, as something natural and organic.[8] That the 1945 newsreel should capitalize on the naturalized process and production of such "truth" is not surprising, given that the same year, the regime adopted its new philosophy of "organic democracy," disavowing in official discourse the primitive reins (not to mention the menacing political associations) of totalitarianism in favour of a more acceptable – because natural – rule of law. Thus, since the camera captures us observing its observations, the logic of the newsreel's opening sequence suggests not only the naturalness of this entire activity (the intricate interplay between observed object and observing subject) but also, and potentially more problematically, its *universal* character as a legitimizing device. Since we all see the same thing, it must therefore all be real and true.[9]

As a cinematic technique, the binocular framing of the NO-DO invites and persuades the viewer to focus less on important current events related to the nation, all of which we are told the camera records, and more on the fact that we too are cameramen, we gradually become voyeurs participating in the production of news. The end result is odd but simple: we watch through the screen's fictitious, illusory frame the actual cameramen, who are already (but again fictitiously) watching and filming us. In terms of the uneasiness I mentioned earlier, this system of double-optics that is imposed on the viewer – the binocular framing that facilitates a two-way vision in which we and they watch simultaneously – is uncanny in another way as well. For it suggests that the viewer's otherwise passive seeing is now transformed into an active watching. While this shift may seem subtle, it is nevertheless remarkably peculiar, suggesting that our vision *is* the camera's and thus engages in the same sort of filming, the same objective, mechanical gaze that the *noticiario* itself purports to have. In Foucauldian terms, it is a seeing whose "spatial nesting" operates in a way that forces us to see *how* we are seen. We literally look through the camera's eyes to see ourselves being observed and captured. This image marks the inauguration of a new way of seeing, one that the newsreel consciously co-opts by taking a familiar device and estranging it, making it work in an unfamiliar and indeed uncanny way.[10]

The mechanics of seeing are precisely what is at work here. The screen, now turned into both an optical apparatus and the object or field of that apparatus's gaze, is no longer the imaginary divider between spectator and moving image; rather, it becomes the material unifier of both, paradoxically establishing and erasing the line that separates them. As the NO-DO's binocular frame converts each viewer into an active individual participant, the tyranny of the camera's gaze becomes our own, and any invention it creates we are complicit in creating, which underscores further the idea that if everyone sees, everyone is in turn seen. This collapse of meaning between seeing and being seen constitutes what Foucault called "hierarchical observation," the first of three "simple instruments" from which undoubtedly "the success of disciplinary power derives" (1995, 170). However, the type of "hierarchical observation" the NO-DO offers verges on a more sinister inversion of the disciplinary surveillance used to train subjects that Foucault discusses in *Discipline and Punish*. The observational technique as presented in the newsreel biography denotes, in fact, a kind of lateral seeing that alters the traditionally vertical (top to bottom, centre to periphery) hierarchy, placing it on a more even plane in which we *all* see on the same level at the same time. The temporal dimension is key. It is important to remember that the newsreel does more than portray the camera as an "all-seeing eye" that captures everything – or, recalling panopticism, as the "eyes that must see without being seen" (171); it also reproduces the mechanism by which the camera (and by extension, the screen itself) becomes an instrument through which the subject's observation is not only disclosed but also self-imposed and knowingly inscribed onto a system of watching and recording. The logic follows. If we all see through the camera's lens – that is, if we all are cameramen who observe and record one another incessantly – then the hierarchy folds in on itself. As such, the notion of everyone seeing everything everywhere at all times becomes a concept the NO-DO co-opts in order to simultaneously stake a claim on "truth" and institute an optical mechanism, one that converts all observation into normalizing, disciplinary, and *self*-imposed behaviour, a sort of autodidactic surveillance in which the viewer willingly (though surely not blindly) participates. We no longer have to imagine an anonymous, omnipotent eye looking down on us in order to correct and train our behaviour; instead, we now see something much more personal and real – our own collective eye, looking out, capturing everything, including our very own actions. Our line of vision is thus coerced into aligning itself with the authority behind the screen, the same one sponsoring the news – in this case, the regime itself. Foucault tells us that all discipline "presupposes a mechanism that coerces by means of observation; an apparatus in which the techniques that make it possible to see induce effects of power, and in which, conversely, the means of coercion make those on whom they are applied clearly visible" (171). In line with Foucault's analysis, it is the *production of visibility* here that marks the presence of the uncanny – the eyes that should see without being seen, the ones that should remain hidden, now suddenly come into the open, framed, as it were, and recognized strangely as our own. Similarly, the subject being observed (the spectator) is now forced also to observe himself, not only to imagine but also to view and indeed position himself *within* the mechanics of one of the regime's most ritualized and politicized propaganda tactics, in which he too now plays a vital role.[11]

The opening sequence of the 1945 newsreel biography is indeed impressive. Within the short time frame of the first ten seconds, we are simultaneously shown and told the veracity of the NO-DO and are made complicit in its totalizing and universalizing observational techniques. After all, what better way to show the viewer the truth of the image than by allowing him to see it for himself? And what better way to convince the viewer that this method of observation is not wrong or intrusive but, on the contrary, powerful and exciting, resounding with the commentator's original rhetoric that the newsreel's methods are "educational" and "popular"? As the binocular camera montage sequence becomes suffused with superimposed images of scripts, typewriters, and silhouettes of radio broadcasters and narrators reading what we assume to be the actual news, the newsreel presents yet another striking montage. This time the focus shifts from meta-cinematic images that reference vision and the act of viewing/filming to images that reference sound and communication. In rapid succession, images of telephones and switchboards flash up, followed by alternating images of men and women talking on the telephone – all signs of technological progress and timely communication of the latest and most important news. Informing the viewer that this "biography" is made especially for him, at his request, the narrator states: "Desde entonces y con la simpatía del público, este noticiario procurado para responder al afecto con que fue acogido y hoy se complace en ofrecer algunos aspectos de su labor" (Since then and with the public's support, this newsreel was made in order to respond to the affection with which it was received and today it is pleased to offer a few aspects of its work). The emphasis on technology is followed by allusions, in both word and image, to innovation, labour, and movement – in other words, to advances in news production. We are further told that the guiding force behind Spain's progress is not only the news itself (i.e., events that are newsworthy) but also directionality – that is, the careful selection of locations where the news can be "found." At this point, the images of telephones and operators collapse subtly into a sequence of three distinct shots: (1) a door that marks the entry to the NO-DO office, with a plaque that reads "Dirección"; (2) three men standing in front of a large map of Spain; and (3) a close-up shot of the map (Figure 1.3). The fact that direction is a key component in the making of a newsreel is further underscored by the images of road signs, highways, and last but not least a car racing across the open Spanish landscape, which together imply not only that the news is "born" from a logical sequence of steps but also that it is "arrived at" after following a specific course involving calculability, predictability, and visibility. One needs only to read the map. The narrator continues:

> Nuestra musa es la noticia, la dirección y la reacción ante el mapa. [*corte*] Los operadores parten al lugar exacto. *Nada puede ni debe escapar a la ágil captación de la cámara.* Para efectuar el rodaje, se busca los emplazamientos y se emplea los medios más eficaces por muy arriesgados que sean. Así los hechos son sorprendentes en sus más vivos y dinámicos perfiles. [*música*]
>
> Our muse is the news, the direction of and reaction to the map. [*cut*] The cameramen set out for the exact place. *Nothing can or should escape the agility of the camera's capture.* In order to carry out filming, locations are sought out and the most efficient, even if very risky, means are employed. Thus the facts are surprising in their most intense and dynamic profiles. [*music*; my emphasis]

We learn too that direction and location are as essential to filming as the news itself, which in theory never "can or should escape" the all-capturing camera eye.[12] After directionality, we are told that the next essential piece in the NO-DO machinery is efficiency. The narrator continues to detail the core properties of each newsreel, declaring that visibility, direction, reaction, agility, and efficiency constitute the five fundamental elements of capturing "intense and dynamic" news and thus of giving the news vitality and "life."

But the true mechanics underlying the "birth" of each newsreel lie, we learn, in the editing process. The narrator informs us that making

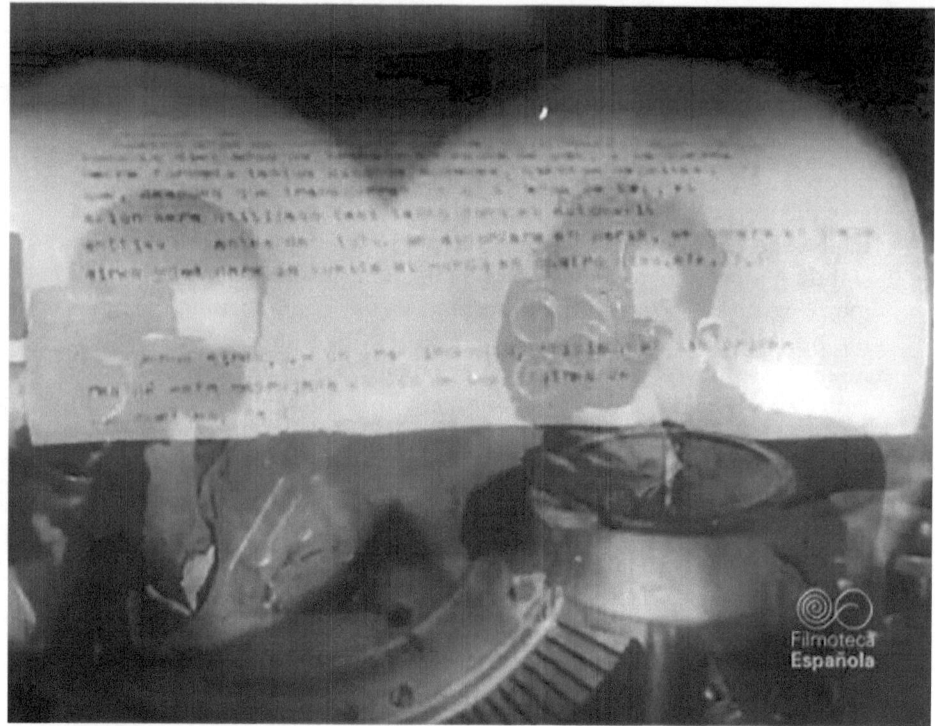

1.2 Cameramen filming the audience superimposed over images of typewriters and scripts. (No. 105A, 1945) Copyright *Filmoteca nacional.*

the news visible involves not only direction but also immediacy and velocity – speed and acceleration are key factors. After reading a map or capturing real events with the camera comes the "speedy" and "necessary work" of arranging filmed images into sequences that will relay the reality of history, making the news appear real, accessible, and current:

> Terminando el trabajo de los operadores el material es conducido *rápidamente* a los laboratorios donde se efectuarán con él *diversas operaciones necesarias.* [*música*] En la truca se revisa el material rodado. *A esto sucede la minuciosa y rápida tarea del montaje.*

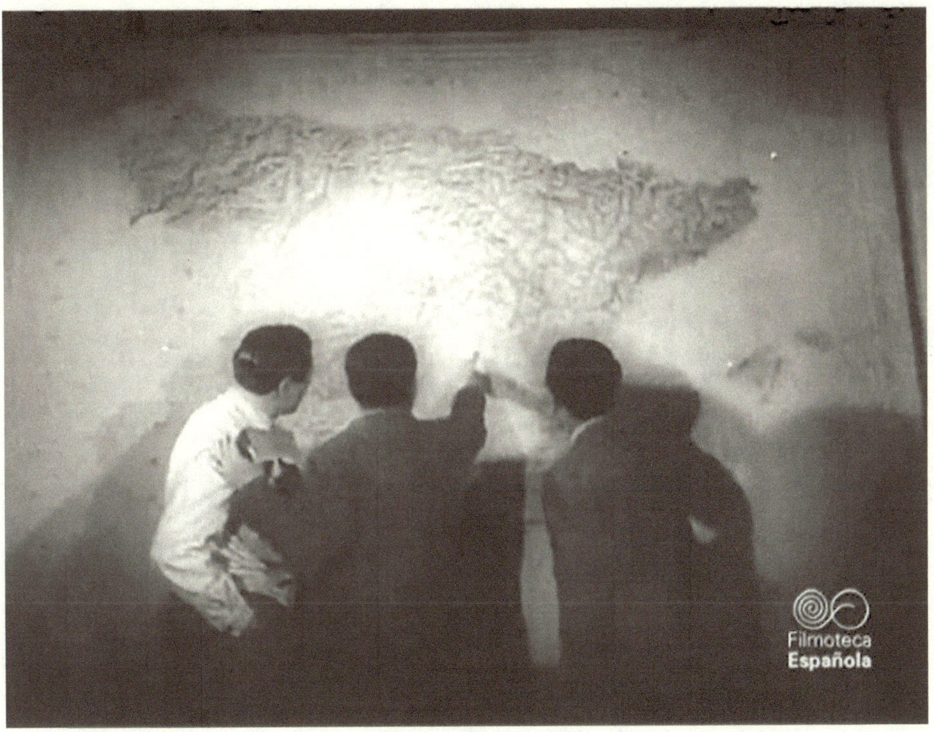

1.3 NO-DO cameramen study a map of Spain. (No. 105A, 1945) Copyright *Filmoteca nacional.*

> Finishing the work of the cameramen, the material is *quickly* driven to the laboratories where a *series of necessary procedures* with be carried out with it. [*music*] In the editing room, the filmed material is reviewed. *This is followed by the* detailed and rapid *task of editing*. [my emphasis]

Following another montage featuring close-ups of various tools of the editing process, such as equipment, switches, light boxes, negative spools, and slides, the viewer becomes witness to the truth of these images – namely, that their visibility hinges on their manufacture, on their "being made." The previous message "everything is and can be captured" now reads something like this: "because we capture and record everything, we can *only* show you some things." In a contradictory move, this NO-DO tells us it is necessary to fabricate the news – to

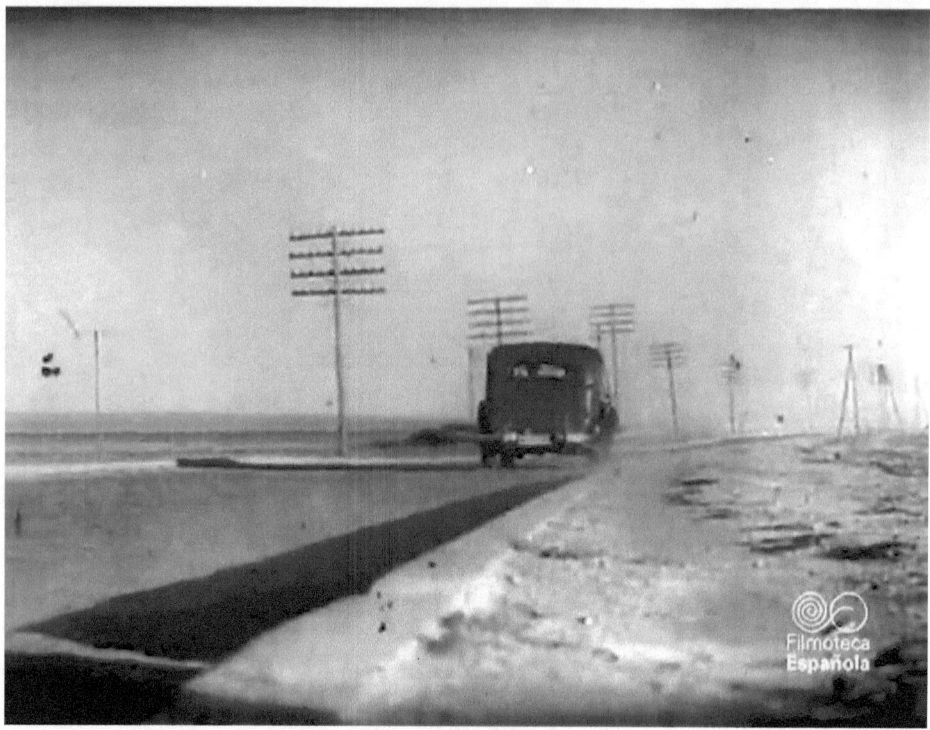

1.4 NO-DO car racing across the landscape in search of the news. (No. 105A, 1945) Copyright *Filmoteca nacional.*

compile the materials swiftly, assemble them into coherent, compact narratives, and review and edit those narratives for proper viewing. In other words, the news is not "found" with the help of a trusty map; it is not captured with the modern technology of the camera; it is not merely sought out; rather, it is invented. One could argue that there is no real mystery here since all filmic texts require an editing process or, conversely, since the editing process is inherent in all forms of cinema. In other words, the modern technology of cinema makes editing possible – it even encourages and to some extent requires that editing be done. But this subjectivity – in contrast to its self-defined objectivity and impartiality – is not the only aspect of the NO-DO that highlights its paradoxical nature. The visualization of production underscores

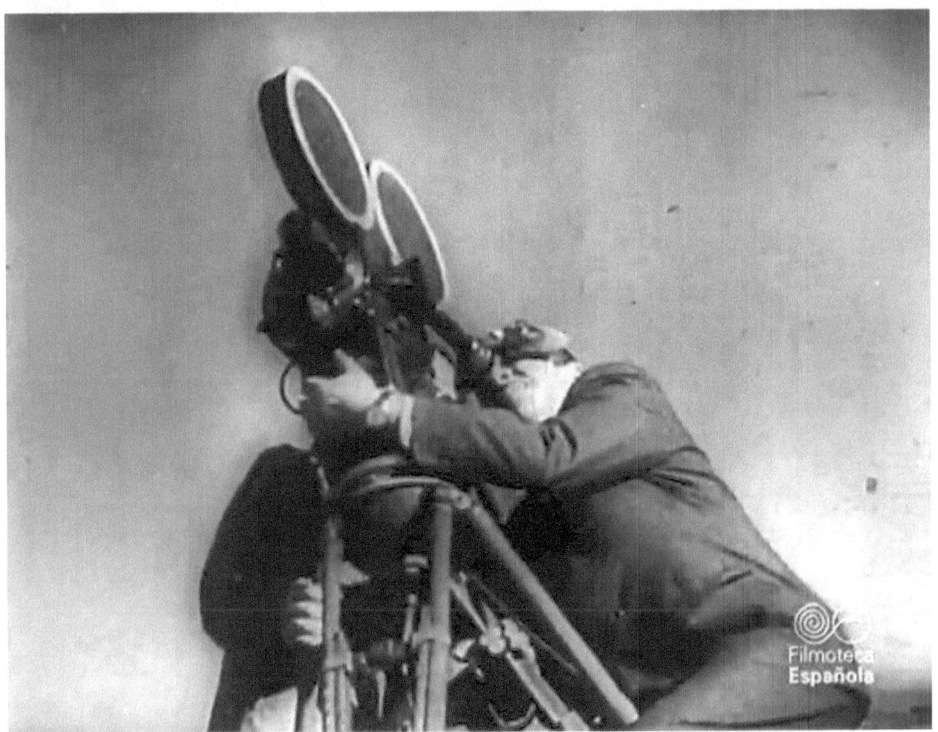

1.5 "Hunting" the news in all places. The newsreels tell us repeatedly that *everything* is caught on film. (No. 105A, 1945) Copyright *Filmoteca nacional.*

this paradox as well. The calculated attention given to the NO-DO's system of editing recalls Derrida's affirmation that "the archivization produces as much as it records the event" (1996, 16–17).

In this NO-DO example, as in the other three newsreel biographies I will be discussing, it is obvious that technology functions as both the means of production and a symbol of progress. Technology is absolutely essential to making the news possible, which is to say, making it accessible and visible. Here, visibility and technology go hand in hand with totality and assemblage. Thus, what the biography is underhandedly suggesting is that technology makes each newsreel real – that each film canister contains within it history and truth and that the assemblage process inherent in making this propaganda machine function

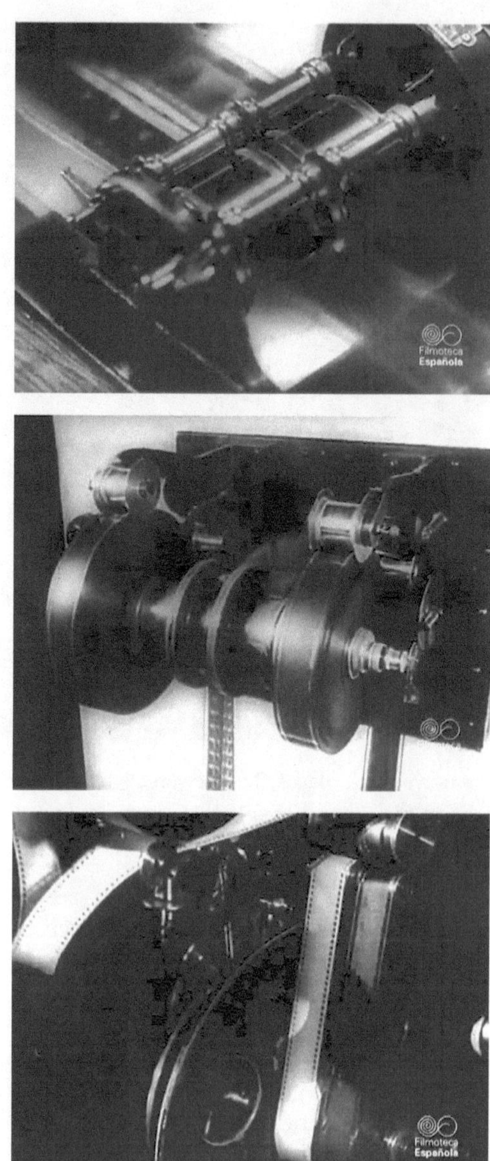

1.6, 1.7, and 1.8 Multiple images of the "news being born." Here a montage of developing and editing machines and strands of film negatives. (No. 105A, 1945) Copyright *Filmoteca nacional.*

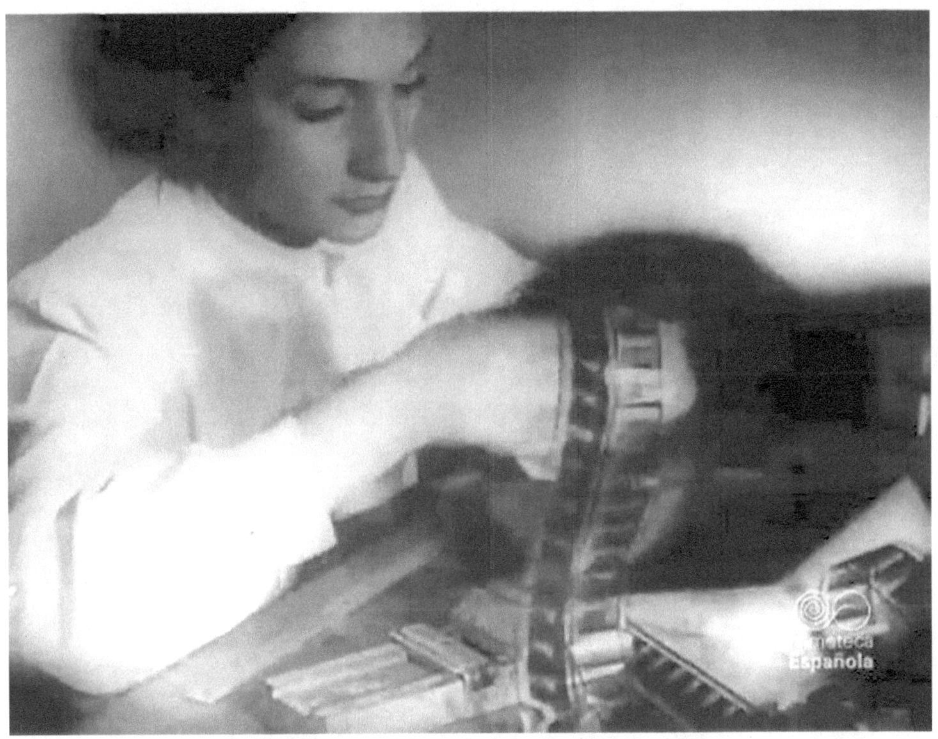

1.9 An editing technician selecting the most important news. (No. 105A, 1945) Copyright *Filmoteca nacional.*

properly (which is to say, operate on us) is authentic and progressive. In fact, that process is the very notion of progress towards which the newsreels so often and so arrestingly turn.

At this point, the biography provides another montage sequence, one that offers the viewer yet another glimpse of its wealth and plentitude – the abundance of news and information that arrives in Spain, all of which needs to be sorted through, organized, and catalogued. We are told that Madrid is the centre of an "ocean of news," the sea into which all rivers of information abundantly flow. This comment is synchronized perfectly with one of the newsreel's most imposing images: the rapid piling up of film canisters to the deadening sound of a marching drum. The narrator asserts:

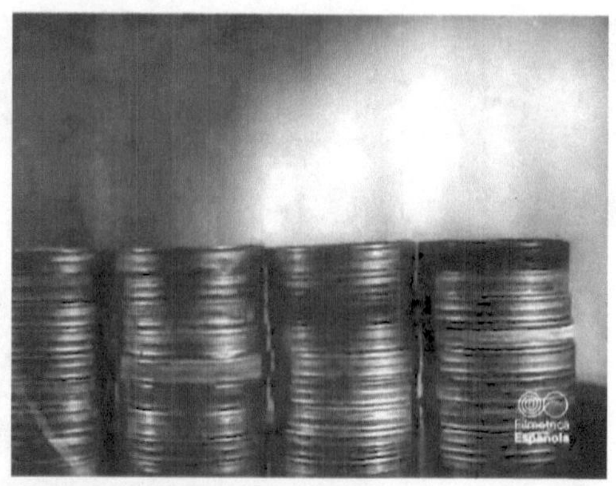

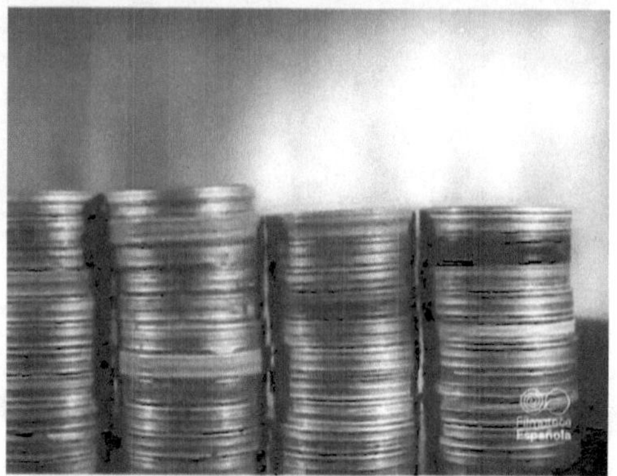

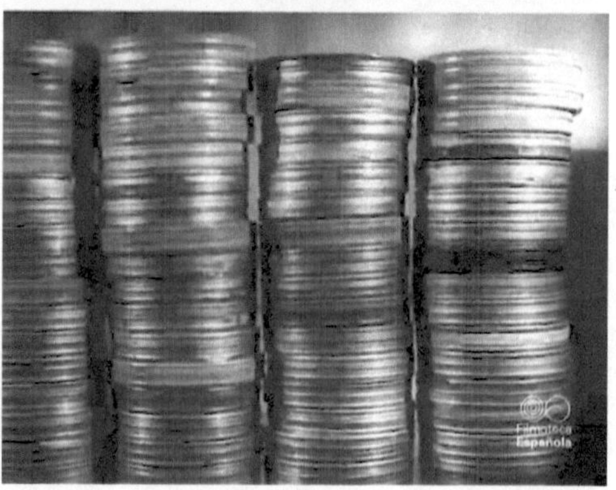

1.10, 1.11, and 1.12 The archive's wealth of information. The accumulation of film canisters. (No. 105A, 1945) Copyright *Filmoteca nacional.*

> De todos los lugares del mundo, llegan las noticias cinematográficas, confluyen en Madrid y se centralizan en el edificio del NO-DO. [*imágenes de tecnología y transporte: aviones, trenes, tranvías, y las máquinas de corte, montaje, etc … todo acompañado por música triunfal*] Los roles extranjeros enriquecen la cinemateca. [*el sonido del tambor de un desfile militar, sincronizado a la imagen de los botes de film que se amontonan*] Elección de la música y los ruidos. Una vez seleccionada estas noticias, se ajusta la imagen y el sonido. Corte y montaje del negativo [*música*] Una vez coordinado el noticiario, pasa al estudio para su sonorización. En el registro, el técnico de sonido efectua las mezclas. El noticiario está terminado y en el laboratorio se realiza la tirada de copias. Obtenida la primera copia, se comprueba en la sala de proyección. Terminado este proceso, los temas nacionales llevan a todas partes las imágenes de la vida española. [*imagen: mapa de España, flechas hacia todas direcciones del mundo*]

> Cinematographic news arrives from around the world, converges in Madrid, and is centralized in the NO-DO Building. [*images of technology and transportation: planes, trains, trolleys, and editing equipment, montage machines, etc … all accompanied by music*] The foreign reels enrich the cinematheque [or cinema archive] [*drum beats, as if in a military parade, to the image of film canisters piling up*] Selecting the music and sounds. Cutting, editing, and mounting of the negative. [*music*] Once the newsreel is assembled, it goes to the studio for sound synchronization. In the office, the sound technician completes the mixing. The newsreel is finished and in the laboratory the print run of copies is made. With the first copy in hand, it is tested in the projection room. Once this process is finished, national topics bring the image of Spanish life everywhere. [*image: map of Spain, arrows pointing in all directions*]

Here, production contributes directly to the newsreel's authenticity and is portrayed visually as a natural part of each reel's making, its wealth of information and veracity. And thus the paradox once again is made visible: the NO-DOs are revealed to us as both fabricated and real documents, shown to us as both assembled and born, artificial and natural. But perhaps the most unsettling aspect of this newsreel's acute attention to production, method, and the particulars of the editing process is something that relates back to the archive – namely, that the totality of the news (akin to the archive's collection) always hinges on ghostliness, on a structure of spectrality. This spectrality is constituted by the double-bind of visibility/invisibility, direction/directionlessness, concealing/unconcealing. The ability to capture everything – a trait supposedly shared by both the archive and the camera eye – comes with the hefty price of always having to omit something.

In this way, the biography "NO-DO por dentro" reflects a fact about the film archive itself – that the archive does not "forget" or leave out through the conventional process of *non-remembering* (*anmesis*), but rather through the process of *hyper-remembering* (filming, capturing, recording, projecting everything). We would do well here to recall Derrida's concept of the archive as an entity or structure defined by the notion of "outside." In the context of the newsreels, the making of the NO-DO is depicted as a historical technology or, better yet, as a technology of narrating history, of giving it "life" (with all the associations that word brings to mind – biology, humanity, natural, organic processes), or of capturing life and "animating" it in the name of education and entertainment. This technology makes history possible by taking those events deemed important to viewers – the news (now history) of "everyday Spanish existence" – and making them available to everyone, everywhere.

However captivating or compelling this NO-DO is, its focus on making its production process explicitly visible creates a certain dis-ease – what I will call here a moment of "uncanny inversion" – that seems to go against traditional tactics of propaganda. In examining itself, the newsreel biography co-opts the very thing it pretends to offer its audience: the possibility of studying and scrutinizing how the news is always already mediated and filtered, literally and figuratively, through the lens of Francoist ideology. It is uncanny because, recalling Freud quoting Schelling, it reveals those aspects of the newsreel's production – the gears of its machinery – or everything that "'ought to have remained ... secret and hidden but has come to light'" (1955, 224).[13] In other words, all of those aspects of production that were obscene (in the sense of "off-stage" or "out of view") are here deliberately exposed and legitimized in the name of propagating the authority of state-sponsored news broadcasting. On a different but related note, we could also say that the biography is based on a moment of "uncanny suspension," since throughout it, we as viewers are positioned in between two seemingly opposite poles of the newsreel. On the one hand, its archival totality makes production of each reel necessary; on the other, the production of each reel undermines that ideal of totality. This is key. The insider glimpse into the newsreel's birth via assemblage translates into the visualization of the aforementioned archival paradox. Importantly, this is also an uncanny moment of the visualization of loss. The newsreel simultaneously calls attention to its totality and wealth and implies the impossibility of that totality. It converts the screen into an optical instrument that invites us to see the process by which we decidedly do *not* see everything that has been filmed. We are told to view select images that relay "objective" news, born from a subjective process of bringing each newsreel to "life," a process involving calculation, direction, speed, filming, editing, cutting, switching, reordering, organizing, synchronizing, and so forth. Since production inevitably omits, since it always marks a loss, it can be said that this NO-DO really only shows the viewer that while everything can be filmed, everything filmed cannot be seen. This is a minor deviation from the newsreel's rather compelling opening statement, if not a somewhat obvious message complicated by the fact that within it another inversion, an asynchronicity of sorts, takes place: the narrator's comments draw attention to omissions while the viewer is shown images of the labour put into production.

In fact, capturing the labour invested in the production of each reel is an aspect all too important to the biography's visual rhetoric. The images lead us to believe that the craftsmanship, time, and skill put into editing equate each NO-DO with the cultural and political capital it purports to project and disseminate throughout the world. Parallel to the images of international news converging on the "information headquarters" located at the news epicentre of Madrid, the viewer is presented with images of exportation – dozens of canisters, made, wrapped, and ready to be mailed to any number of foreign destinations. Drawing on its distribution power and international circulation, the newsreel's final segment highlights two important and final features of the NO-DO. First, the newsreel makes the universal local; second, it visually documents the greatness of the nation under the dictatorship. The narration concludes:

> Semanalmente, los cines exhiben el noticiario haciendo realidad el lema de 'poner el mundo entero al alcance a todos los españoles.' Así NO-DO puede ofrecer los más variados aspectos de la actualidad en las distintas manifestaciones de la misma; registra los hechos importantes y en cuanto constituye una expresión constructiva o conmemorativa. [*música/montaje*] Imágenes de la existencia nacional que reza y gobierna Franco, Caudillo de España y jefe del estado ... siempre en trabajo y en desvelo constante por la unidad, la grandeza, y la libertad de la patria. [*últimas imágenes de la cruz en la pared que tiene colgado una tapicería medieval, y de Franco sentado, escribiendo*] [*Nota de la imagen de cierre: Lema con el símbolo del águila encima del mundo: "El mundo entero al alcance de todos los españoles."*]

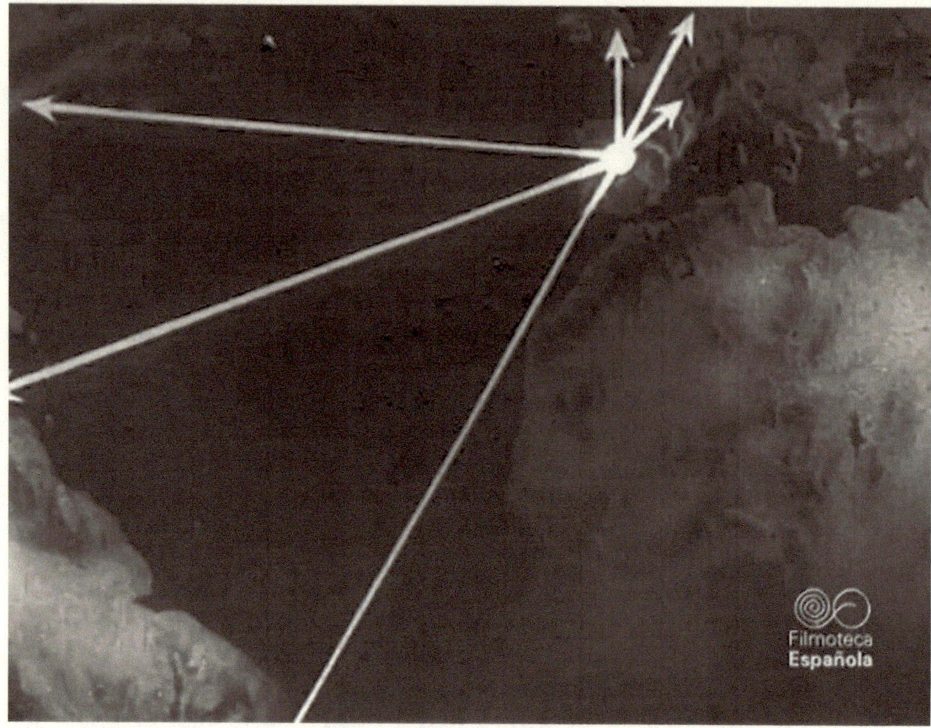

1.13 Spain's exportation of NO-DO. Global dissemination. (No. 105A, 1945) Copyright *Filmoteca nacional.*

Weekly, theatres show the newsreel, bringing certain reality to the motto: "making the whole world within reach of every Spaniard." In this way, *NO-DO* can offer the most varied aspects of current events in all their different manifestations; it records important facts and represents a constructive or commemorative expression. [*music and montage*] Images of the national life that Franco, *Caudillo* of Spain and head of state, prays over and governs ... always working and constantly doing all that is possible for the unity, the greatness, and the freedom of the nation. [*Final images of a cross on the wall with a medieval tapestry hanging, and of Franco seated, writing. Cut to* NO-DO *slogan with the symbol of eagle on top of the globe. The caption below reads: "The entire world within the reach of every Spaniard."*]

The viewer is led to believe there is a reciprocal relationship between the surplus of images that arrive in Madrid and the weekly newsreels that Spanish movie houses screen for public viewing. Moreover, the narrator tells us not only that these images circulate true stories ("historias") assembled by film technicians but also that they disseminate the political work of Franco all over the globe, exporting images of his own efforts to unite and build a free nation. The newsreel's final images of a crucifix and a medieval tapestry, figuring a battle scene in the background, complemented by the presence of the dictator himself, pensive and working diligently at his desk, all coincide with the description of Franco as "siempre en trabajo y en desvelo constante" (literally "always working and constantly awake") for the well-being of the nation. In this way, the NO-DO both reproduces the means of its own production and reinforces the command and control of the regime, simultaneously validating its own work and substantiating the state's supreme authority.

In fact, work and authority are quite appropriate concepts with which to close the newsreel, given that they are woven throughout the entire biography, from its first images of cameramen risking their lives to film the news, to sharp details of the tedious but necessary labour of editing, to the final scene depicting Franco, as the seat of power, tirelessly working for the nation. In the end, this newsreel biography narrates its own production, which is reinforced both by the opening images of scripts and writing apparatuses and by the closing image of the dictator writing, and it does so symmetrically, linking mechanical optics and the technological writing of history to the image of historical (and in the final images, religious) grandeur, embodied not in what is written down but here in the image, and body, of Franco himself.

What knowledge is the viewer to gain from a document that visualizes its own "life cycle" of production and in doing so perpetuates its own uncanny logic, making the invisible seen while conversely making what is seen strangely invisible? What sense can be made of this literary reading of a historical document that uses the mechanics and technology of cinema to reproduce and propagate its own paradoxical rhetoric? More importantly, and returning for a moment to the relationship between the means of production and the economy of visibility, what can we as cultural critics understand from a system that shows us how, why, and with what means it *does not* show us – that is, a system that "writes out" as much as it inscribes crucial parts of the news and thus of history?[14] What can be theorized from the type of authority, quality control, and mechanical observation that the NO-DO offers? All

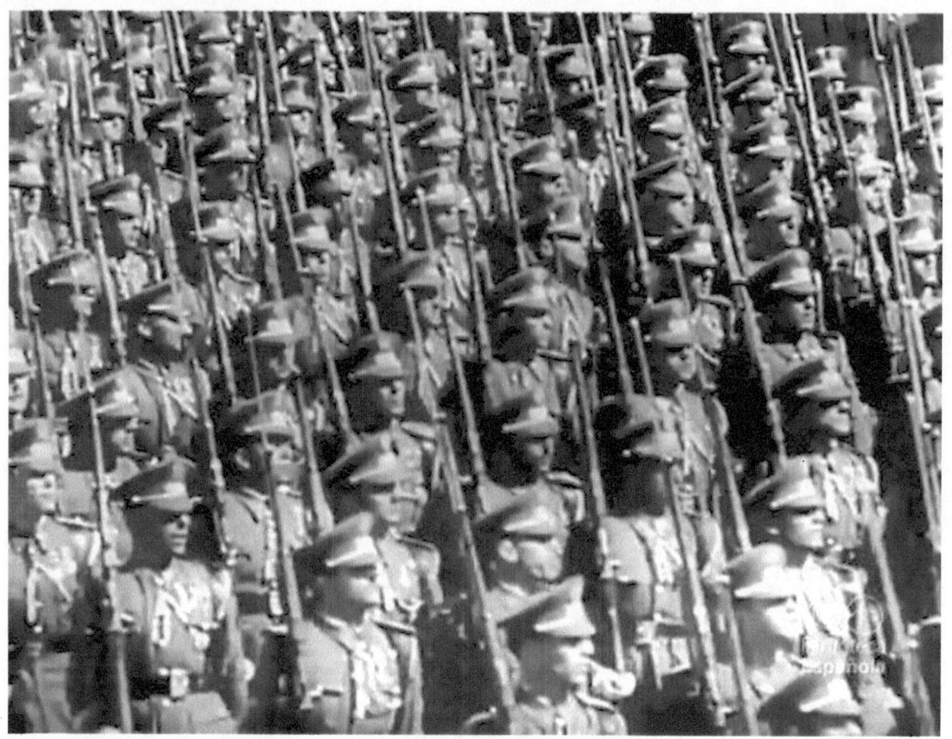

1.14 The masses symbolize unification of a "free" nation under Franco. (No. 105A, 1945) Copyright *Filmoteca nacional.*

of these questions inevitably lead us back to the paradox of the archive – how it "works against itself," its spectral logic that simultaneously conceals and unconceals.[15] In the end, it is a system of production and reproduction that draws closer to its limit the more it looks at the magnitude of what it contains. The deeper it looks inside, the less it "sees." The newsreel biography, like the archive, *always exceeds itself.* It is an accumulation that always requires and relies on omissions. As such, it is on the one hand a place of origins and indeed a place that originates (i.e., "births") power and history, and on the other a place of desire, imagining, and fiction.

The "machinery of propaganda," as Spanish historian Vicente Sánchez-Biosca has appropriately described the NO-DO, no longer functions as a secret ploy but rather as a quotidian device (Tranche and Sánchez-Biosca

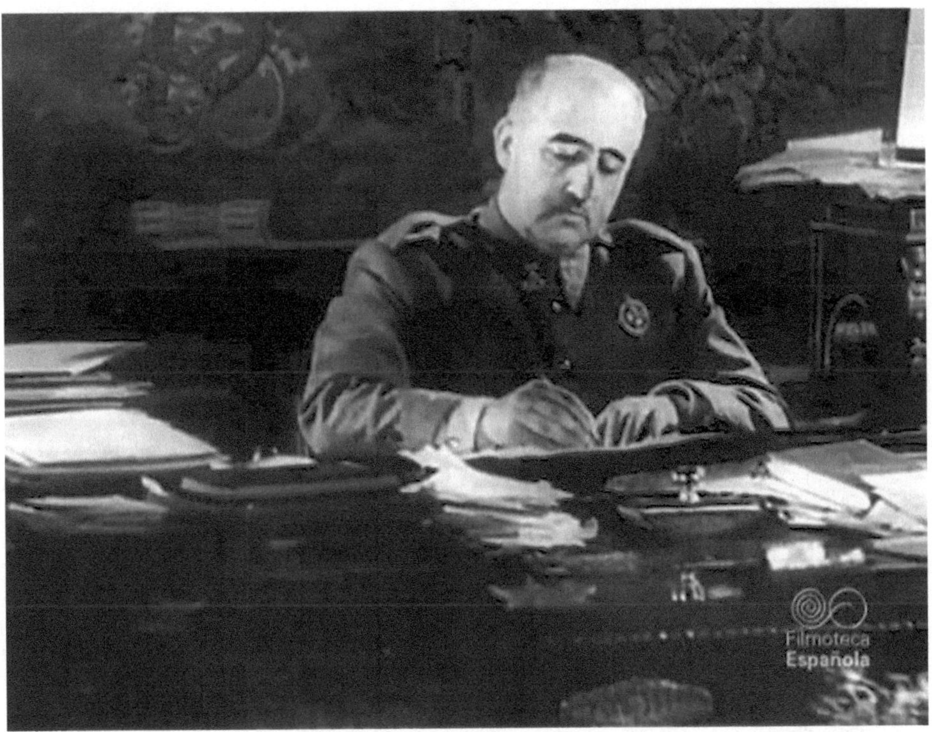

1.15 Franco at his desk, "always working" for the nation. (No. 105A, 1945) Copyright *Filmoteca nacional.*

2005, 43). The camera explicitly and cinematically inserts the viewer into its hierarchical structure and uses the screen to conflate reality (here, everyday Spanish life) with the constructions of that reality. The NO-DO simultaneously images and reproduces the mechanics of state ideology under Franco. It performs for the viewer while also making him a complicit spectator. It relates and reproduces an architecture that surveys its own interior – its contents and the mechanics of its operation – in order to make the state's ideal image of the nation appear natural and real through a tailored and elaborate web of images. Following the Althusserian theory of ideology and ideological state apparatuses, the Spanish state, in this context, reproduces its "machinery of repression" through all newsreel production. But the crucial difference here is that spectators ostensibly (if consciously) become sutured into this machinery not by a covert system of representation, but rather – as I have been showing in closely reading the meta-newsreel – through the unmasking and dissecting of that very system. Through careful self-examination and visual scrutiny, the biography's "surgical gaze" – or the tactic of autopsy, opening itself before our eyes and showing us where the national news is stitched together to portray that ideal image of an ordered, disciplined, and progressive Spain – is ironically the same one that undermines our seeing and manipulates our viewpoint so that ideally, we falsely understand each newsreel to be completely seamless. In the end, the newsreel is to the national film archive what the prosthetic limb is to the body – in Derridean terms, it acts as "a[n institution of a] prosthesis of the inside," or the mechanical instrument that maintains and strengthens the effectiveness of the organism as a whole but in reality proves to be nothing more than a supplement, something artificial that creates an illusion of a totality that does not exist (and by definition can never exist) (1996, 19).

"El mundo entero al alcance de todos los españoles": The Whole World within Reach

> Lo que no se puede si quiere sobrevivir es intentar detener el reloj de la Historia en una hora determinada ... La política que no se renueva es política que se muere.
>
> What one cannot do if one wants to survive is try to stop the clock of History on a specific hour ... A politics that does not renew itself is a politics that dies.
>
> Excerpt from "Franco's End of Year Message" (New Year's Eve, 1961)

So far I have been discussing the ways in which the 1945 meta-newsreel, or "newsreel biography," captures, narrates, and reproduces an uncanny archival logic. I also have been suggesting that this logic, in turn, can be used to theorize a larger structural and topographical concern – namely, the nature of the archive in general and the nature of visibility in the film archive in particular. Building on the concept of the archive as a structure whose totality is not only visually but also practically impossible, and drawing on Derrida's notion of the archive as both a place of history and a site of production – that is, a place of memory, inscription, and writing – I propose the following: that the notion of the archive, presented in the 1945 NO-DO biography, is, drawing on Althusser's terminology, an ideological apparatus that operates through a matrix of visibility, temporality, and technology. In this way, it is as much a place of materiality and visibility (real images contained within real film canisters) as it is one of spectrality and invisibility (we never *really* see all of the images the newsreel tells us it possesses). As such, it is a place of presence and substance as much as one of absence and emptiness. Through the capture and subsequent representation of the film archive as a productive, authoritative, cumulative, and indeed totalitarian structure, the biography highlights those characteristics that create maximum accessibility, allowing the news to "reach all."

As I have been arguing, the introspective examination of the NO-DO's production underscores a logic of self-awareness that, on the surface, seems uncharacteristic of conventional fascist propaganda strategies. Why should the public see how the news is made or know how images are manipulated to construct a perfect, progressive portrait of the nation? Would this not seem "counter" to showing things as they "really are"? This uncharacteristic introspection (what I referred to earlier as the newsreel's "surgical gaze") functions as an uncanny inversion (we could say an incision of sorts), in which what we, as spectators, expect to see actually folds in on itself. The newsreel takes the familiar format of the NO-DO, inserts a "new way of seeing" how the state's technological aptitude brings information "within every Spaniard's reach," and then co-opts the very space of possible opposition and resistance that it purports to offer. In a sense, we do not have to "read" the newsreel since it "reads" and interprets itself. Put in different terms, we could say that the meta-newsreel incorporates binocular vision (a two-dimensional perspective in which both eyes see the same image) in order to construct stereoscopic vision (a three-dimensional perspective created by showing slightly different perspectives of the same image), which in turn co-opts spectatorial freedom through the negation of any valid interpretative space. Through the narrator's commentary, we are reminded that the biography ostensibly offers the possibility (for the first time!) to see, study, and scrutinize NO-DO's infrastructure, its use of editing and arrangement of images in documentary form to produce truth, and that it then turns again, robbing us of the very opportunity it provides. Likewise, the way the newsreel analyses the technology behind and labour put into the newsreel images (all of which, no doubt, generate a coherent, rational, ordered, and total image of Spain and Spanish national identity) is, I suggest, nothing more than a way of paying attention to the possibility of *altering history*. Thus, simply, what the 1945 newsreel biography establishes is an equation between the regime's cinematic production power and the machinery of ideology. Making the machine visible, in other words, is not only a way to write history, manufacture memory, and discipline subjects, but also, and perhaps more powerfully, a way to inscribe and fortify a rhetoric that aligns the means of production with the manipulation of reality and that uncannily links the manipulation of reality to truth.

At this point, we might be inclined to ask how the newsreel succeeds in binding viewers to its discursive system, given its attention to its own manipulative processes. I have already suggested one way – through the co-opting of spectatorial vision. But I would like to offer another possible answer to this question: through the presentation of the archive as a matrix of virtualities whose principal function is to show the mechanics of seeing and writing the news, the meta-newsreel conflates its own self-imaging (and imagining) with our seeing it as an all-powerful, all-present machine. A machine that, we are shown, assembles visual histories through innovative technological process, control, discipline, visibility, and objectivity. In this labyrinth of production, two sets of questions arise that directly implicate us as spectators, as viewers called upon to take an active part in the newsreel's life process, to witness it. The first set of questions involve points of access: How does one enter? Under what assumptions? Where does one begin? And, where does one end? The second set relate to structures of concern: How is the archive made? Why? How do *we* make it? For what purpose? How does it inscribe history onto culture? And how does it omit culture from its production of history? And all of these questions, as I have been attempting to address them, boil down to one: What does the newsreel's self-inquiry reveal about the unmaking and subsequent remaking of historical narrative?

It is no mystery that the newsreels were used for nationalist propaganda and therefore functioned as material instruments employed by the state ideological apparatus to propogate a uniquely Francoist image of the nation – an image that fit the model resurrected during the 1940s of unified national pride, emanating from the belief in Spain as free and progressive, and that promoted, among others, the slogan "la Patria, el Pan, y la Justicia" (the Nation, Bread, and Justice) during the infamous "years of hunger" (Tranche and Sánchez-Biosca 2005, 191). The very idea of Spain as a great imperial nation resonated in another famous slogan from the same era: "España: Una, Grande, Libre" (Spain: One,

Great, Free), which was cleverly embedded in the NO-DO, as we have seen, with images of the map placing Spain at the centre of the world, preceded by images of transportation indicating mobility and freedom within Spain's borders, as well as images of technological wealth concentrating on Spain's cinematic plentitude and prominence. Beyond propagating state political slogans, the newsreels operated, more generally, as the regime's primary means to centralize and control the audiovisual information that both entered into and exited from the public sphere. In this way, the NO-DOs also told visual narratives that went hand in hand with censorship laws and practices instituted under the dictatorship. Their main objective was twofold: to censor subversive, liberal ideals; and to preach Francoist ideology to the masses, "para silenciar toda discrepancia y edificar, al tiempo, un eco permanente sobre la bondad de sus acciones" (in order to silence all discrepancy and to raise, at the same time, a permanent echo over the goodness of their actions) (185). Historian and NO-DO expert Rafael Tranche discusses how the newsreels functioned as one of the main channels through which the regime proclaimed its doctrine, which included, as part of a laundry list of objectives, two main goals I wish to highlight here. The first was to buttress Francoism's totalitarian model of information and efficient communication for the explicit purpose of rationalizing and disseminating its ideology, which originated with "La Ley de Prensa de 22 de abril de 1938" (the Press and Printing Law of 22 April 1938).[16] Directly quoting part of the law in his analysis, Tranche states:

> esta misma Ley de Prensa sentará las bases de un modelo informativo totalitario (al que, obviamente, no escaparía NO DO) donde la prensa es tutelada para que se convierta en una especie de sistema aleccionador, de intermediario entre el Estado y la sociedad: "siendo la Prensa órgano decisivo en la formación de la cultura popular y, sobre todo, en la creación de la conciencia colectiva, no podía admitirse que el periodismo continuara viviendo al margen del Estado."

> This same Press Law would lay the foundations of an informative, totalitarian model (from which obviously NO-DO would not escape) where the press would be protector so that it could be converted into a kind of exemplary system, a mediator between the state and society: "the Press being the decisive organ in the formation of popular culture and, above all, in the creation of the collective consciousness, could not allow journalism to continue living at the margin of the State." (184)

Systems of mass communication were to take centre stage after the inauguration of the newsreels; the news, as such, was to be treated as the "decisive organ" (the essential rather than "prosthetic" component of the organic body), which first and foremost would establish an exclusive tie between the state and the people, between the machine of propaganda and the construction of modern Spanish culture. This, of course, was all for the express purpose of unifying Spain's national body, which had been broken by the Civil War. The second goal involved validating the state's natural origins by developing an official discourse – one that would infiltrate public life and the cultural consciousness of the nation through the camera, the screen, and, ultimately, the archive.[17] This official discourse, however, would come to be haunted by its own rhetorical and visual strategies. As we will soon see, those archival (and iconic) images of early 1940s Spain that permeated the public sphere through the NO-DO's information "assembly line," sewing images of everyday life in Franco's Spain to emblematic representations of Spain as a mighty imperial force, would be repeated endlessly despite strong political and cultural changes during the regime's tenure. Images such as the "asphyxiating presence" of Franco – *el Caudillo* – and his predecessor José Antonio Primo de Rivera as righteous leaders, and the recycled religious iconography invoking the regime's moralistic "civilizing Catholicism," remain virtually unchanged between NO-DO's different political and economic ages. In this regard, according to Tranche, the newsreels comprised

> [un] ejercicio retórico que vuelve a trazar una idílica conexión entre tradición y futuro, entre la recuperación del pasado y un confiado destino. Todas estas medidas fueron un importante caldo de cultivo para establecer los ingredientes de los que se nutriría en adelante la doctrina franquista. Con ellas se edificará además una especie de retórica oficial, que toma sus normas de composición del falangismo e impregnará, como decimos, todos los órdenes de la vida pública. Pero si hay un caso donde se plasman buena parte de los anhelos propagandísticos de esta primera etapa ese es el *Noticiario Español*.

> [a] rhetorical exercise that turns to sketch out an idyllic connection between tradition and the future, between recuperating the past and an entrusted destiny. All of these measures were an important cultural breeding ground for establishing the ingredients of all that would nourish Francoist doctrine in the future. With them, moreover, a kind of official rhetoric,

> takes norms from the composition of the Falange and impregnates, we could say, all orders of public life. But if there is a case where a good part of the propagandistic desires of this first era (of the Regime) are captured, that is the *Noticiario Español* (Spanish newsreel). (188)

The NO-DO thus was not only a crucial part of the state's machinery of propaganda but also a propaganda machine in and of itself – it was, in a quite literal sense, the eyes, mouth, and mind of the nation. It simultaneously sought to synthesize the Spanish nation as an organic, progressive, free, and mobile body and to combine its historical imperial power with the myth of its fascist heroism. (This is also evidenced in a number of newsreels from the 1940s depicting Franco's triumphant and glorious reign in Africa during the Morocco invasion and subsequent Spanish occupation.) So what we have throughout the newsreels is a double-interest: first, as Marta Bizcarrondo has pointed out, "las imágenes y las locuciones de los Noticiarios buscan ante todo imponer un sujeto colectivo, España, central e indiscutible, en torno al cual se articula jerárquicamente toda la sociedad española" (the images and narrations of the newsreels seek beyond anything else to impose a collective subject, Spain, central and indisputable, in which the whole of Spanish society is articulated hierarchically) (cited in Tranche and Sánchez-Biosca 2005, 198). And second, NO-DOs tried to inscribe cinematically those ideals that had founded the regime and "sanctified" Franco as supreme leader, whose project

> pretendía insertarse biológicamente en las entrañas de la tradición española, suprimir violentamente, arrasar, siglo y medio de historia y colocar en el inmenso vacío provocado por esa destrucción instituciones que devolvieron a un pueblo español acéfalo el sentido de la unidad, el orden y la disciplina que partidos y sindicatos habían trastocado.

> pretended to biologically insert itself in the bowels of Spanish tradition, to violently suppress, destroy, a century and a half of history and place in the immense void created by that destruction, institutions that returned a sense of unity, order, and discipline to the leaderless Spanish people, which political parties and unions had disturbed. (Santos Julia, cited in Tranche and Sánchez-Biosca 2005, 180)

Simply put, the newsreels were intended to fashion images into narratives that conflated the real world ("the years of hunger" in postwar

Spain, for example) with its ideal counterpart (images of a fascist Spain bringing justice with every loaf of bread, to give an official counter-example).[18] This amalgamation is most evident in the opening and closing headliners, which always featured the official newsreel logo, also known as *la cabecera* (or *genérico*). Each *cabecera* mixes the epic (i.e., the worldly, mythical, and fictional) with the national; this can be seen with the closing image of the eagle, a symbol of the regime and of the Falange, sitting on top of the world, which it has surely conquered and which is labelled, not coincidentally, "NO-DO" (figure 1.16). Streamered below the globe is the slogan "el mundo entero al alcance de todos los españoles" (the whole world within the reach of every Spaniard), echoing the 1945 newsreel's (and countless others') closing comments. In earlier newsreels, instead of this popular catchphrase for the regime's progress and omnipotence, there was an opening image of the eagle soaring through the sky against a backdrop image of the world, whose "estética arcaizante" (archaic aesthetic), according to Tranche,

> junto con su mensaje anacrónico (aunque en sintonía con la visión 'ucrónica' de la Historia que postulará el Régimen) la alejan del afán de contemporaneidad (esa voluntad de situarse permanentemente en el presente) propio del discurso informativo. Porque el universo que se evoca y recorre en la cabecera no es el mundo actual, sino el que idealmente querría el Régimen para petrificarse: el reinado de los Reyes Católicos.
>
> together with its anachronistic message (although in tune with the "uchronic" vision of History that the Regime would seek) shifts away from the desire of the very contemporaneity (that will to situate itself permanently in the present) of informative discourse. Because the universe that is evoked and traversed in the opening credit sequence is not the real world, but rather that which the Regime ideally wanted in order to petrify itself: the kingdom of the Catholic Kings. (Tranche and Sánchez-Biosca 2005, 97)

Though perhaps obvious, it is worth mentioning that in terms of NO-DO's crucial role in facilitating state propaganda, newsreels like the 1945 biography manipulated images to accompany constructed narratives that were not exactly in sync with the real world of a wounded, divided, and recovering postwar Spain. Take for example the enormous gap between the images shown in the 1945 newsreel and those of its literary counterpart from the same time period. The newsreel represents Spain as a technologically developed (even advanced) and

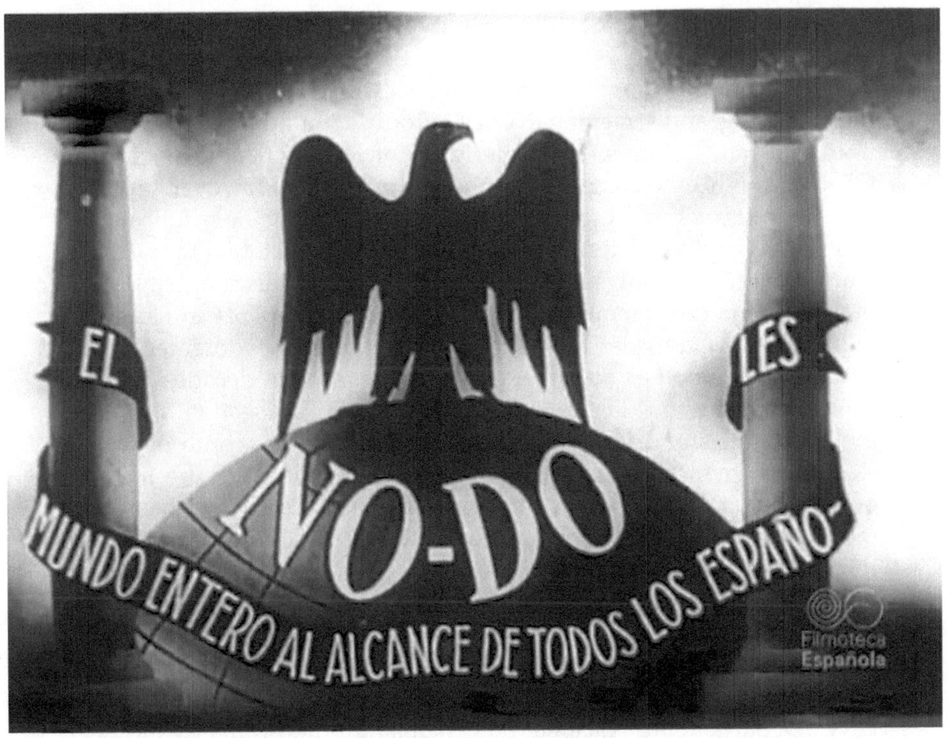

1.16 NO-DO logo. "El mundo entero al alcance de todos los españoles." (No. 105A, 1945) Copyright *Filmoteca nacional.*

independent nation that is graciously bestowing its knowledge on the world; by contrast, the literary representations of the era offer a contrary vision, that of a weak (in fact, crippled) and economically underdeveloped postwar society, as evidenced in canonical works such as Camilo José Cela's *La familia de Pascual Duarte* (1942), Carmen Laforet's critically acclaimed *Nada* (1944), which won the Primer Premio Nadal, and Dámaso Alonso's poetry collection *Hijos de la ira* (1944), to name only a few examples. The crucial though no doubt less obvious question has to do not only with *what* images were used to further Francoist doctrine, but also with *how* they were used and *why*. And that question brings us back to the archive, to the uncanny inversion of the newsreel biography's uncanny introspection, visual autopsy, and "self-dissection," as well as to the relationship between visibility and production, seeing and knowing.

The Editing Room: Assembling Sight

Over the course of nearly forty years (1943–81) of filming, documenting, archiving, and screening, NO-DO produced hundreds of newsreels from thousands of images, which its technicians meticulously crafted, whether behind the camera or in the editing room. However, archival records indicate that in those decades, NO-DO made only four newsreels in the style and format of a biography (or, autobiography, as it were) like the one analysed in the second section of this chapter. Rather than examine the remaining three newsreel biographies in close detail, I will now consider the relationship between the aforementioned 1945 text and another newsreel produced nearly two decades later, in 1968 (the fourth and last newsreel biography). This section discusses the continuities and variations between the two texts, both of which examine the newsreel's mode of production as a means to spotlight an ordered, disciplined, and quality-controlled Spain. A look at their common features and at the economic and political discontinuities between the dates of their production – 1945 and 1968 respectively – will open new territory for understanding how NO-DO simultaneously propagated and undercut its own authority.

If we consider Stanley Payne's analysis of the early years of Spain's "post-fascist era," an era he dates from 1945 to 1977 and in which the DNC (Departamento Nacional de Cinematografía) produced the 1945 "NO-DO por dentro," then those uncanny aspects of the meta-newsreel that I discussed earlier now appear more plausible and begin to crystallize. Payne characterizes those initial years of post-fascism as "the beginning of the cosmeticization of the Regime," a time when the regime took an unexpected interest in concealing what would eventually be remembered as its most complicated period of "defascistization" (1999, 407). The political turn the country took would come to be defined in large part by economic leniency and as such would involve Spain's opening itself up to more liberal economic policies. In fact, the first stage of "defascistizing" Spain would set the stage for the Opus Dei technocrats of the 1950s to come to power following the country's entrance into the United Nations (1955) and Franco's restructuring, two years later, of the regime's sixth government (1957).[19] Both events played a crucial role in widening Spain's economic aperture, a widening that resulted in a strong influx of foreign investment as well as foreign tourists.[20] The same liberalism that the regime had built up as the main ideological threat (both morally and politically) to national unification and to its own greatness was now, paradoxically, a fundamental component of Spain's political (post-fascist) reformation.[21]

Given this historical context, it becomes clear why the 1945 biography depicts the production of the news as an orderly, progressive, and innovative process of technology and assemblage. The main purpose of this was to mask the dismantling and disassembling of the regime's "fascist economics" (Payne 1999, 408). While largely descriptive in its narration, the newsreel is in effect "selling," through a kind of cosmetic veiling, Spain's resourcefulness and wealth of information. As we have seen, this newsreel in particular uses optical techniques such as the binocular screen and carefully crafted montages of transportation and machinery to detail its own labour and, I would argue, its own value as a system that always *produces in excess* of itself. The objective seems fairly clear: not only for Spanish audiences to "buy in" by seeing and believing these images as truths, but also for the rest of the world to which this news is being exported to "buy in" as well. Who, after all, was going to question the NO-DO's harnessing of Francoist national ideology when the newsreel itself treated that very topic as an object of its own inquiry, prominently and publicly displaying it for all to see? Newsreel production, then, appears as labour-intensive, and its end result appears seamless and masterful; all of this serves to disguise a regime that is using the medium of film to co-opt a space of opposition and that has surrendered (without declaring as much) to the very opposition it had constructed during and immediately after the Civil War.

By 1959, the year that President Dwight Eisenhower visited Spain to re-establish its diplomatic ties with the United States and to announce an economic stabilization plan, Spain's entrance into the 1960s was a virtual certainty.[22] But even while the country was opening its doors to foreign influences, including Western democracy and economic liberalism, the dictator maintained a strong discursive stance against radical political changes, especially those that would undermine the regime's political doctrine. In October 1961, in a speech to the National Council of the Movement to celebrate his twenty-fifth year in power, Franco declared that

> the great weakness of modern States lies in their lack of doctrinal content, in having renounced a firm concept of man, life, and history. The major error of liberalism is its negation of any permanent category of truth – its absolute and radical relativism – an error that, in a different form, was

> apparent in those other European currents [of Fascism and Nazism] that made "action" their only demand and the supreme norm of their conduct ... When the juridical order does not proceed from a system of principles, ideas, and values recognized as superior and prior to the State, it ends in an omnipresent juridical voluntarism, whether its primary organ be the so-called majority, purely numerical and inorganically expressed, or the supreme organs of power. (cited in Payne 1999, 431)

The same fascist discourse resorted to in the early 1940s is being recycled here, some twenty years later. Franco is reaffirming what we already know from the 1945 newsreel – that the state as the supreme "organ" of power uses action and discipline to arrive at totality and truth. If looking inside the archive in 1945 becomes synonymous with both assembling the underlying principles of Franco's autarchic system (a national policy of isolation and self-subsistence based on "looking inward") and concealing the disorder and impracticalities of fascist politics (the "cosmetic" approach), then what are we to make of the 1968 newsreel biography (1304B), which is haunted to some degree by the same rhetoric, albeit an increasingly and explicitly anachronistic one? While it may seem at first glance that this later NO-DO's biographical inquiry into the archive and newsreel production is a mere replica of its 1945 precursor, I argue here that it does in fact reveal small yet striking differences that merit interpretation and critical analysis.

The text opens with the facts: "Nacimos hace veinticinco años. NO-DO apareció en las pantallas españolas en enero de 1943" (We were born twenty-five years ago. NO-DO appeared on Spanish screens in January of 1943). After briefly addressing the purpose of the biography, the narrator concisely lays out NO-DO's hierarchy of production:

> Por una vez, nos vamos a permitir explicar a Uds. cómo trabajamos. [*música*] El director recibe al jefe de producción y pasa a comunicarle las noticias del día. Ambos seleccionan las más importantes y acto seguido se pasa aviso a nuestros operadores. Rápidamente, éstos se disponen a efectuar las órdenes recibidas. En uno de nuestros vehículos salen dispuestos a cazar la información, porque la verdad es que en muchas ocasiones hay que atraparla poco menos que por los pelos.

> For once, we are going to allow ourselves to explain to you how we work. [*music*] The director meets with the head of production and informs him of the day's news. Both select the most important news and immediately

> afterwards they communicate this with a note to our cameramen. Quickly, they prepare to carry out their orders. In one of our vehicles they set out determined to hunt information, because the truth is that on many occasions one has to catch the news before it slips away.[23]

The former hypervisibility and multidirectionality of the 1945 newsreel now translates into a description of the chain of command and control that governs all news production and efficiency (figure 1.17). Moreover, what the earlier text considered dangerous and risky work is now defined as a calculated "hunt" for information, invoking strong overtones of masculine determination, will, and aggression. No longer is the news something to be captured by the all-seeing eye of the camera; now it is a specific target of the cameramen's fierce and swift pursuit. As the optical illusions and montage of images of technological devices are swapped out here for images of young, valiant operators, we are reminded by the narrator that the omnipresence of NO-DO is quantifiable:

> NO-DO cuenta con dieciséis operadores distribuidos entre Madrid y Barcelona, mas con correspondientes en Alicante, Baleares, Canarias, Coruña, Lugo, Málaga, San Sebastián, Sevilla, y Valencia. Aquí les tenemos en plena acción por toda la geografía española. [*música*]

> NO-DO counts on sixteen cameramen stationed between Madrid and Barcelona, and with correspondents in Alicante, Baleares, Canarias, Coruña, Lugo, Málaga, San Sebastián, Sevilla, and Valencia. Here we have them in action throughout all of Spain's geographical terrain. [*music*]

Before, we were shown both a long shot and a close-up of a map of Spain; now, the focus is on specifying exact locations and accounting for the precise number of cameramen stationed throughout distinct (and again quantifiable) cities. The visual mapping of NO-DO's vast terrain has turned into a numerical conquest that shifts the focal point from a total image of the nation to the various parts that make up the whole. Directionality and totality, while still important characteristics of the newsreel, give way to multiplicity and particularity; likewise, geographical presence replaces the notion of visibility along with the importance of surveying unexplored territory, such that being in several different places removes the emphasis from "seeing all things" and places it on ubiquity – on "being everywhere" at all times.

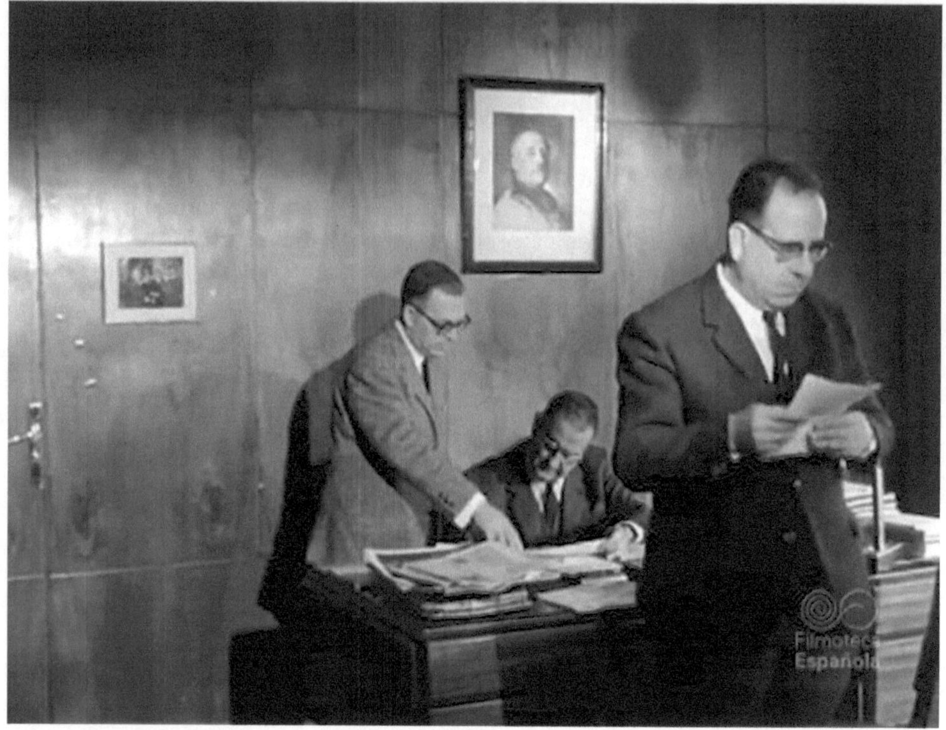

1.17 Inside NO-DO. Chain of command and control for news production. (No. 1304B, 1968) Copyright *Filmoteca nacional.*

The 1968 newsreel biography nuances the shift from optics to operational conquest and from studying the map to occupying specific locations; what remains familiar is the narration's detailed explanation of the editing, assemblage, and montage process. This is, curiously, exactly where the text *could* highlight new NO-DO technology or improvements in film development – that is, the place where it *could* distance itself from its 1945 predecessor, highlighting its cultural advances and technological achievements. Instead, it employs images of numerous technicians working side by side in the editing room and presents us with a repetition, almost verbatim, of the 1945 text:

> Una vez rodada la noticia, se lleva al laboratorio donde se procede a su revelado y depositivado. [*música*] El movio listo que viene a ser como un

> borrador de trabajo vuelve a NO-DO. Hay que seleccionar los planos y escoger los más expresivos para montarlos y dar forma al montaje. [*música/editar*] En la truca, se realizan los títulos y los efectos especiales. Y concluido el montaje de positivado, se escriben los comentarios, cuidándole ajustar los textos a la imagen. Después, son puestos en limpio a máquina. Simultáneamente, hay que preocuparse en preparar y ajustar las bandas sonoras correspondientes a música y efectos. Y, casi simultáneamente también (*porque NO-DO trabaja contra reloj*), hay que cortar y empalmar los negativos de acuerdo con el copio-depositivo que viene a ser el patrón básico.

> Once the news is filmed, it is brought to the laboratory where it proceeds to be developed and stored. [*music*] The moviola is ready and will be a working draft that turns into the NO-DO. The shots need to be selected and the most expressive chosen for assemblage and to give form to the montage. [*music/images of editing process*] In the editing room, the titles and special effects are made. And when the editing and mounting of the print is done, the commentaries are written, being careful to adjust the text to the image. Afterwards, a clean copy is written by typewriter. Simultaneously, preparing and adjusting the soundtracks needs to be taken care of so that they are in sync with the music and effects. And, almost at the same time too (*because NO-DO works against the clock*), cutting and splicing the negatives needs to be done corresponding to the stored copy that becomes the basic pattern. (my emphasis)

A crucial and perhaps intriguing difference is that rather than images that evoke speed and acceleration (remember the newsreels' earlier use of any number of shots of trains racing across the landscape with the NO-DO logo superimposed on them), now the narrator reports to the public that time is not an asset but rather an always pressing factor – echoed in the parenthetical note "because NO-DO works against the clock." As if directly anticipating the outdated features on which both the meta-newsreel and the regime continue to capitalize, this strange narrative insertion calls attention ironically to the very change taking place on screen as well as behind it – that is, from NO-DO as an ideological tool to NO-DO as a temporalized rhetorical one (Tranche and Sánchez-Biosca 2005, 195).

At this point, it would be a gross oversimplification to say that the 1968 newsreel functions as a mere reflection of the politics and economics of the decade, which I believe to be true but is perhaps too obvious. While I would not disagree that this visual text marks "changes of the

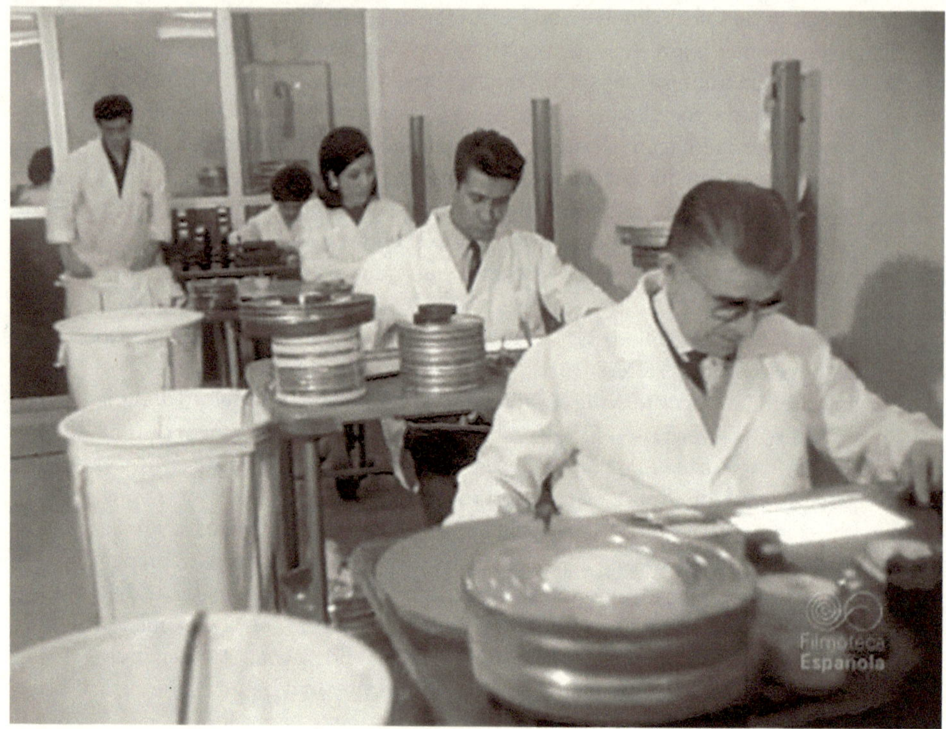

1.18 In the editing room, technicians hunt for the news too. "NO-DO works against the clock." (No. 1304B, 1968) Copyright *Filmoteca nacional.*

times" (noted also in its trendy music and stylishly dressed operators), I think what can be gained from evaluating its rhetoric both visually and discursively is a deeper understanding of how its uncanny inversion repeats and recycles itself – that is, how it registers a rhetorical haunting. Consider, for example, the following passage from a 1943 issue of the Spanish film magazine *Primer Plano*, in which the author defines the goal of modern Spanish cinema in terms of its indoctrinating power, which is fully supported by and completely in line with the regime's political agenda:

> Nuestro cine actual debe estar en juego con la formación de la conciencia nacional. Ha de recogerla en las manifestaciones – poderosas y vitales – del Estado nuevo y en el exponente de todas sus actividades y,

simultáneamente, debe informar esta conciencia llegando a todos los espectadores con la eficacia que tiene la pantalla, en el reflejo del mosaico de valores gráficos, espirituales y materiales que encierra España. Debe ser información y debe ser formación. Debe ser noticia y debe ser documento.

Our cinema today should be involved in the formation of national consciousness. Having to collect [it] from manifestations – powerful and vital – of the new State and from the example of all its activities, simultaneously, it should inform this consciousness, reaching every spectator with the efficiency that the screen brings, in the reflection of a variety of graphic, spiritual, and material values that Spain encompasses. It should be information and it should be formation. It should be news and it should be a document. (anonymous source, cited in Tranche and Sánchez-Biosca 2005, 194)

Reflecting the regime's characterization of the media and of all forms of news communication as its "decisive organ," this commentary has no qualms about overstating the state's ideological role not only in cinematic production but also in the formation of a national consciousness. Returning to the 1968 newsreel for a moment, the sharp rift between image and text cannot be overstated either. While the narration does reflect the "mosaic of graphic values" – spiritual and material – that encompass Spain, it also remains stuck in the proverbial hinges of early Francoist discourse, a discourse that in the context of the late 1960s does not convey the state's political project as flawlessly as it may have done twenty-five years prior. In other words, the 1968 text presents a kind of double-bind. On the one hand, we see images and listen to descriptions that are all too similar to those of the previous newsreel biography, which by now is over two decades old. On the other, the text produces new perspectives on the country's economic and political evolution, as well as on its increasingly liberal "conciencia nacional" (with its focus on quantification, breadth, and expansionary power). It offers images of a production capacity that are consistent with the political and economic climate of the 1960s while providing textual analysis that is repetitive and dissonant at best, inconsistent and untimely at worst. The "pre-emptive rhetoric" of the 1945 newreel – the way it "claims" that newsreels are constructed before viewers can see it for themselves – has turned into a "haunted rhetoric" in the 1968 text. The repetition of discourse is borrowed and belated; it has no logical purpose except to atemporalize the very idea of Spain's production power

– that is, the power to halt and at the same time paradoxically set into motion its machinery. In short, we see Spain producing – indeed reproducing – the same means, methods, techniques, control, discipline, and ideological coercion. But in producing the same discourse, the NO-DO produces *nothing* new; instead, in 1968, it is simply producing *more* of it. It accumulates to the point of excess. The once cosmetic approach (recalling again the optical illusion of the binoculars) now adheres to a capitalist model (quantifying production and "scoring" news footage). The narrator continues:

> Aquí se archivan todos los NO-DOs y multitud de noticias extranjeras. Editamos cada semana cuatro noticiarios – dos para España, uno para Portugal, otro para Hispano-América – además de imágenes y de otras producciones especiales. Concretaremos afirmando que en estos veinticinco años hemos producido dos millones tres cientos mil metros de informaciones y documentales. Nuestro servicio del intercambio asegura la difusión de las realidades españolas por todo el mundo.

> Here all the NO-DOs as well as the multitude of foreign newsreels are archived. We edit four newsreels each week – two for Spain, one for Portugal, another for Latin America – apart from images (another subset of NO-DO production) and other special productions. We will conclude [by] affirming that in these twenty-five years we have produced 2,300,000 metres of information and documentaries. Our exchange service ensures the distribution of Spanish realities throughout the world.

The images of machinery have been exchanged for ones of accumulation. The close-up montage of film canisters piling up to the beat of a drum has been replaced by no less than seven different shots of the archive's totality that show its shelves overflowing with canisters. The virtual buying (formerly "co-opting") of the spectator's vision has been converted into the virtual sale of hand-selected images. The principal tenets of the NO-DO's mechanics of production are still present – visibility, objectivity, totality, labour, truth – but the approach is less panoptic and more overtly capitalist. Another crucial difference is encountered at the end of the newsreel. The 1968 text concludes not with the mythic image of a heroic Franco inscribing himself on the nation's wealth of information, but rather with the cumulative amount and precise quantification of actual newsreel footage – we are told the *exact* amount, "2,300,000 metres," that NO-DO has produced over the past twenty-five years.[24] Instead of the map of Spain that had indicated the regime's

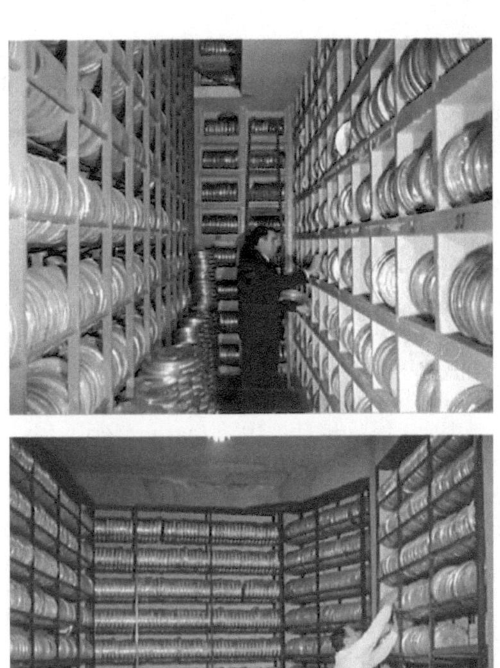

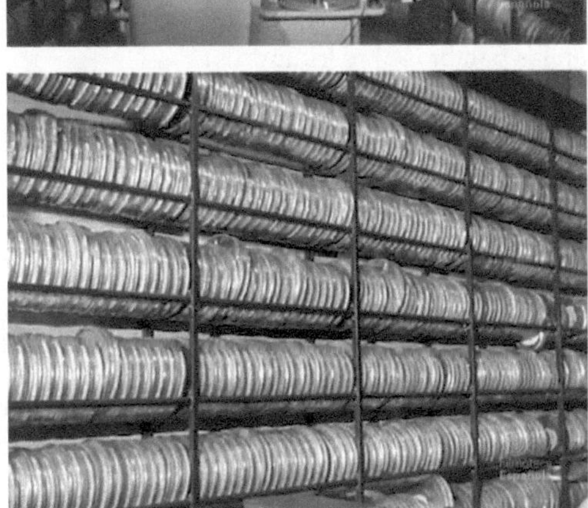

1.19, 1.20, and 1.21 The viewer is invited into the archive to see NO-DO's power of accumulation. Here the totality of news captured is stored, catalogued, and measured. (No. 1304B, 1968) Copyright *Filmoteca nacional.*

global reach by visualizing the newsreels' ability to branch out all over the world, we are provided with metrics – that is, with the specific length of total footage captured. By calculating in metres rather than reels, the NO-DO quantifies the distance of that "branching out" in spatial rather than temporal terms. Finally, the hyper-remembering of the 1945 reel now turns into an exercise in hyper-forgetting in the sense that numbers replace actual events and the news privileges statistics over substance, measurable form over content. In this way, the previous message that "the archive contains a reality" has morphed into "the archive contains a fixed number of reels." Rhetorically and visually, this registers as a shift from the archive's ability to totalize through capture to its capacity to be exportable and sellable. The newsreel's concluding statement sums it up best. Where the 1945 text ended with the resounding albeit introspective statement "el mundo entero al alcance de todos los españoles" (the whole world within reach of every Spaniard), the 1968 text boldly affirms the inverse: "la difusión de las realidades españolas por todo el mundo" (the dissemination of Spanish realities throughout the whole world).[25] This powerful statement endorses the exporting of Spanish reality (here, "realities" in the plural) around the globe – at once upholding the regime's ideological stance and actively rewriting it.

NO-DO as Spectacle: Ghostly Landscapes and the Birth of Spectrality

Pero ¿qué pueden las palabras ante los muros?
¿Qué es la oratoria ante estas gloriosas cicatrices?

But, what can words do before the walls?
What is oratory before these glorious scars?

Francisco Franco before the ruins at the Simancas Barracks

Restaurar una falsificación, una apariencia. Por eso nuestra misión y nuestro orden era no la de restaurar sino la de instaurar, la de crear, la de fundar, asumiendo la sustancia viva y válida de la tradición y ordenando su instrumentación de acuerdo con las necesidades y con los imperativos de nuestros tiempos.

To restore a falsification, an appearance. For this reason our mission and our order was not to restore but rather to install, to create, to establish, assuming the real and valid substance of tradition and ordering its instrumentation in accordance with the necessities and the imperatives of our times.

Francisco Franco, New Year's Eve Address, 1961

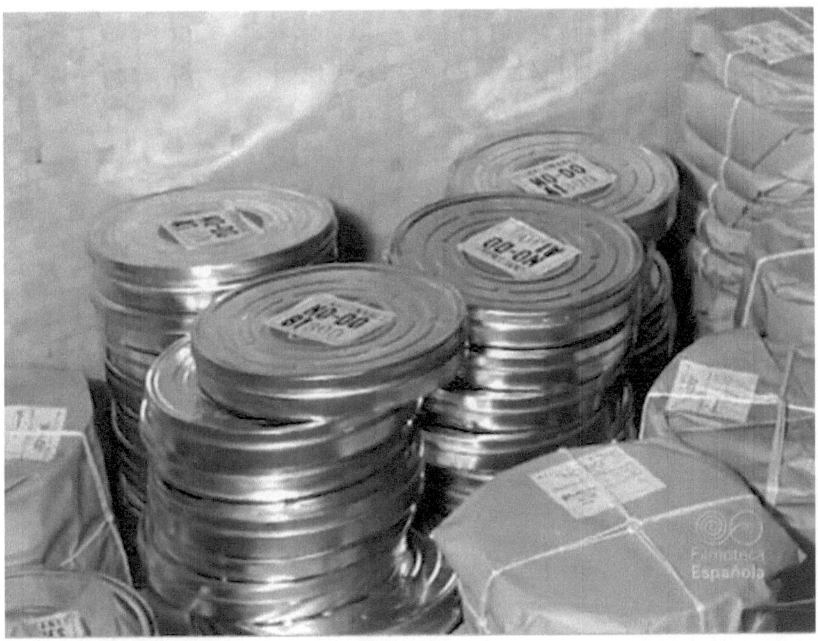

1.22 NO-DO reels ready for exportation. (No. 1304B, 1968) Copyright *Filmoteca nacional.*

> The spectacle creates an eternal present of immediate expectation: memory ceases to be necessary or desirable. With the loss of memory the continuities of meaning and judgment are also lost on us. The camera relieves us of the burden of memory. It surveys us like God, and it surveys for us. Yet no other god has been so cynical, for the camera records in order to forget.
>
> *About Looking* (Berger 1991, 59)

I close this chapter with a discussion of the relationship between news reels and spectacle, a discussion that to date has been given curiously little attention in scholarship on NO-DO as an institution, an industry, and a genre of propaganda. If the camera, and by extension the screen, the newsreel, and the archive, became ideological apparatuses, optical mechanisms employed under Francoism to indoctrinate and discipline subjects by conflating real with imaginary experiences, then what did the newsreel biographies (i.e., the reproduction of their production) accomplish as spectacle? Did they *perform* as spectacles? Did they operate

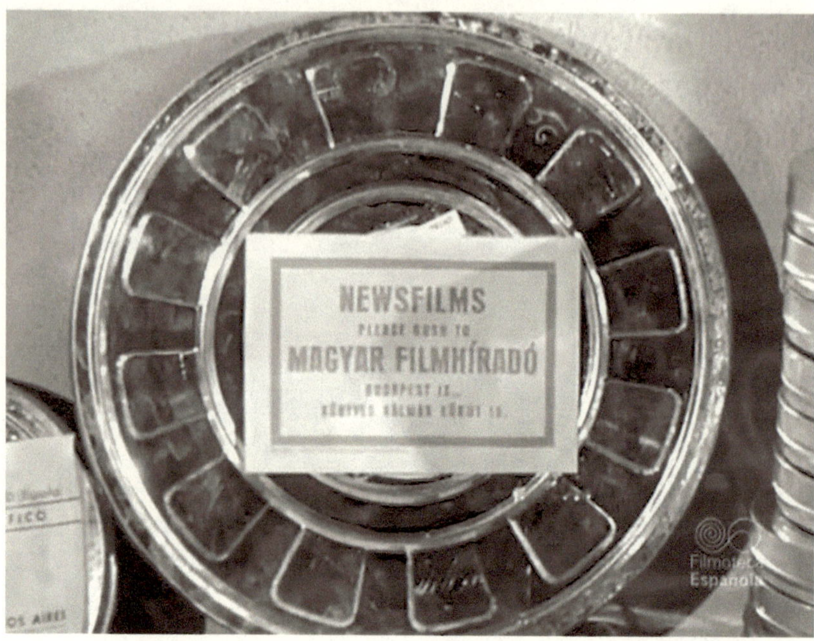

1.23 "La difusión de las realidades españolas por todo el mundo." (No. 1304B, 1968) Copyright *Filmoteca nacional.*

in what Guy Debord called "spectacular time" – which is to say, time produced for mere consumption rather than contemplation?[26] Might we consider them, moreover, to be spectacles in themselves? Similarly, how might spectacles under Francoism (in forms other than the newsreels – mass celebrations, stadium rallies, syndicalist demonstrations, etc.) also have acted as optical mechanisms, or tools for expanding and inflating images of the masses by assembling individual subjects into ordered accumulations of shapes and patterns, creating what Siegfried Kracauer called a "mass ornament"? More specifically, given NO-DO's concern with documenting its own totality and assemblage, how can we rethink its "biographical approach" as one that unveiled the relationship between spectacle and state machinery under the dictatorship? To what extent did the newsreels capture (in the twin sense of "filming" and "depicting" or "representing") the relationship between filming spectacle and making the machine (or reproducing the machine, as is the case in the meta-newsreels)? More intriguing for the purposes of this study, what do these newsreels reveal about the relationship between spectacle and *spectrality* – a question I will return to at the end of this chapter. How are we to theorize the production value of this machine by examining via the newsreels the relationship between the visible and the invisible, or that mechanically reproduced ideology that filters into the present, allowing history's ghosts, ruins, and scars to go virtually unseen? And lastly, what role did the fascist spectacle play in Spain's proverbial theatre of ideology and culture of consumerism, in which the paradoxical yet inevitable marriage between traditional political values and modern economic principles was thoroughly scripted out in the double-sense of being both "written" and "omitted"?

Though the aforementioned questions are many, it is not entirely impossible to sketch out some answers here. At least, it is not entirely impossible to pose them and to begin thinking about how these relationships shaped politics in Spain – the rapidly increasing depoliticization of fascism under Franco towards the end of the 1950s and into the early 1960s, the injection of commodity and consumer culture into the country's new market economy, and, above all, the contradictions of a dictatorship that in its waning years privileged both autarchy and pluralism, both totalitarianism and liberal democracy, both fascist economics and capitalism. In a sense, the questions listed above boil down to two. First, in what sense did the newsreels constitute spectacle? And second, how can spectacle itself (such as those epic stadium, commemorative, and anniversary events filmed by NO-DO) be read as texts, or as textual evidence attesting to the relationship between an always hidden image of Spain's fragile and fragmented social reality, and an accessible and strongly overexposed image of its unity and strength? In an attempt to synthesize the role of fascist spectacle with my own analysis of the newsreels, I offer a concise overview of how spectacle – both as a theoretical point and as a concrete object of study – fits in to the production of history as visible in the NO-DOs.

In his seminal work *Lenin and Philosophy*, Althusser posits that a system of authority "never works only by force, by sheer violence; instead, it works through ideology, through some meaningful procedure" (Ricoeur 1994, 69). And in defining ideology, Althusser concludes that it is first and foremost a system of representations always based in material existence.[27] Ideology always manifests itself in and through material culture and operates through the framework of an apparatus. In this way – through apparatuses – ideology creates and sustains its own reality: "the reality of the illusory," which both transcends time (historical time) and distorts the subject's relation to the real conditions under which he exists (60). Althusser states:

> All ideology represents in its necessarily imaginary distortion not the existing relationships of production (and the other relationships that derive from them), but above all the (imaginary) relationship of individuals to the relations of production and the relations that derive from them. What is represented in ideology is therefore not the system of the real relations which govern existence of individuals, but the imaginary relation of those individuals to the real relations in which they live. (Althusser 1970, 111, cited in Ricoeur 1994, 155)

In a critical synopsis of Althusser's theory, Paul Ricoeur beautifully summarizes this powerful yet somewhat dizzying passage by asserting that ideology operates on a system of images in which "the so-called real causes [of our conditions of existence] never appear as such ... but always under a symbolic mode" (1994, 61). Guy Debord takes this idea one step further, arguing that the most powerful material manifestation of ideology as a "system of representation" operating under a symbolic mode occurs in the spectacle. In his pioneering work *Society of the Spectacle,* Debord contends that spectacle is "the materialization of ideology brought about by the concrete success of an autonomised system of economic production – which virtually identifies social reality with an ideology that has remoulded all reality in its own image" (2005, 116). The place where ideology and illusion meet, for Debord, is in fact in the spectacle itself, which always bears the uncanny burden of making spectral – that is, both emulating and obscuring, making visible and invisible – the mode of production under which it arises. As such, the spectacle is the visual reflection of the ruling economic order, but portrayed through a "pseudo world" that despite all appearances is nothing but illusion; the spectacle is thus both representation and reality, both image and mediation, both fiction and fact – an apt description that could not better illustrate the NO-DO. Consider also the following contention offered by Debord:

> The spectacle presents itself as a vast inaccessible reality that can never be questioned. Its sole message is: "What appears is good; what is good appears." *The passive acceptance it demands is already effectively imposed by its monopoly of appearances, its manner of appearing without allowing any reply.* (9–10, my emphasis)

This is precisely the main strategy of NO-DOs' discourse; more specifically, it is the underlying objective of the 1945 and 1968 newsreel biographies – to offer the *appearance* of a detailed inquiry into their composition and production by means of a pre-emptive rhetoric that eventually turns into a rhetoric of haunting, one that "can never be questioned" since the newsreel supposedly interrogates itself and thereby co-opts any possible space of opposition or public investigation through its imposed "manner of appearing without allowing any reply." Visually, it asserts itself as a "monopoly of appearances" that simultaneously subsists by and maintains Francoist ideology. The newsreels offer an illusion – a total image of Spain comprised of fragmented, isolated images strung together through a selective and labour-intensive editing process. In other words, the NO-DO operates in exactly the same way as a spectacle: it simulates its own production power through an abundance of filmed material (which afterwards is stored away safely in the archive for future use and reuse), then fashions that material into captivating images, compelling the viewer to see a powerful, all-knowing information machine. Each newsreel, like the spectacle, "is *capital* accumulated to the point that it becomes images" (Debord 2005, 17). In sum, the NO-DO is the place where ideology and spectacle meet; it acts as both ideological apparatus and system of spectacular imaging. Of course, the newsreel biographies take spectacle to a whole new level – they spectacularize themselves and in doing so walk the fine line between granting and denying the spectator access to the "real" relations of production. What is more, drawing on Althusser's argument, the meta-newsreels in fact *do* show those "real relations" of production (remember that they supposedly give us access to the inside: we enter and see the editing room). But they employ spectacular optical tactics to create an illusory relationship between the individual spectator and that system of production. The example of binocular vision illustrates this point well: a fixed perspective is imposed on the viewer, instilling in him a sense of powerlessness yet simultaneously fostering a perceived sense of complete authority and control.

At this point, we can identify three modes of spectacle with the NO-DOs. First, the newsreels themselves operate as spectacle by collecting individual images of important national events and grouping them together to form a contrived portrait of the nation, which is then presented to Spanish audiences weekly, monthly, and yearly. Second, through a detailed yet uncanny process of self-examination and dissection, the newsreels convert themselves into spectacles by offering a series of biographies that purport to study their own production. And third, the newsreels capture certain events that are commonly known *as* spectacles; this amounts to yet another stratum of mirroring and uncanny self-reflection in the Francoist propaganda machine, one to which I now turn. For if we assume that the newsreels operate *as* spectacle, then their filming *of* spectacle stages a sort of mimicry – a kind of meta-spectacle in which one form of imaging production (a weekly newsreel) presents and imitates another form of imaging production (a commemorative parade, military exercises, or the exhumation of the previous dictator, José Antonio Primo de Rivera, to give only a few examples).

If the NO-DOs' form emulates and therefore constitutes spectacle, then what are we to make of spectacles that are filmed and thus form part of the newsreels' content? Here I turn to another newsreel to consider this question: the 1968 Anniversary Documentary, which, like the newsreel biographies, offers a specific kind of inward gaze. On the surface, this special-edition NO-DO presents nothing new. Stringing together highlights from Spain's "twenty-five years of peace with Franco," the documentary traces various spectacles, starting with a speech delivered by the dictator in 1943 in front of a massive public gathering of supporters, who listen attentively to his discourse on the reconstruction of the nation under three main tenets: "Orden, Dios, y la Justicia" (Order, God, and Justice). The documentary continues with an impressive range of images of the most important and noteworthy events from each year leading up to 1968 – images of Franco's benevolence and concern for Spanish culture, his cultivation and practice of tradition, his authority and command, his life as leader, *Generalísimo, Caudillo,* father, and grandfather. All of this serves to spotlight not only his political supremacy but also, significantly, his humanity. The spectator is being presented with a series of spectacles that frame Franco as a peaceful, caring, and attentive leader, from his 1945 concern for the protection and maintenance of the Real Academia Española's collection, in which he is filmed surrounded by books in its library, to his emotional reaction to the 1947 "Ley de Sucesión," to his familial bliss at his daughter's wedding in 1950, to the no less than six mass-scale spectacles performed in his honour, including the epic 1958 "Mundo de Trabajo" syndicalist event at the San Bernabéu stadium, in which an entire football field is covered in mechanically synchronized rows and circles of hundreds of men performing gymnastics and eventually forming themselves into a giant human tower.

But perhaps the most curious (and definitely the most absurd) example of spectacle that I have come across is the documentary's featured highlight from 1963. It shows Franco as a family man in what the narrator refers to as an intimate setting: *El Caudillo* taking part in "his favourite sport with his grandchildren." What starts out as a simple, innocuous family outing – a day of fishing – quickly and violently turns into a spectacle of whale watching in which the NO-DO just happens to catch the frail and aging Franco in a historic moment as he catches a giant sea mammal. In a feat of near Melvillian proportions, we see what appears to be the mechanical harpooning but sadly turns out to be the merciless and horrific machine-gunning of a whale.[28] Needless to say, the whale is killed, and as it is dying in the ocean, the camera records several different shots (striking long shots and painful, claustrophobic close-ups) of the animal's blowhole closing and opening as it gasps for air. We then see an image of the whale laid ashore (on the dock) with Franco standing beside it – suggesting that the small dictator is as powerful and aggressive as he had appeared humble and gentle only moments earlier on deck while playing with his grandchildren. Arguably, no newsreel image captures the *essence* of spectacle under Francoism better than this one, which measures the event with one very impressive detail: the whale weighs "forty tons." The whale, literally, is a spectacular catch, but besides this, the event exemplifies what spectacle does best – it creates an illusory thread, one that connects Franco not only to this large beast but also to a feat of conquest that can in turn be commodified, quantified (as the newsreel footage was), and appear larger than life.[29] The suggestion is quite clear: despite all impracticalities, Franco's appearance is all that matters, and precisely *because* it matters, it appears to us, in the form of a spectacular victory.

The NO-DO documentary shifts almost without transition to the 1964 highlight event: a military parade celebrating "La Victoria." Of course, the lack of transition may in fact be the point. The text slides from one year to the next and sews the previous family fishing expedition to a colossal commemorative ceremony all too common under Francoism in the 1960s. As the images glide between monumentalizing aerial shots of the event and closer, ground-level shots, the audience is placed in the same position as the parade's spectators, watching thousands of jeeps, tanks, and foot soldiers pass by, each representing different branches of the military. Planes, helicopters, and even knights on horseback proceed down El Paseo del Generalísimo Franco in Madrid (today known

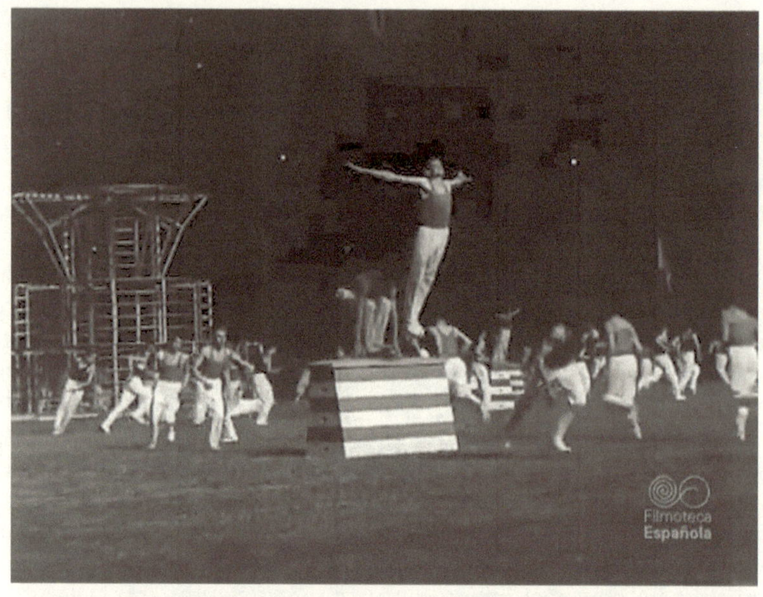

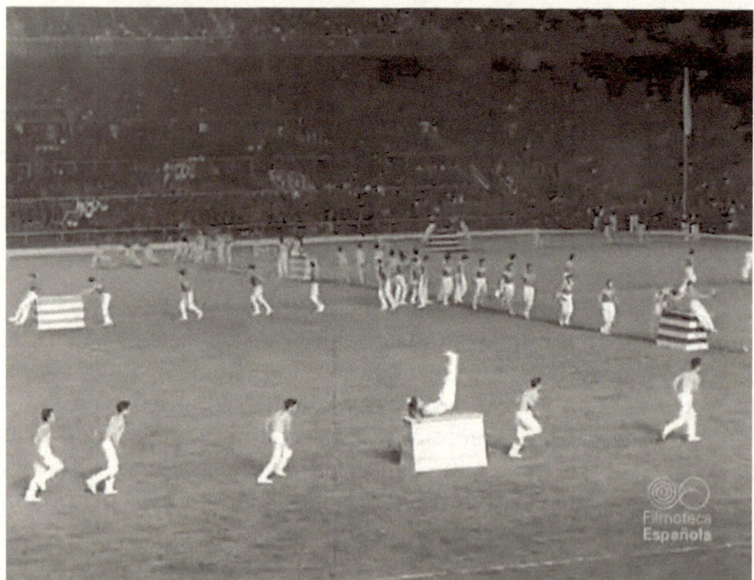

1.24, 1.25, 1.26, and 1.27 (above and facing) "Mundo de Trabajo." Syndicalist spectacle at the San Bernabéu stadium. Male workers perform choreographed

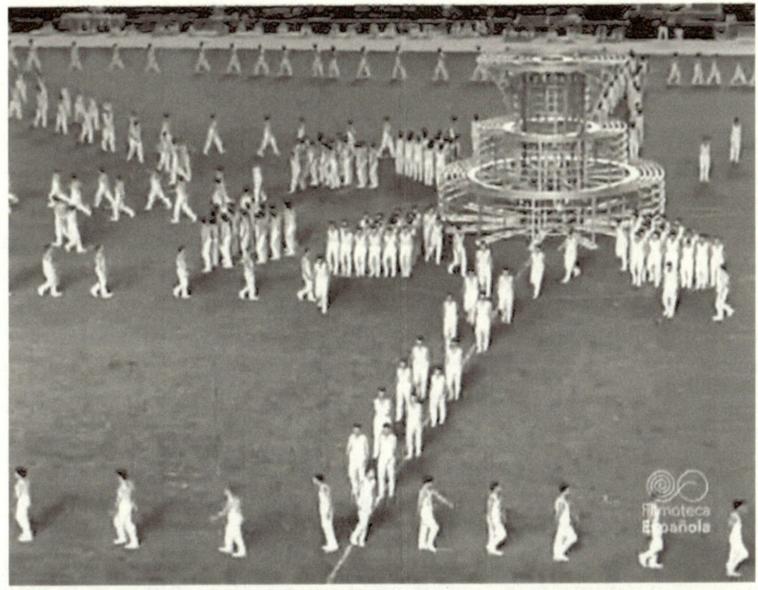

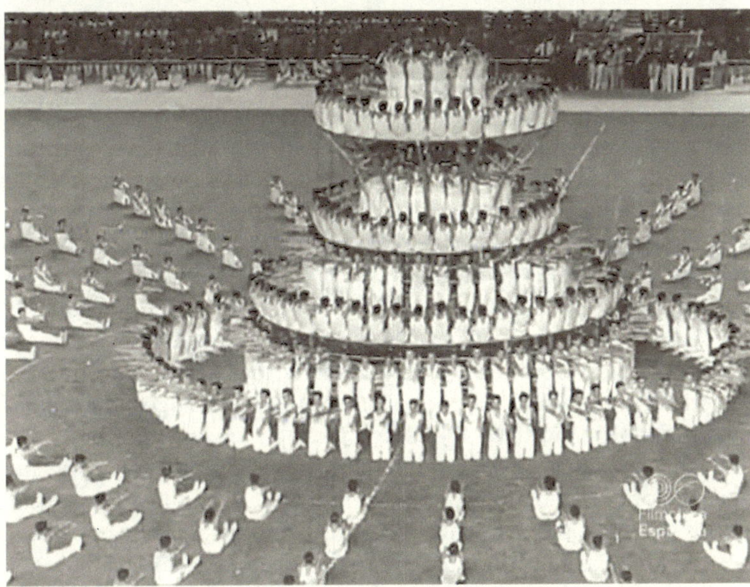

calisthentics and eventually assemble themselves into a giant human tower. (No. 801A, 1958) Copyright *Filmoteca nacional.*

as La Castellana) in honour of the peace and progress that Franco has brought to a formerly chaotic and "unruly" Spain. The various phases of the parade are meant to suggest to the viewer that it was Francoism that ended the destructive anarchy in 1939 and that is responsible for today's order and unity. In this nearly three-hour commemorative ceremony, it is Franco who dominates all aspects of the nation, in all venues – land, sea, and sky – in both the present (marked by parading the latest military tanks and weaponry) and the imperial past (most notably, with the fully armoured knights evoking the Crusades). In Tranche's words, this use of spectacular show was intended to "asimilar e identificar el franquismo como una consecuencia lógica de los tiempos imperiales" (assimilate and identify Francoism as the logical consequence of the imperial past) (Tranche and Sánchez-Biosca 2005, 185). Francoism staged and performed itself as a "logical consequence" (or rightful successor) of its historical imperial power; the newsreels capitalized on this spectacular image of the nation and, to a great degree, fossilized it in almost every aspect of public and private life under the dictatorship.

From showing the masses spectacular images to showing the masses *as* a crystallized image of spectacle, the newsreels captured yet another vital aspect of Francoism's ordered, disciplined, and rational organism: the making of the masses into a machine. From the impossibly absurd (killing the whale) to the intoxicatingly hypnotic (perfectly choreographed stadium calisthenics and orderly military exercises), and everywhere in between, the NO-DOs filmed spectacles to fix the public eye not only on Franco but also on itself; this allowed the public to watch itself being fashioned into not only cameramen or editing room technicians but also human assembly lines that, all too like the newsreel biographies, reproduced an image of their own self-manufacture. The aforementioned 1968 commemorative event held at the Bernabéu stadium offers the pre-eminent example of this machinery at work – that is, the mechanical operation of engineering the masses into flawlessly executed constellations, abstractions, and ghostly images. Based on the regime's idea that the state-sponsored trade unions should replicate the nature and structure of the nation's "organic democracy," spectacles such as the one staged at Bernabéu were meant to equate state syndicalism with strength, mechanical production, and disciplinary power – all under the guise of sensational illusion, or, to be more exact, the illusion of turning subjects into ornate cogs in the production wheel. The image of extraordinary physical discipline and talent was to be representative of Spain's population at large. Synchronized to a stream of anonymous uniformly dressed men zigzagging across the field as they twist, twirl, run, and jump, the narrator informs the viewer:

> En una elección pública de cómo en las empresas se cuida la cultura física de los productores, ochocientos hombres de la empresa nacional ("Bazan") realizan una extraordinaria demostración gimnástica ... Sus desplazamientos y sus ejecuciones exactas y disciplinadas se acomodan en cada instante al más perfecto ritmo ... La exhibición de la tabla gimnástica se caracteriza por su precisión y armonía.
>
> In a public demonstration of how companies maintain the physical culture of their employees, eight hundred men from the national company ("Bazan") perform an extraordinary gymnastic demonstration ... Their movements and precise and disciplined execution adapts to the most perfect rhythm each instant ... The display of the gymnastic stage is characterized by its precision and harmony.

The mass of workers then transform themselves into a gigantic human tower intended to epitomize the nation's peace, progress, and order, to resurrect literally and figuratively a monument to national unity and strength. The narrator concludes: "Remata estos ejercicios la composición de una torre humana que se alza como un símbolo de la Olimpiada Laboral sobre la tierra española donde los Juegos Deportivos Sindicales han significado expresión elocuente de la paz y disciplina de la patria" (These exercises complete the composition of the human tower that is erected as a symbol of the Industrial Labor Olympics on Spanish soil where the Syndical Sporting Games have signified the eloquent expression of peace and discipline of the nation.)

Only three years later, in his 1961 "fin de año" address to the nation, Franco would publicly declare the syndicalist role in politics as crucial to the creation of necessary illusions:

> El sindicalismo necesita penetrar y establecerse directamente en las plataformas de las decisiones y de las iniciativas políticas del estado. Responsabilitarse ... será capaz de servir y no de fraudar la confianza que hay de tener y las ilusiones y esperanzas que se despierta ... sólo así se podría cambiar.
>
> The State syndicates need to penetrate and directly establish themselves on the platforms of decisions and political initiatives of the State. To make

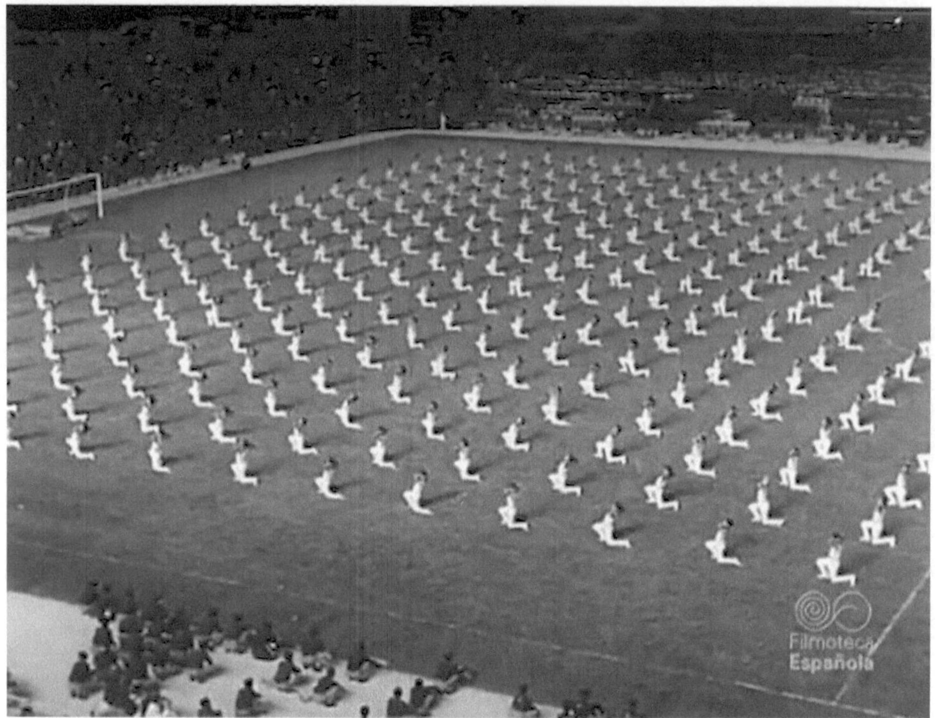

1.28 Rows of workers flawlessly execute a series of exercises, becoming constellations, abstractions, and ghostly images. Here the image of the field evokes that of a military graveyard. (No. 801 A, 1958) Copyright *Filmoteca nacional.*

> themselves responsible … They will be capable of serving and not breaching the trust that must be made and the illusions and hopes that it awakens … Only in this way will it be able to change.

The transformative and performative power of the syndicalist body, then, is much more than suggestive. That body is exploited by the state to simulate the political body through spectacle – to *aestheticize politics* by converting the social mass into a generic geometric form that is emblematic of the national and political organs of power. In theoretical terms, Francoism's use of syndical workers to create spectacles of this magnitude constitutes a "mass ornament" – one that reproduces on a larger geographical plane (the stadium field) exactly what the meta-newsreels reproduce on a cinematic one (the screen): the ideological and economic conditions of production, which fuse the reality of a fragmented social body with the illusion of a cohesive total structure. Spectacles of this sort offered a visual representation of politics as an organic edifice – a tower that could be built, rebuilt, commodified, and sold.[30] Interestingly, the mass ornament, like the newsreels, assembles its totality before our eyes, resulting in an image that alters our mode of seeing as we watch. What is so disturbing about these forms of fascist spectacle is that they constantly cross over that fine line between situating the spectator as an objective observer and converting him into a complacent participant. Tranche writes:

> El otro ámbito de este fenómeno [el espectáculo] es su utilización como mecanismo organizativo de masas, donde se combina el acto político y el espectáculo, la demostración del esfuerzo colectivo y la unidad en torno al líder. *Los actos políticos, en los que las masas eran simultáneamente actores y espectadores bajo la dirección del jefe, fueron una de las formas de plasmarse la política franquista.*
>
> The other influence on this phenomenon [the spectacle] is its utilization as an organizing mechanism of the masses, where political action and spectacle – the demonstration of collective strength and unity towards the leader – are combined. *Political action, in which the masses were simultaneously actors and spectators under the direction of the dictator, was one of the ways to express (and capture) Francoist politics.* (Tranche and Sánchez-Biosca 2005, 217; my emphasis)

Mass spectacles like the event at Bernabéu collapse any distance between individual subjects and the indistinguishable mass, and what the newsreels offer in filming them is a bird's eye view of this collapse that effectively welds together man and state by aligning our visual perspective with that of the regime – more specifically, with that of Franco. Tranche offers an interesting reading of this that is worth quoting at length:

> Tanto espectáculo como reportaje, está construido en función de la mirada del Caudillo. De hecho, *el espectáculo sólo alcanza su pleno sentido si es contemplado desde una posición superior con un punto de vista cenital* … La misma retórica falangista de antaño, glorificando el deporte y el trabajo como símbolos del esfuerzo colectivo, y los mismos gestos perviven aquí: *la*

> *"masa actora" vertebrada por obra y gracia de una geometría unificadora construida para la visión de conjunto, para la mirada del sumo hacedor: el Caudillo.* Es decir, más allá del culto a la educación física y de su escaso interés como espectáculo, esta representación viene a ser una prueba de obediencia a Franco.
>
> As much spectacle as news report, they are constructed through the Caudillo's gaze. *In fact, the spectacle only reaches its full meaning (or culmination) if it is contemplated from a superior position with a high vantage point …* The same Falangist rhetoric of the past, glorifying sport and work as symbols of the collective strength, and the same gestures survive here: *the "acting masses," backbones of the work and grace of a unifying geometry constructed for the vision of their togetherness, for the gaze of the supreme maker: el Caudillo.* In other words, beyond the tribute to physical education and its sparse interest as spectacle, this representation proves to be a test of obedience to Franco.[31] (Tranche and Sánchez-Biosca 2005, 208; my emphasis).

Unlike the parade spectacle, these gymnastic drills composed of parallel lines and units do not access patriotic feelings or commemorate a specific historical event; instead, they impose a multidimensional ornament on an otherwise flat landscape. As such, the mass ornament resembles, in Kracauer's words, "an aerial photograph" (such as those captured by NO-DO), an image that "does not emerge out of the interior of the given conditions, but rather appears above them," towering over the surface of reality (1995, 77).[32] As such, the mass ornament blurs the distinction between surface and depth, between theatre and stage, between spectator and actor. Aesthetically speaking, these fascist spectacles edify the commodity culture of politics under Francoism; they reconfigure and colonize public space not only by co-opting spectator vision but also by making visible ornate, spectacular, and ritualized forms of political palimpsest.

Where do all of these spectacles leave us? I propose that in the case of Spanish fascism, and as I have been discussing in the case of documentary and totalitarian optics, spectacle and spectrality have a unique, causal relationship. For as much as we see the physical, organic, and spectacular representation of politics at the Bernabéu stadium, and in the meta-newsreels themselves, we also have to consider what we do *not* see. Spectacles do not highlight ruptures, breaks, discontinuities, or differences (such as the enormous political changes between 1945 and 1968). Rather, spectacles emphasize cohesion, unity, continuity, and

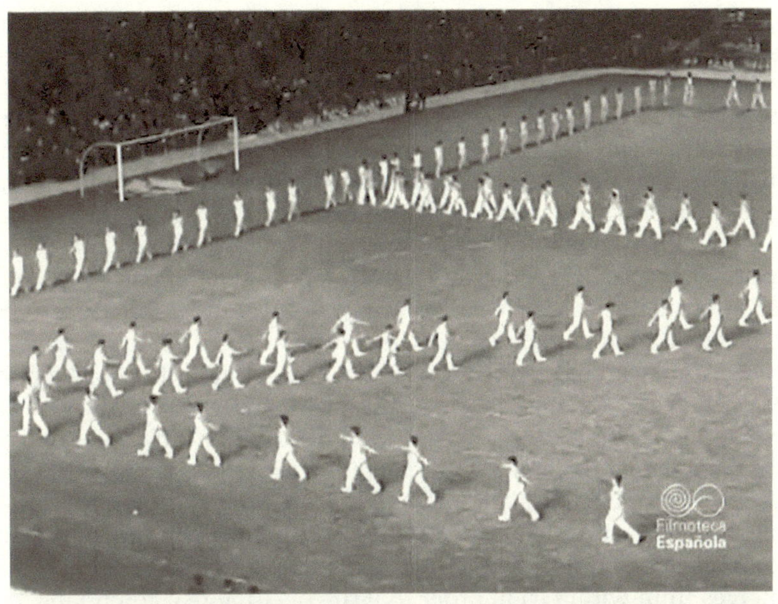

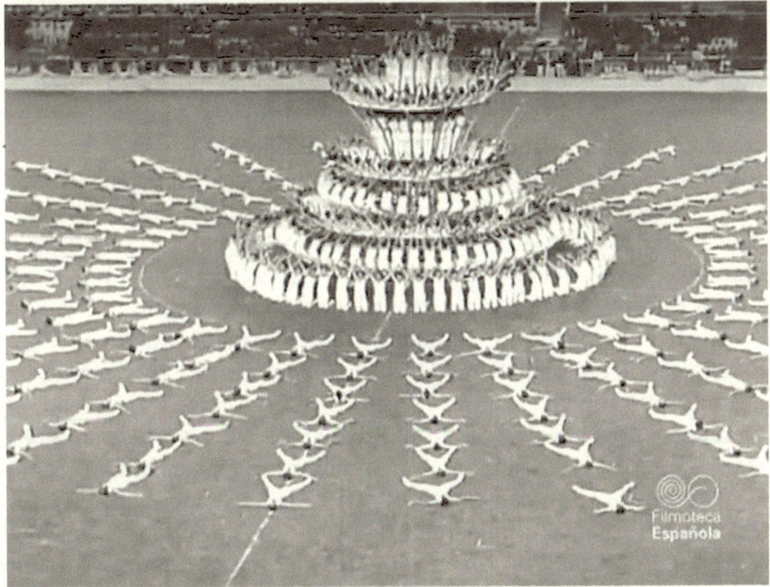

1.29 and 1.30 Individual men fashion themselves into the mass ornament. (No. 801 A, 1958) Copyright *Filmoteca nacional.*

sameness. Insofar as they co-opt vision, it is not only through the camera lens, or in the newsreels, or in the editing room, but also in real life – in the stadium, on the street, over the radio, or on a television set in someone's living room. *Spectacles change the landscape.* They negate difference and contemplation, they create images without openings – no small feat, and perhaps nowhere better exemplified than on the grand scale of the mass ornament, in which landscapes are altered to appear dazzling, vital, dynamically rhythmic, and foundationally sound. In a sense, what spectacles do is overshadow spectral remnants. In the context of Spain, they took the devastating effects of the Civil War – ruins, scars, social impoverishment, poverty, exile, hunger, destruction, mass graves, and even battle wounds, which Franco himself called "gloriosas cicatrices" – and made them all disappear, tucked them away under brilliant and extraordinary tapestries that could be, and were, willed or summoned at the regime's command. Spectacles operate as the aesthetic other to ruins, cultural and otherwise. And in this way, spectacles construct a specific historical, cultural, and political narrative that imposes an image onto the national landscape (as opposed to one that emerges from within it) in order to write over the real conditions that lie there, replacing them with illusory "special effects." Spectacles, in this sense too, function as the counterpart to spectral evidence – they continue the newsreel's rhetorical project, which empties landscapes, images, texts, and language of meaning precisely by flooding them with an *excess* of illusions.

Like the newsreel biographies we have examined, spectacles operate on a tenuous system of visibility and invisibility, through a system of concealment and exposure as well as through a process of making and unmaking ways of seeing the real and the utterly fabricated. For all their attempts to saturate and control vision by atemporalizing space, spectacles under Francoism created untimely political and ideological landscapes; the fantastic, kaleidoscopic illusions of totality would later be haunted by the underlying reality of a still isolated, fractured, and traumatized postwar culture. If the newsreels both *as* and *like* spectacles were complicit in inaugurating a new vision for a unified, "peaceful" nation under Franco – one predicated on assembling and stylizing images of landscapes rather than digging into actual ones – and if the regime used spectacle to turn Francoist ideology into art, and consequently the masses into mechanized abstractions, then it was up to artists and intellectuals to create a space where landscapes could be excavated and where new horizons could be found. Landscapes where the loss inaugurated by the regime's visualization of the nation could be redressed and mourned. One such space was the countercultural movement that came to be known as New Spanish Cinema (*Nuevo cine español*).[33] Through it, filmmakers would use experimental cinema to survey and "dig into" otherwise illusory and seamless landscapes. They would use spectacle not to transform subjects into machines, or to suture spectators into the discursive threads of ideology, but to show them already transformed into phantoms, spectres of Francoism destined to wander aimlessly in Spain's cities and villages, gardens and fields. Francoism had converted politics into art; now, the young, politically engaged artists of the NCE movement would use their works as political weapons to critique the regime's ideological corruption of Spanish society. In action, image, and cinematic discourse, this artistic production would refute the state's long-standing tradition of aestheticizing and spectacularizing its political platform. These films, in short, would speak to a ghostly, haunted, or wounded culture, placing at the centre of their cinematic stage the social realities of a nation and culture haunted by its history yet programmed (as we have seen) to perform spectacular illusions that actively suppressed and excluded those realities. These films, above all, would offer alternative yet *real* landscapes, writing back into their scripts a place for Spain's ruins, offering new ways to see and name the country's "glorious scars," and proposing a new kind of social memory, one in which loss could now be unmasked and addressed. One artist in particular would use the medium of film in this new wave climate to generate a whole new genre of innovatively countercultural and politically conscious works – ones that depicted the social realities of defeat, trauma, denial, repression, failure, impossibility, and haunting. Ones that made "ghostly landscapes" as visible as they were real. His name, Carlos Saura.

Chapter Two

Cinematic Apertures: Carlos Saura's Untimely Landscapes

Visibility is a complex system of permission and prohibition, of presence and absence, punctuated alternately by apparitions and hysterical blindness.

Ghostly Matters (Gordon 1997, 15)

A fruitful approach to landscape would be to start from its claim that it is a complete record of evidence and to inquire why that claim is effective – while demonstrating how much the scene demands that we not see. By picking apart seen and unseen, we begin to get at the variety of human experience in a way that shatters the landscape's pretenses. This conjunction of seen and unseen, then, draws our attention to the experience of landscape as well as its initial creation. It emphasizes the relative roles of vision and the intangible in the interpretation of landscape.

Understanding Ordinary Landscapes (Upton 1997, 176)

Holding Time in Place

How do images allow us to understand a place, what a place means and what it, in the gently evocative words of John Berger, "holds dear"?[1] How might moving images change that understanding by calling to mind the passage of time in a place, or by placing time in different spaces – the camera, the screen, the theatre? How do we gain knowledge of a place's meaning by looking at its landscape, which, like the moving image, is always shifting and settling and taking new shape? How do we experience a place, a place's sense of and relationship to time, by viewing how its landscape is narrated? And how do we grasp that sense and that time by seeing how a landscape is framed, by contemplating what in it has been made visible and what, subsequently, has remained invisible? The scope of these questions – admittedly large – has to do, in part, with the landscape "problem" or question, which conventionally in cultural and human geography has referred to man's impact on the land and on nature. In the previous chapter, I looked at the ways in which the politics of constructing the national Spanish landscape were entangled with the problem of the archive and, we could say, its architecture of invisibility and erasure, its drive towards memory and total capture, and its omissions, limits, and failures at such a totalizing project. The impact of cameramen on the Spanish landscape, in a concrete sense, was not that they encountered it in its natural state, but that they constructed it through a specific ideology of editing and production. In this chapter, I am interested in the somewhat opposite question – the land's impact on man and how we are impacted by its veering and colliding planes of history and desire, its affective qualities, its ontology, and what we might call its psychology and its phenomenology. In other words, the way a place feels, which is also to say the way *we* feel and experience a place. Distinct yet related to this interest is the question of how such an ontological–psychological-phenomenological conjunction reveals (or restrains) a place's mode of being and existing – a line of inquiry that inevitably brings to mind the *presencing* and *absencing* qualities that every place bears. How might surveying landscapes, then, inform experiential knowledge of a place? How do landscapes store away information or histories while, conversely, making other stories or artefacts visible, placing them, so to speak, before our eyes? In sum, how do landscapes –here, specifically cinematic ones – invite us to see things or, conversely, obstruct our sight?

A common understanding of landscapes for humanists is that they function as containers or archives of history in that they stratify and solidify time, holding in place, as it were, concrete evidence of the past. While the archival logic that structures studies of what landscapes reveal about time and how they index history is certainly important to recognize, the readings presented here shift away from forms of sedimentation or historical preservation to focus instead on the concept of *resurfacing* and on how resurfacing visualizes, concretizes, and in a way opens a window onto otherwise abstract desires and fears – "permissions and prohibitions," recalling Avery Gordon's alluring phrase – of coming into knowledge of the past. For the cultural geographer and the literary critic alike, landscapes not only carry the weight of the past beneath them – literally in the geological strata of time or figuratively in the sense of the burden (or gift) of certain legacies – but also can grant us *access* to the past, to those strands of time that linger, the same ones that may leave an impression on the present in which we live and experience the world.

A key concept throughout this chapter then is, naturally, landscape, which I draw upon repeatedly for its unique capacity to evoke both place and space and for its ability to intertwine the specific with the general, the local with the global, the vast with the infinitesimal, the natural with the constructed, and perhaps most importantly, the seen with the unseen. For as immense as landscapes may be or may appear to the onlooker, the layers, crevices, and canyons of the unseen that comprise their foundations are as present and noteworthy as the mountain ranges, open fields, and lines of trees that may at first sight catch the eye. Thus, in centring my argument on landscapes as both conceptual and material sites of knowledge, my readings seek a deeper understanding of how they act as containers or archives of both the invisible (that which is inscribed yet subterranean or ob-scene, meaning, we recall, "off stage" or "out of sight") and the visible (that which surfaces, emerges, and comes out into the open).[2] This task will involve looking at different landscape representations and exploring how their scenes ignite or extinguish that fine line between the seen and the unseen. More specifically, in the works discussed in the following pages, these representations take different shape – the former battlefield, the *campo* or hunting ground, the open road, as well as the theatre of death. My readings are meant to be not prescriptive but interpretive, aiming to offer a new angle on each work by weaving together the question of landscape with notions of place and temporality, historicity and in/visibility. I engage with how landscapes provide patterns and coordinates that constellate cultural and historical information that we, as spectators or participants, must learn to read and interpret. This approach to reading landscapes implies thinking about them not only as texts (or textual places) but also as locations of a visible illegibility or obversely a legible invisibility, in which we must negotiate constantly between the visible and the invisible, between the hidden and that which is in plain sight. Apertures – whether literal or metaphorical – prove to be particularly instructive in gauging this kind of in/visibility, or il/legibility, since they are, by definition, openings or entryways through which light passes, as diffused or as concentrated.

Beyond the general interest in what landscapes *do*, what and how they "perform," and how they instigate thought and movement, this chapter is primarily concerned with how cinematic representations reveal landscapes as haunted. Throughout my readings, I understand haunted landscapes as those places, whether natural or constructed, that simultaneously exude symptoms of the conditions that create them – censorship, violence, or, to borrow another of Avery Gordon's striking phrases, "hysterical blindness" – and project spectral qualities, or remainders of a time that is out of joint, one that emerges yet is non-contemporaneous with the present. I understand such landscapes as affective places constituted by *untimeliness*, or a mode of temporality in which the double-bind of emergence and disappearance is the governing logic that allows the past to make the present waver, shifting the weight of the former into the continuum of the latter.

On the one hand, this requires looking at the ways in which cinema, and specifically here Carlos Saura's cinema, constructs a vision of history in which the past is not divorced from the present but always continuously emerging and re-emerging in and through it. By extension, this also means observing how the language of cinema, and in particular New Spanish Cinema, instructs our line of sight towards that point of emergence and disappearance (at times, a point of uncanny convergence between the two) through interruption and fragmentation that breaks our sight, in a sense, in order to open it to the multiple layers of time that inform the moment of the image. On the other hand, and perhaps somewhat simpler, to examine the relationship between what certain films *do* and what certain landscapes *are* (or what they hold) is to question the latter's relationship to the former. How are landscapes represented not as static, dead places but as fluid, animated sites in films from a specific time period and geography (here, Spain during the final years of dictatorship)? And how can spectators view and engage with those landscapes in ways that are akin to reading and interpreting film, or in ways that might enhance the film experience?

Of course, landscapes are not new or unique to cinema. Indeed, they comprise an entire genre of representation in their own right (painting, photography, not to mention subgenres within cinema, such as the western). That said, a central question in this chapter is not how landscape is something uniquely crafted by the cinematic apparatus, but rather how it is that specific figurations of landscapes in cinema – here, we might refer to "modern Spanish landscapes," to give them a categorical label – repeatedly reveal a tendency towards an indexing of time that positions history not as something lodged "in the past" but rather as that which opens in and to the present, that which both crystallizes and obscures the present, that which paradoxically arrests and instigates what Walter Benjamin calls "this particular now" by stopping time and, conversely, setting it back into motion (2002, 463).[3]

Whereas my previous discussion on the connection between landscape and spectacle sought to relate the construction of landscape to ideological forms of erasure and omission, here I want to think about what is brought to life or what returns *through* the landscape. To consider not only the temporal but also the indexical nature of cinematic landscapes means then to think about how the past comes to inscribe itself on a specific place or site through repetitions and how that inscription (a kind of writing that is itself an act of repetition, and an act of presencing and absencing – a point to which I will return later) comes not only to shape but also challenge and disrupt the present. Building on this idea of disruption or disturbance, to consider a place "untimely" means then to ask how such inscriptions – traces of a former time that surface in a place always "other" or out of sync with its own time – yield a structure of inheritance that burdens the present. That a place bears the burden of untimeliness because something remains unsettled or is disturbed implies that that something is *wounded*. This wound or temporal fracture – itself an aperture or opening of sorts, as we will see – is the space of haunting and the very site and situation of ghosts. Cinema too is constituted by a logic of temporal fracture – it operates on the basis of capturing place in one time and projecting it in another; it manoeuvres through and sculpts time at the threefold conjunction of locating, dislocating, and relocating time.

This question of place's – and cinema's – relationship to time, and indeed to multiple coexisting temporalities, is also, at least in part, a question about space. How does the specificity of place as an object of representation hinge on the generality of space as a mode of presentation, projection, and production? What connection can be drawn between place as the location of a certain time (or times) and space as movement, freedom, expansion? Put somewhat differently, what happens when something already imbued with meaning (place) is made visible through something designed to create meaning (space)? What is at stake in figuring or imaging a place as stilled time, arrest, or "pause" (drawing on Yi-Fu Tuan's idea), understood here as the space of movement and fluid time?[4] This is undoubtedly a larger question of cinema's ability both to *show* place and to *make* places from that showing or "window" onto the real – its ability to work through space *and* create space simultaneously. In line with these questions arises another – what is the relationship between cinema and landscape? Like landscape, cinema captures places and the spaces between those places – both place and space, together or separate. Unlike landscape, however, which traditionally hinged on linear perspective to draw attention to fixed points in time and place, to "arrest the flow of history at a specific moment" in order to make it "a universal reality," cinematic representation works against this approach by creating movement and space, thereby activating the flow of time and liberating history from linearity so that it may course through time openly and freely (Upton 1997, 165). This means, most importantly, that where landscape operates synchronically by framing and drawing our vantage point (inward, to set the eye), cinema works diachronically through a system of expansion, by freeing those otherwise anchored viewpoints so as to open the eye and let it wander.

Ultimately, I am suggesting that while landscapes are not unique to cinema, cinema can and does have the potential to reveal things in landscape that, for instance, a sixteenth-century Dutch or Italian landscape painting, in its one-dimensionality, stasis, and flatness, simply cannot. Cinema thus accesses the darkest and most difficult-to-reach corners of landscape's narrative by loosening or freeing it from the confines of linear understanding of historical time. In what follows, I draw on a two films that I see as working in dialogue with each other. My readings of their narrative and visual components aim to think about how the cinematic landscapes in each, as complex sites of visualizing loss, memory, silence, and trauma, offer particularly instructive and insightful ways of revealing history as an *assemblage* of fragments – that is, an understanding of history *as cinematic*. I draw on the notion of cinematic apertures as openings and also wounds in connection with "untimely landscapes," which too denote a kind of wound related to time.

Mapping Untimeliness (Landscapes Tell More than Time)

Carlos Saura made his remarkably gritty debut film, *Los golfos* (*The Hooligans*), in 1959, but it was not shown in Madrid theatres until 1962. That delay reminds us that many Spanish films faced a difficult cultural and political climate in the late 1950s. Interestingly, though not surprisingly, the film's narrative hinges almost entirely on the problem of debt, not only monetary but also temporal. The main protagonists – the "hooligans" of the English title – do not have enough money to escape the streets for a better life (Juan, the "star" of the gang, dreams of becoming a bullfighter), and all of them, collectively, have only a short time to pay their way out. The preoccupation with temporality and latency that begins in *Los golfos* marks only the beginning of what will become a strong thematic thread centred on the question of untimeliness – a thread that undoubtedly extends from the narrative content to the very real social and political conditions influencing that content.[5]

Though this anxiety over latencies, egregious lapses in time, and the general climate of untimeliness and stifling insularity under the dictatorship was shared by many of Saura's contemporaries, what perhaps most differentiates him from his peers can be condensed into the single driving question at the heart of so much of his work (arguably in all of his films up until the late 1980s): How do splinters of non-contemporaneity embed themselves in the present? In my interpretation, Saura's cinema treats seeing as a political act and attempts to shed light on the question of non-contemporaneity. His cinema is profoundly indebted to and profoundly concerned with the problem of wounds – how they open spaces of possibility for imagining an alternative history, but also how they cast light on and sometimes sustain injury.

The term "cinematic apertures" is not random or accidental. Rather, I draw on it deliberately for its cultural as well as optical connotations of an opening or prelude (to something larger or external) and as a metaphor for the political, social, and economic changes that flowed from Spain's belated entry into modernity and capitalism. In part, this is simply a function of my broader interest in understanding how the experience of non-contemporaneity develops from a supposedly contemporary or contemporaneous context. In the economic and political sense, in Spain, "aperture" signified an open door policy to the outside world, which until the late 1950s had been understood culturally as everything beyond Spain's national borders. Inasmuch as apertures, like overtures, are openings or spaces through which light enters, they are importantly aligned with visibility and perception. Thus, my turn to "cinematic apertures" suggests a double line of thought – on the one hand, new modes of seeing and perceiving social and historical realities (the twin legacies of indebtedness and inheritance), and on the other, the visualization of spectral affects and wounds.

Saura's political films – those that fall into his early period, established with *Los golfos* and commonly equated with the beginning of Spanish cinema's "transition to the post-Franco era" – do not dedicate themselves exclusively to portraying or protagonizing landscapes; but they do draw compellingly on them, and craft them in specific ways that, as I hope to show, heighten spectatorial awareness of cultural hauntings by mapping the spectrality of place (D'Lugo 1991, 123). Saura's early films often visualize compelling if disturbing narratives of the fragile yet flailing social bonds among men, as well as within families caught in webs of anachrony and networks of silence, unable to articulate what haunts them. Notably, these films share another trait: their narratives are structured entirely around untimely returns and departures punctuated by loss.

In this chapter, I begin with a close reading of the filmic "precursor" to Saura's early cinema: Juan Antonio Bardem's *Muerte de un ciclista* (*Death of a Cyclist*, 1955); I then analyse what is widely considered to be Saura's masterpiece – *La caza* (*The Hunt*, 1965). I read this work as a detailed and intricately designed portrait of loss. I ask how *La caza* poses crucial questions: How can memory be understood as the condition of finitude? And how might breaks or fractures in that memory produced by cinematic apertures challenge this notion of finitude? How might cinema offer an opening into the inner workings of memory – its blind spots and areas of perceived illumination – but an opening that is also a wound and a process of wounding?[6] Like film itself, which in *La caza* constitutes a kind of landscape that captures place and creates space, memory becomes a kind of landscape in these works, a place out of time, and a time uprooted, without a stable place. And it is this juncture – memory becoming landscape, landscape unfolding time – that Saura's work especially, even radically, stages.

Across these readings, I trace the wounds of place, beginning with the battlefield or *campo,* which I connect to the twin tropes of traumatic experience: repetition and return. In these landscapes the scars of the past reopen in the present, revealing themselves as wounds, or signs of unhealed injury, which in turn expose place as symptomatic of a visibly anachronistic Spanish modernity. Thus the landscape surveyed is a place of violence, disease, and death, yet also one of longing and desire, a place where one encounters fatality with no hope for reconciliation or redemption. Finally, these battlefields embody and exude the symptoms of war; as places of profound loss, they repeat the logic of war by other means. This repetition creates (or re-creates, as it were) a proscenium of death, a kind of resurfacing that sets the stage for death. I am interested here in film *as* landscape and the treatment of landscapes *in* film as two distinct yet related ways to *place memory* within (or outside) the boundaries of linear, historical time. Reading the movement through varying settings and scenes, from the natural to the artificial to the oneiric, I analyse Saura's use of natural landscapes to express the "grammar" of place. That is, how the visualization and temporalization of place expands or condenses social bonds and iterates power relations, and how it symbolically calibrates and differentiates subjective experience and collective access to the past. I explore how Saura uses natural settings as stages, in a sense, on which to "act out" the inability to live in a present rid of its traumas, wounds, and ghosts. On the one hand, this translates visually into the cinematic transformation of such settings into repressive spaces that confine and debilitate subjects; on the other, it means narrativizing ostensibly natural places in a way that conjures and destabilizes the memory of the past and denaturalizes and redirects the force of historical knowledge.

Muerte de un ciclista (1955), Reconciliation on the Battlefield

Este lugar es el más importante del mundo para nosotros.

This is the most important place in the world for us.

Death of a Cyclist

In many ways, the precursor to Saura's *La caza* – not to mention one of the most poignant if not relentless treatments of landscape to come out of New Spanish Cinema, is Juan Antonio Bardem's 1955 classic feature-length film *Muerte de un ciclista* (*Death of a Cyclist*). The film's visual logic is governed by the persistent presence – the cycling and recycling – of places that function as both reflexive and reflective windows onto the world of the main characters and secret lovers, Juan and María José. In fact, from the opening shot to the last, the spectator is brought full circle from the framing of a lone country road during the day to that of a similarly desolate road at night. This temporal cycle of the road (daytime to nightfall) marks the film's *mise en scène* from beginning to end. It is difficult to miss Bardem's visual repetitions of symbolic landscapes, so often represented through cyclical places (racetracks, round tables, etc.), and his repeated framing of circular images that may not constitute landscapes in any traditional or geographical sense but that do come to occupy the space of the screen in its entirety – crisp close-ups of glasses, eyes, faces, mouths, wheels, mirrors, and broken windows. Interestingly, this spatial configuration finds its narrative equivalent in the temporal configuration of return.

After accidentally hitting a cyclist and leaving him for dead on the side of the road so as to avoid exposing their adulterous affair, María José reunites with Juan at the film's conclusion to find out his plan of escape. He tells her that, inconsistent with her own plans to never "come clean" of the crimes she has committed, he has decided to turn himself in to the authorities. In an intriguing parallel of life and death cycles, the lovers have rendezvoused at their usual place – a hotel on the outskirts of town. Afterwards, moments before their fateful ending, they return to the scene of the accident where the cyclist was killed. Apart from the particularly sombre use of light mixed with sharp, contrasting shadows that visually anticipate Juan's immanent death at María José's somewhat ambivalent yet ultimately murderous hand, what marks this scene as unique is its refiguring of temporal scenes – specifically, traumatic events from the past – within the physical boundaries of the bleak and seemingly limitless landscape before them. Through the confessionary tone of an exterior monologue spanning alternating point-of-view shots of him positioned in and absorbed by the landscape, Juan speaks the film's extraordinary final words, worth quoting here at length:

> Las trincheras estaban allí mismo. Yo pensaba en ti. En todos los ratos que habíamos pasado juntos ... en el último veraneo ... entonces tenía fe en muchas cosas. Te quería. Hacía grandes proyectos para el futuro ... Es curioso, este lugar es el más importante del mundo para nosotros ... ¿Te das cuenta? Siempre ha habido algo nuestro aquí. El recuerdo cuando la guerra y luego ... fue aquí mismo, no? [María José: "Sí"] ... Aquí mismo matamos a un hombre ... le dejamos morir porque nos estorbaba ... ¿Tienes frío? [María José: "Sí"] ... Me gusta [este tiempo] el crepúsculo hay un momento en que todo calla. Tengo tantas ganas de vivir ... como nunca. Es duro empezar otra vez, pero es bueno. ¿Ves? La tierra está en orden ... Es el silencio, la paz.

> The trenches were right over there. I thought of you. Of all those times we had had together ... that last summer ... back then I had faith in a lot of things. I loved you. I had big plans for the future ... It's curious, this place is the most important place in the world for us ... Do you realize that? There's always been something of ours here. The memory of the war and later ... it was right here, wasn't it? [Yes] ... Right here we killed a man ... and left him for dead because he got in our way ... Are you cold? [Yes] ... I like the twilight, there's a moment when everything is quiet. I am so

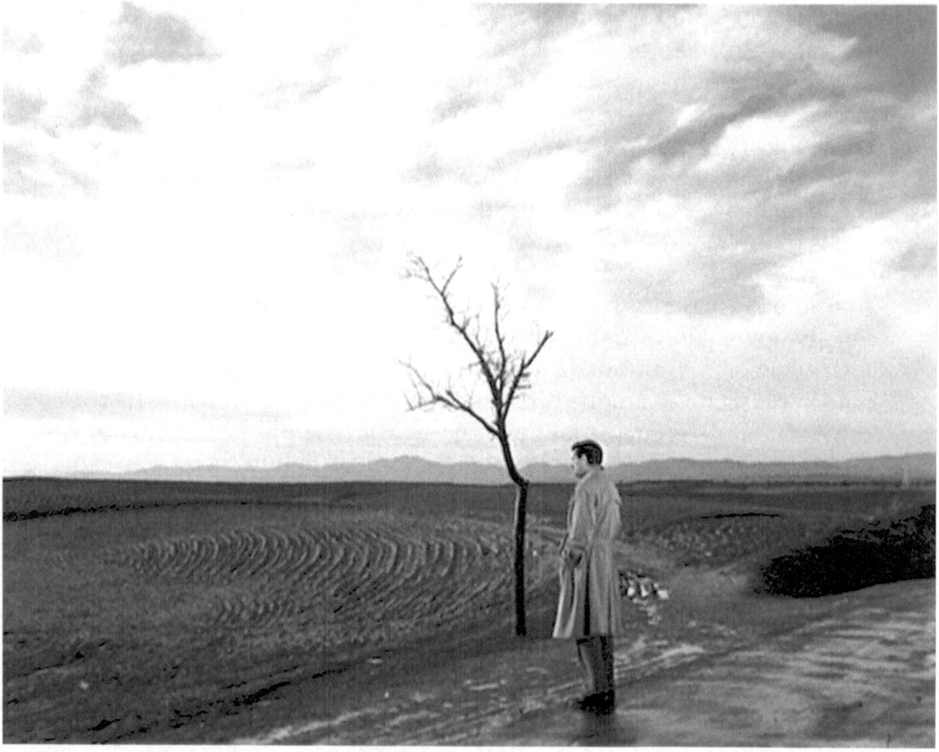

2.1 Juan embedded in the desolate landscape in *Muerte de un ciclista* (1955).

> excited to live … like never before. It's hard to start all over again, but it's good. See? The land is in order … It's the silence, the peace.

We must not overlook that the final lines of Bardem's film are about the landscape – "the land is in order … it is the silence, the peace." In this scene, Juan's verbal expression of feeling whole, clean, and purified through his encounter with the land (he now wants to live "como nunca") is curiously coupled with his physical return to the place that marks death threefold: the film's original crime (the war), secondary crime (the accidental death of cyclist), and final crime (Juan's own untimely death at the hand of his lover). It is the landscape that he draws on in order to evaluate his moral existence and to acknowledge his sins, the very place where war, love, and death are all intertwined.

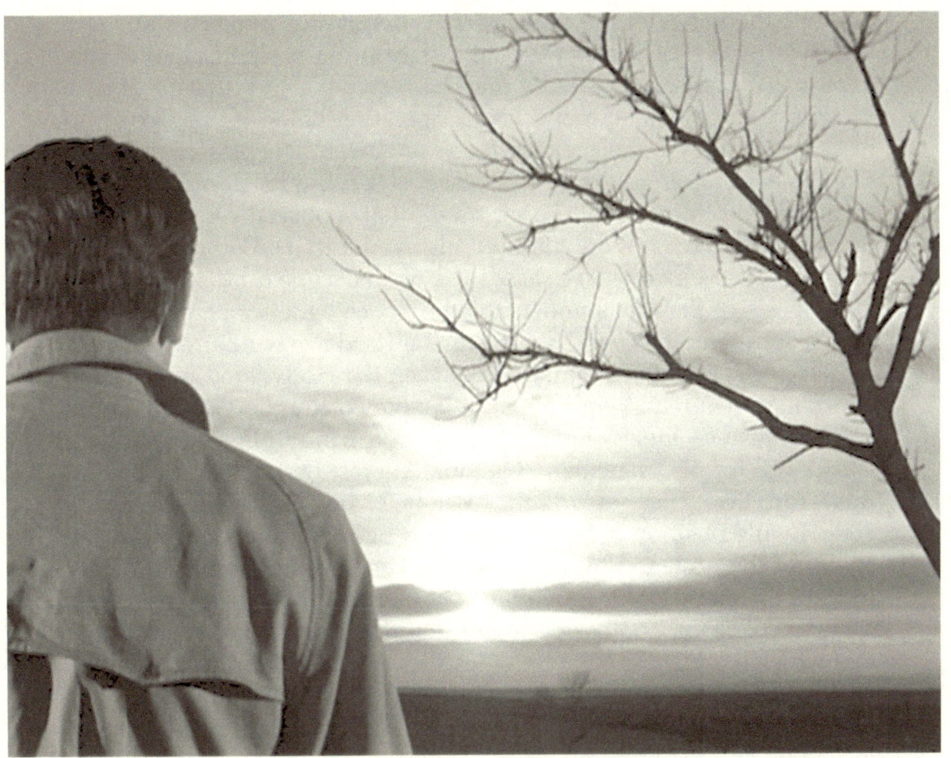

2.2 Juan against the landscape at dusk. A new horizon. *Muerte de un ciclista* (1955).

Of course, this intertwining, for Juan, signifies a site of profound loss – of his youthful innocence, of his love for a woman who will betray him repeatedly and unexpectedly, and much later of the cyclist's life, the lovers' secret, and his own dignity and self-worth. Juan's mental and emotional journey through the past – a journey "back to himself" as he alerts Matilde, the student he unjustly fails and who subsequently becomes his guiding light and the sole inspiration to correct his wrongdoings – implies coming to terms with the mistakes that defined his former life. The return to this particular and intensely personal landscape necessarily implies, for Juan, a return to painful memories of the war, of a love that once was, of hope now lost, and of what has remained unspoken but nonetheless haunts him, that which has staked a claim on his directionless and thus meaningless life.

While the image of the open, barren countryside remains static and unwavering, as spectators we gain insight into the significance of this exact place that has repeatedly marked Juan's life and thus are able to imagine the various temporal layers operating under its surface without ever having them visualized for us on screen. The present moment, like the act of going back to this place, observing its significance and magnitude, is imbued with a "pastness" that is unseen yet real and felt (and in this scene, not only felt but also verbalized). Without wanting to overcredit *Muerte de un ciclista*'s use of landscape (or discredit other key aspects of the film's undeniable brilliance – the script, cinematography, sound, editing, and what Marsha Kinder has referred to as its mastery of subversive mediation between the Hollywood melodrama and Italian neo-realist traditions), it is noteworthy that Bardem chose such an austere, lifeless terrain to contain the multiple layers of lived experience for his tragic hero. Of equal interest perhaps might be that this return takes place at twilight, an in-between, ghostly time that parallels Juan's position between starting a new life, liberated from the chains of the past, and his all too sudden and seemingly unjust death. Indeed, the crepuscular time that Juan likes because "everything falls silent" evokes yet another cycle in the film's narrative of repression – that which has been spoken becomes silent again, just as before. In and through this cycle of silence, the former battlefield is reiterated – indeed, rehearsed – as both a site of loss and enunciation, and one of mourning and redemption.

Also worth noting is that Juan's open confession is presented neither as a guilty plea nor as a disavowal of his past crimes; on the contrary, it is an avowal, a life-affirming declaration before nature. He approaches wholeness again – reclaims his dignity, as he had told María José back in their hotel room moments earlier – by recognizing the past and cleansing his spirit of the impurities that past bears, by taking action to correct the injustices he has done. It is safe to say that the landscape holds a certain authority over him, both commanding him towards this recognition and demanding disclosure and revelation. The link between landscape and confession here is indeed compelling. In discussing the qualities of landscapes that commemorate the past, Dell Upton writes "the unseen forces the scene [the landscape] to confess" (1997, 177). While this place is not recognizable as a site of commemoration, Juan's will to live, articulated as an act of enunciation on the road, as he stands before the open *campo,* both ascribes a narrative to the landscape and functions as an act of memorialization. Interestingly, it is not the landscape that reveals to him this history of injustice; rather it is he who, in a sublime, almost hypnotic moment of clarity and resolute determination, reaffirms history in this place by listing the events that have played out there and that have scarred his life. In many ways, his personal confession *is* the monument never erected on this site, but it is also the wound, an opening of sorts back into what otherwise would have been a long-forgotten past. Strikingly, the act of naming past crimes and injustices both repeats those unconscionable acts committed, thus invoking the suffering endured, and also, as Benjamin might say, conjures a "presentiment of mourning," a space where that suffering might be put to rest (2009, 224).[7]

Bearing in mind, then, the confessionary, commemorative tone of Juan's monologue, we could say that Bardem's landscape, at once called upon and returned to, is not only a repository of sins and crimes, a place that literally and figuratively grounds a past cycle of violence and killing, but also a site of reconciliation. This is key, for reconciliation connotes both an agreement and a resolution, both a "settling" and a coming to terms. That Juan should feel a sense of harmony ("la paz") and balance ("la tierra está en orden") after contemplating the landscape is no coincidence; after all, that landscape is a place where things have been "settled" (physically) and where the earth must "come to terms" with the hostility, disorder, and destruction enacted upon it. Perhaps even more telling is the etymology of "reconcile" – it comes from the Latin *reconciliare, re* meaning "back" (and also expressing intense force) and *conciliare* meaning "to bring together." Juan's confession displays a kind of "bringing back together" since it suggests an attempt to attune his former life to his newly discovered and identified self – he will be "master of his destiny," someone who for the first time has something to "believe in" because he will start again "limpiamente" (cleanly), "away from so many dirty things." "Iremos de tantas cosas sucias, y esto también," he promises María José. "Jamás … empezaremos limpiamente" (We'll get away from so many dirty things, and this too. Never … We'll start cleanly). Embedded in the logic of reconciliation, we should remember, is not simply a return to the past, but a notion of futurity – the idea that in returning and bringing back together former sufferings and losses, there may be forgiveness and redemption.

In a film so indebted to cycles, not least because of its title, it is only fitting that the ending should return to its beginning – to the road that has traversed the lives and deaths of the main characters. It is equally fitting that the definitive scene of narrative closure should be represented through an intense openness – a scene that brings back into view for the spectator what was not made visible before and hence what we did not see in the film's opening shots. For it is only in these final shots of *Muerte* that the landscape's meaning is fully expressed, through the physical openness and desolation but also the visceral and psychological force that the former battlefield bears for the main characters.

Nearly ten years later, in *La caza,* Saura would take this same image – of a man returning to a battlefield after the war to confront the spectres that haunt him – to explore a similar narrative strategy. But rather than being peripheral to the main action, as in Bardem's work, the battlefield would take centre stage, a stage on which the trauma of the past once concealed is made visible, materialized in the form of symptoms, wounds.

La caza (1965), Memory's Desert, Landscape's Wounds

Ahora solo han quedado los agujeros.

Now only the holes have remained.

La caza

It may come as no surprise that Saura first came up with the idea for his third feature, *La caza* (*The Hunt,* 1965), when he visited the very place that would become the film's main setting: "the scenery of the game preserve impressed me from the start: without a single tree, gypseous and dry, crossed only by a shallow stream and lined with rabbit den holes, as well as the caves and trenches from the War" (quoted in D'Lugo 1991, 56).[8] As with Bardem's *Muerte de un ciclista,* the landscape where *La caza* was filmed had been a real Civil War battlefield, containing both physical and psychological traces of Spain's violent and subsequently silenced history under Francoism. As an homage and intertextual reference to Bardem's work, the narrative space of *La caza,* like its predecessor's, evokes both the origins of those traces (bloodshed and war) and the temporal displacement of the original event (its continuation, decades later, in the present). As Marvin D'Lugo has noted, this setting "implies that the *mise en scène* of all contemporary action is necessarily the suppressed battlefield of the Civil War, not merely as a passive setting to action, but as the absent cause of all the personal and collective moves we witness" (1991, 57). Yet even as origins and

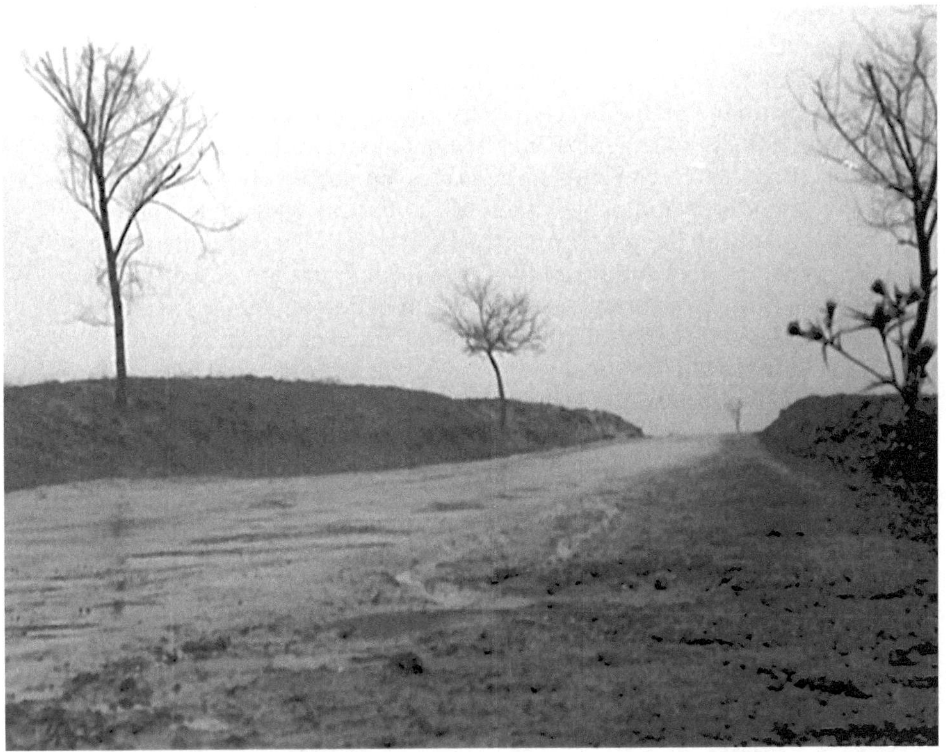

2.3 The open road. *Muerte de un ciclista* (1955).

traces are revealed, the war's screen presence in the form of residue on the landscape is matched unevenly with its diegetic absence. The war is alluded to but never really "spoken about" or narrated in any intelligible way. Perhaps most unlike Bardem's perfectly still yet disquieting place of reconciliation is Saura's infernal landscape of perpetual and inexplicable suffering, of incessant blindness, due in large part to the scorching light of the sun as well as to pervasive, immanent disease, asphyxiation, and death. The main characters of *Muerte,* in one way or another, reckon with the past by returning to it physically and emotionally; the protagonists of *La caza* are unable to do so, and thus the hunting grounds that surround and besiege them come to epitomize a place of entrapment and condemnation with no hope for redemption or posterity.[9]

To date, scholarship on *La caza* has tended to highlight two important yet limited aspects of the film: its multifaceted levels of allegory, and the sedimentary aspects of the *campo* where the film's main action takes place (Kinder, 1993; Kovács, 1990; Ochoa 2009; Pillado-Miller 1997; Wood 1999; Zunzunegeui 2003).[10] My detailed reading here stresses the subtle ways in which Saura's landscapes are deeply but also paradoxically rooted in static preservation of the past as well as its uprootedness, or the way the past drifts in and out of frame (eventually filling it completely). I concentrate on the film's reconfiguration of the legibility of place through a complex visual system of detotalization, fragmentation, and interrogation. Ultimately, these interrogations of the visible and of vision itself can be understood as rhetorical devices that synthesize what is arguably the main conflict in *La caza* – the desire to know at odds with the inability to access that which is in plain view. Of course, much of the film hinges on the constraints of knowledge – whether desired or undesired, whether collective or individual; not insignificantly, this is expressed (as with Bardem) through careful alternating shots between the vastness of the ultimately inhospitable landscape that engulfs the film's main action and the one that catalogues and anticipates the return of a catastrophic experience.

Plotting Spectrality

¿En qué guerra?

In what war?

La caza

Arguably Saura's most political film to date, *La caza* tells the story of four men – the older José, Luis, and Paco (three longtime friends and business partners), and the younger, more impressionable Enrique (Paco's brother-in-law) – who get together for a day of leisure and rabbit hunting. At José's invitation, they set out for the remote hunting grounds (the campsite, or *el campo,* as they refer to it) in what at first glance appears to be an innocuous exercise in male bonding. As the narrative unfolds, so does the group's mysterious and troubled past, which gradually unveils itself in scenes of escalating tension and mutual antagonism, which swell to the film's climactic moment: a massacre. It is

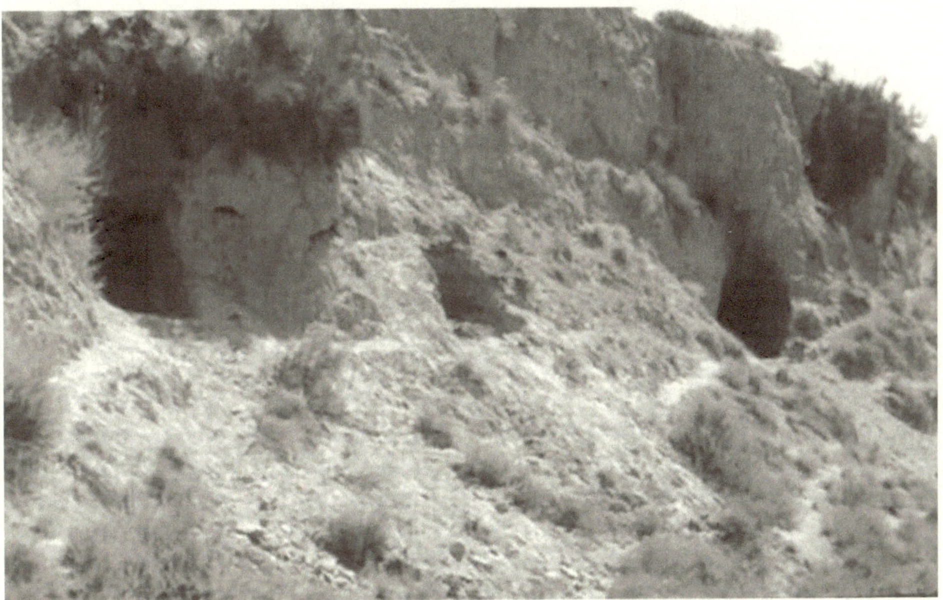

2.4 The hillside holes, wounds from the war. *La caza* (1965).

clear from the outset that the unresolved conflict between the four men, though largely unspoken, is rooted in their common past – that is, their shared but silent history, which is mirrored in the landscape. Male aggression and hostility are at the heart of *La caza*'s narrative, but so is the unspeakability of the past, which continues to wound the present and finds visual parallels in the high-contrast black-and-white long shots of the arid, infested hunting grounds where the main action takes place, grounds that engulf and absorb the protagonists and that are themselves replete with markings and scars, later revealed to be traces of a Civil War battle where thousands were killed.[11]

Several visual and audio prefigurations of these tensions occur in the first few minutes of the film: the opening credits feature the camera's steady zoom into a close-up of two restless ferrets caged in a beehive wired box, the relentless pulsing "heartbeats" of drums interspersed with the agitated ringing of bells (presumably on the collars of the ferrets), the image of a jeep racing across the screen towards the audience and then stopping abruptly, and finally the first image of the modernized yet unpromising landscape, seen from the perspective of Paco, who scans the power lines sprawling across the near-moonscape. Horns blare as two cars nearly collide off screen. These first few moments distil the film's overarching narrative and audio-visual architecture, connecting the problem of unnatural, domesticated enclosure to a heightening sense of danger, angst, and general dis-ease, all of which will culminate in a rapid suspension of movement that doubles as a premature breaking point and an "exit strategy," eventually sealing the protagonists' common fate – entrapment.

In one of *La caza*'s earliest scenes, the men arrive at a bar on their way to the campsite. This initial encounter between the four is where we first witness their internal conflicts: José nervously self-medicates due to his "stomach issues," Paco feigns a relaxed, collected composure though he is extremely anxious to get to their destination, Luis's second round of bourbon and overall malaise signal his alcoholism and general discontent, and Enrique is left in the proverbial dark, shrouded in boyish innocence and his desire to belong to the group, accentuated by his constant and eager questioning of the three older men. Besides foreshadowing the events to come, this scene establishes a set of rules and regulations, prohibitions and taboos, all of which allude to a shared but uncanny past, one that has become estranged and unfamiliar in the present, a past that is perhaps unreconciled, or unreconcilable. As the law is laid down, so too are the parameters for this social hierarchy – silence, distrust, anxiety, and longing, all traits that cast a shadow of doubt over the supposedly amicable reunion that is to comprise the remainder of the film's diegesis. After leaving the bar, the men arrive at Juan's house, where José's *cojo* (literally "crippled"), and in this scene absent, servant will help them prepare for the day's hunt. It is here that the themes of disease and contamination first surface. As José enters the house, looking for Juan, he is confronted with the abject poverty in which the farmhand and his family live, evidenced further as José stumbles upon Juan's seemingly delirious and bed-ridden mother, beside her a cage housing hungry, wily ferrets (an image that undoubtedly recalls the opening credit sequence and that echoes, once again, feelings of imprisonment and agitation). Afterwards, José suggests that they get started without Juan, and the four continue their descent into the infernal valley of the *campo*. The camera, now distant, in a striking long take followed by a slow tracking shot, follows the jeep as it plummets into the belly of the desert – a precursor to the steep descent that will ensue.

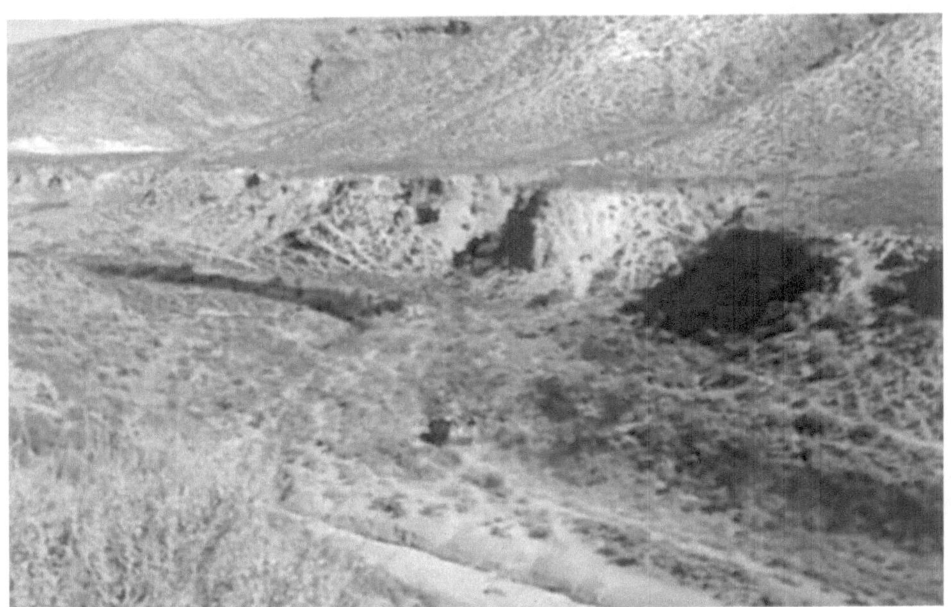

2.5 The desert landscape of the former battlefield. *La caza* (1965).

The Language of Violence, Shutters

Buen lugar para matar.

Good place to kill.

La caza

Violence pervades *La caza*'s narrative scheme both through carefully placed omissions in the dialogue and through images that force the spectator's sight open, creating visual and temporal incisions on the body of the film. Upon arrival at the campsite, José's question to Enrique – "¿Te gusta el sitio?" (Do you like the site?) – prompts the latter to gaze upon the land, taking a visual inventory of its weathered, arid "scenes." Enrique's gaze comes to rest on the caves carved into the surrounding hillsides, and it is from this point on that a curious (and endless) chain of inquiries and speculations arise regarding the location's history. Luis's answer to Enrique's question – "¿Eso es de la guerra?" (Is that from the war?) – suggests the presence of a historic event that cannot be named but remains "open" and thus one that the film, in turn, is opening (or reopening, as it were) for us, the spectators: "Aquí murió mucha gente. A montones murieron aquí. Y ahora solo han quedado los agujeros. Buen lugar para matar" ("Many people died here. A lot died here. And now only the holes have remained. A good place to kill).

After various ellipses and ambiguous references to "the war" – allusions that no doubt co-emerge with the camera's glimpses of the campsite's distinctive pockmarked soil, strangely shaped caves, vast shooting range, and exceptional field of visibility – the four hunters take out their respective weapons for cleaning and oiling. The three older men inspect their rifles while the "muchacho" ("boy," as Enrique is repeatedly called) attends to another kind of weapon – his camera. In referring to the film's "highly complex ensemble of dialectic images," Marsha Kinder has concentrated her reading of *La caza* largely on the stylization and fetishization of violence that, in this sequence in particular, visually binds the gendered rituals of the hunt to what she calls the "artificial powers of the cinematic apparatus" (1993, 161–2). Indeed, the montage of alternating close-ups of the guns and long shots of each hunter "shooting" gives the first impression of their individualized aims regarding one other; now the original target (the rabbits) has been substituted for a human one (the hunters themselves). Rhetorically reinforcing this visual substitution is the fact that the hunting instruments double as instruments of war, a point doubly underscored by Luis's comments about Enrique's vintage pistol – "Made in Germany" and "Más de uno ha muerto por esto" (More than one have died by this). These observations segue into Enrique's childish fascination with the gun and eventually into the group's collective discussion about the nature and purpose of the hunt. According to Paco, the "natural law" that exterminates the weak and the sick becomes the same law that dictates the "beauty" of the hunt. To José's explanation – "Cuánto más sensación del enemigo, más bonita la caza. Se lucha de poder a poder" (The greater the sense of the enemy, the more beautiful the hunt. It's a fight of power against power) – Luis calmly replies "Por eso, alguien dijo que la mejor caza es la caza del hombre" (That's why someone said that the best hunt is a manhunt). Of course, rather than a meaningful defence of the hunt, what this discussion generates is a fascist, pseudo-Darwinist discourse on the aesthetics of violence, aesthetics rooted in asymmetrical power relations. The fact that for these men, opposition creates aesthetic pleasure is a crucial point, one that strikingly sets the tone for the first phase of the hunt.

Setting aside Enrique, who remains an interested observer, the group's collective desire to gain a sense of power through the hunt – that is, through their spoken though senseless "rationale" for engaging in acts of violence that "no tiene ningún interés" (are of no interest) – emerges at the same time as their inability to discuss their past. Their common (and we might assume traumatic because unspoken) experience of the war is something that the hunt undoubtedly invokes even though (or perhaps *because*) it remains taboo; the result is the beginning of a systematic substitution of violent acts and "actings out" for meaningful language. In sum, the hunt is not so much naturally justified as it is revealed to be disproportionately and arbitrarily legitimized by the laws of man, which here aestheticize laws of violence pertaining to the natural world.

As a film that draws on the very device it critiques, *La caza* both reveals censorship as a form of violence and reproduces mechanisms of censorship as an operative narrative strategy within the text, on the characters, as well as outside the text, on the spectators. According to Marvin D'Lugo, this is one of the many innovative ways in which Saura equates cinematic spectatorship with social spectatorship, both subject to a cultural and historical deficit of knowledge (1991, 59). The unspeakability of the past comes to dominate the group's encounter both with the land and with itself, producing an outbreak of violence that articulates a shared sentiment that – in contrast to Bardem's work, for instance – cannot be named. This unspeakability is matched by a certain degree of visibility, summed up neatly in Luis's casual comment, "Now only the holes remain." In effect, the visual language of violence that begins with simple observations of the land, first through Paco's gaze and then Enrique's, now "utters" the unutterable, what cannot be expressed with words. This places the interpretive burden on the spectator to discern what such an utterance signifies.

Of course, it is not just images but actions that come to "fill in" the holes where language fails. Insofar as both action and image replace language, gaining credence as the dominant forms of expression, we could say that Saura's hunt doubles as a performative fiction as well as a figurative screen on which the symptoms of censorship and untimeliness are played out, simultaneously exposed and set in motion. This occurs through the ellipses and dangling questions left unanswered that pepper the dialogue as well as through stark glimpses of the dry, weathered landscape that has remained untended even though, as the servant Juan explains to his niece, "la tierra es buena. Se podría sacar una cosecha buena. ¡Pero eso a él que le importa!" (the land is good. It's possible to harvest it. But what does he care!). The substitution of spoken language for discriminate violence (the hunt as symbol and practice) and violent images (ones that interrupt the narrative and thus require interrogation) is crucial to Saura's own cinematic language – it is an absence (in this case, that which is not said) that contributes to the quality of his visual system, in which a probing of the landscape – at times literally, placing it in the crosshairs – must transpire in order for us to recognize the signs that mark this deficit.

But as much as this language of violence binds the protagonists together, eventually it causes their separation too, a separation we see played out as they "divide and conquer" under the blinding glare of the sun during the initial stages of the rabbit hunt. After José assigns positions as if the event were "una operación militar" (a military operation), each man goes on a distinct path alone. Here, the spectator gains access for the first time to their inner thoughts, which take the form of interior monologues communicated through voice-overs. While José contemplates his dire financial situation, Paco ponders his fear of disease and death, and their banal self-absorption becomes the focal point of these unspoken reflections. But it is perhaps Enrique's interior monologue, just moments before we hear the others, that is most revealing. He feels both drawn to and estranged from the land: "Tengo la impresión de haber estado aquí otras veces. Me gusta – el calor, el olor del tomillo" (I have the feeling of having been here other times. I like it – the heat, the smell of thyme). As an uncanny feeling overcomes him, he asks himself rhetorically: "Qué sensación más estraña … ¿Cuando he estado yo en un sitio como este?" (What a strange sensation … When would I have been in a place like this?). This raises an important concern – one that can, in part, be addressed by his desire to produce memories through the tangible, material evidence of photographs; as he explains to José, he brought his camera to "llevarnos un recuerdo" (for us to have a souvenir). The question of whether he has in fact been to the campsite before is relatively insignificant. Instead, this inquiry suggests an inexplicable sensation that situates Enrique in a temporal fog or displacement – a feeling that perhaps drives him to create evidence of the "once was."

Shortly after this sequence, we are presented with a second montage in which the "real-time" rabbit hunt is presented to the viewer as a succession of jarring images that imitate the firing of the guns in a rhythm of convulsionary violence, all marked by quick cuts and rapid, disorienting camera movements. We are shown the scorched hillside, the rabbits, the dog ("Cuca") fiercely running and retrieving, cross-cut with close-ups of the sweat on the hunters' brows and their smoking rifles. These images allude to and visually reinforce the fragmentary, divisive nature of the hunt rather than the solidarity or camaraderie it might create. Interestingly, the collaged chaotic movements that characterize the hunt swiftly conclude with the "click" of the camera shutter after two "static" images are shown. The first shows the four hunters triumphantly posing, waiting for their picture to be taken; the second shows a full-frame shot of a Yashica camera lens, aperture open wide for a few seconds before the timer stops. First we see the photograph before it is taken, then we watch the photograph *as* it is being taken – a double viewing that equates spectatorship with both seeing and being seen. In the end, *a seeing how things are seen.* Worth noting too is that Saura reverses the logical order – camera–point–shoot – that yields (and thus would conclude with) the photograph itself. Here, he presents us with the reverse order of this process – the soon-to-be tangible "product" of the machine's gaze, followed by the origins of that gaze, which in this case is the camera's view of the camera itself. In essence, Saura is inserting into his cinematic text a footnote or parenthesis of sorts that synthesizes two divergent temporalities: on the one hand, he is pointing to the future tense of the photograph not yet taken; on the other, he is bringing into view the constructedness of our viewing of that yet-to-be photographic image, which is presented not as natural or seamless but as mechanical and staged. It is the moment when the present image turns towards a future action and simultaneously recalls the past scene.[12] This displacement situates – indeed, *draws* – the spectator deeper in the hunt's oppressive and repressive logic. Here, literally, our eyes must "make" the image appear; seeing becomes an event, an opening of the spectator's eye onto the camera eye. It is up to the spectator as well to keep the previous cinematic image (the photograph before it is taken) in mind, which is to say to keep it present as the film moves forward in time. Rather than forcing the spectator to experience a cinematic shot as real or chronological, such a reversal invites us to see the otherwise "naturalized" event as contrived by the camera and by extension the screen.

Also related to the image's contrivance is Saura's careful placement of Enrique, not just as eager interlocutor, but also, indeed especially,

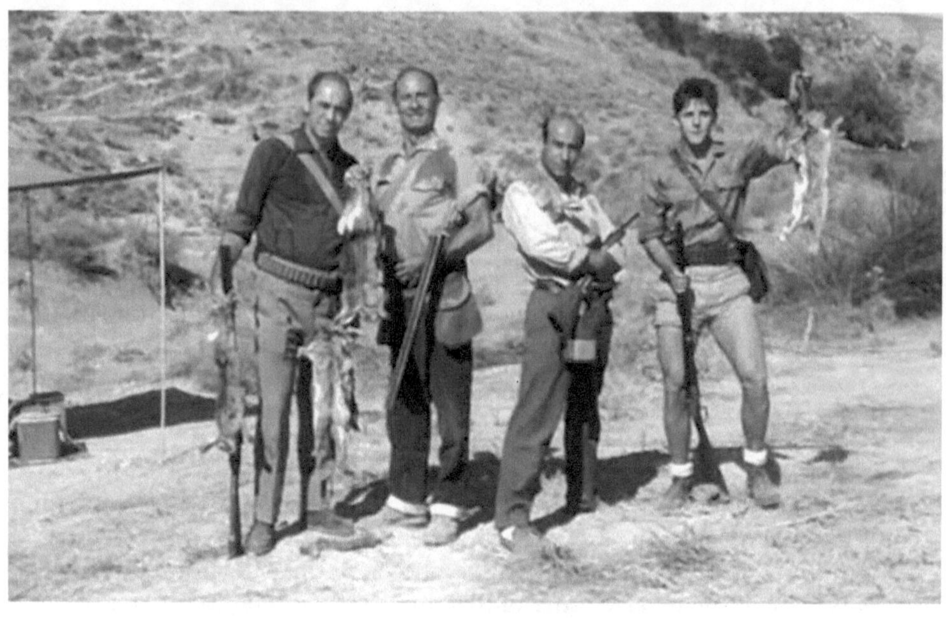

2.6 Snapshot of the four hunters. *La caza* (1965).

in the role of photographer. Whereas Kovács has likened Enrique to a "complicitous bystander, trapped in ways of seeing that he has inherited from his elders," Marvin D'Lugo has noted Enrique's importance as photographer and hunter, interrogator and participant (and here, I would add, producer and product), as a dual role that actively and paradoxically places him both in and outside the frame and at times in and outside the text altogether (1981, 24). This ambivalent positioning is critical, not only because it anticipates the film's final freeze-frame shot, in which Enrique is unambiguously "captured" and remains *in* the screen, but also, and perhaps more importantly, because the camera's aperture is positioned cinematographically to "capture" the four men ("present" but now off screen) even while it is also perfectly open, ready to capture us, the spectators of this spectacle in the making.

Contamination, Emergence of the Symptomatic

Ese Juan se alimentará solo de conejos, conejos apestados.
Por eso está cojo.

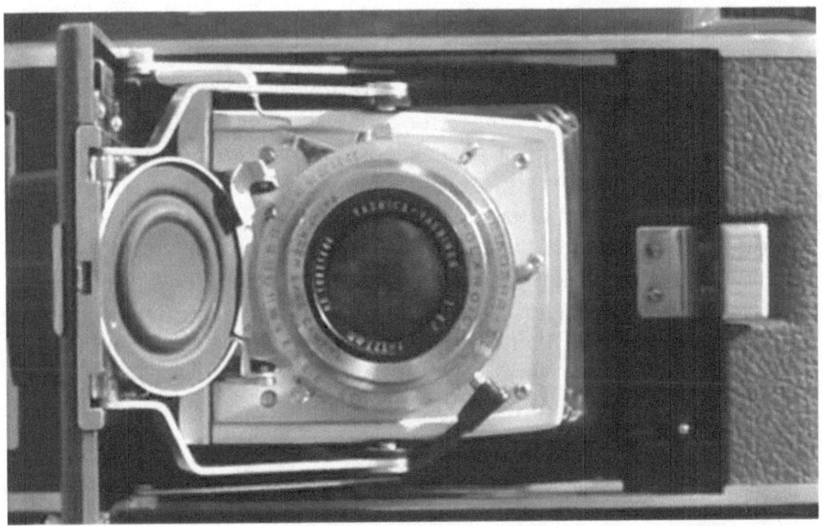

2.7 Enrique's Yashica. Close-up of the camera's aperture. *La caza* (1965).

Juan surely eats only rabbits, infected rabbits.
That's why he's crippled.

La caza

We should not forget, though, that the relationship between what is unspoken and what is acted out, between that which is censored and violent acts, is inextricably linked to a third concept circulating throughout *La caza*'s narrative: disease. Indeed, symptoms that call attention to both bodies in dis-ease (pain, illness, blindness, exhaustion, anxiety) and the diseased (literally plagued) body of the *campo* are alluded to repeatedly.[13] Juan's bad leg and bed-ridden mother, José's weak stomach, and Luis's bad nerves and sore finger are only the first signs of corporeal affliction. As the film's narrative progresses, we learn of Paco's fear of and outright disgust with these ailments, which he believes are contagious. This partly echoes Enrique's revulsion at the sight of a dead rabbit – "No parecía un conejo, ni siquiera un animal. Era como un monstruo" (It didn't look like a rabbit, not even an animal. It was like a monster) – that José later identifies as having been infected with the same incurable plague that has ravaged the land: myxomatosis.

A common tendency throughout scholarship on *La caza* has been to read the rabbits as a metaphor for Spaniards and thus to interpret the hunt as an allegory for the regime's tyranny over a weak, defenceless, and ill-struck populace. Margarita Pillado-Miller, for example, reads the figure of the "enfermo" (or "sick") as a subversive narrative strategy in that it erases any structural difference between victims and victors (2010). She argues that the representation of the diseased body collapses boundaries between these two opposing groups in order to highlight the ways in which they are mutually afflicted. This reading can certainly unpack a powerful, albeit at times obvious, understanding of *La caza*'s cultural and political critique. But it seems equally important to note that while the film might collapse certain differences between victims and victors, at times it also highlights those differences. Paco's svelte physique and financial security place him in a vastly different social and economic position than José, who we learn is struggling financially, or Juan, who struggles physically to take care of the land. I suggest here that what the film calls attention to is not, in fact, that everyone is sick (or at least, they are not sick in the same way), but that the *origins* of their ailments can be traced back to the land, which Saura compellingly and stunningly visualizes for us through an inventory of images of the landscape.

It is perhaps an important detail that the plague affecting the rabbit population should be myxomatosis, a fatal disease that came from abroad (José explains that a doctor in France used it to combat rabbit overpopulation, and it crossed over the Pyrenees from there). Katherine Singer Kovács has read this inheritance as an allegory for repressive Francoist ideology, which "feared contamination not by epidemics or diseases but by foreign ideas and movements" (1981, 24). Setting aside allegory, however, the significance of the plague can be found perhaps along more literal lines. The plague (an "infestation" but also, given the word's etymology, a "wound," from the Latin *plaga* and Spanish *llaga*) indicates that the land is wounded, not only in a metaphorical sense, referring to the indelibility of the war and its traumatic aftermath, but now also in a medical sense that references real, quantifiable, and thus visible injury. Plague in a general sense produces monstrous but unspecified wounds; in a more explicit sense, myxomatosis – which paralyses its victims before killing them – taps into broader themes of immobility and stasis. It is perhaps to Saura's credit that the symptoms of this disease should perfectly reflect the conditions in which the characters live and interact (social paralysis) *and* precisely what they fear (widespread infection and contamination). Just as paralysis is, in a sense, the inevitable result of the men's being "captured," as much by the land and the hunt as by the photographic apparatus, the inability to move brought on by the plague and its subsequent invasion of the land constitutes a kind of wounding that is at odds with the nature of cinematic movement as well as with the "chase" that is at the heart of the hunt itself. This point is all the more dramatized in the famous "siesta sequence" in which a voice-over relaying to the audience José's unnerving dream says "Ayudame. No puedo moverme. El brazo me quema. No puedo moverme" (Help me. I can't move. My arm is burning. I can't move).

The notion of capture – as condition rather than symptom – warrants particular examination, especially when we connect visible symptoms of wounding such as the abundant abrasions on the terrain, the visible sores on the rabbits, and the weathered, waning masculine bodies of the older hunters, to invisible ones. For however recognizable or exposed such symptoms are, there is also a sense of the subterranean reserve of these "outpourings," realized at two key moments – first, when Saura's camera enters one of the rabbit holes, literally penetrating the landscape; and second, when it enters, along with José and Paco, one of the hillside caves, which is actually an old bunker from the war. In effect, entrance into the land's subsurface illuminates a double layer of wounding, most disturbingly resulting in the "discovery" of another symptomatic body: José's secret cadaver.

Keeping Secrets

Entre nosotros no puede haber secretos.

Between us there can be no secrets.

La caza

Secrets place a particular demand on the film's narrative economy, one that magnifies the burden of representation (and, for that matter, the burden of interpretation). At first, this manifests itself primarily in the form of abstractions – the unnamed but repeatedly mentioned war, José's real motive for inviting the men to his game preserve (which we find out is to ask Paco for money), and what significance the reunion bears for each member of the group. The monumentality of these abstractions

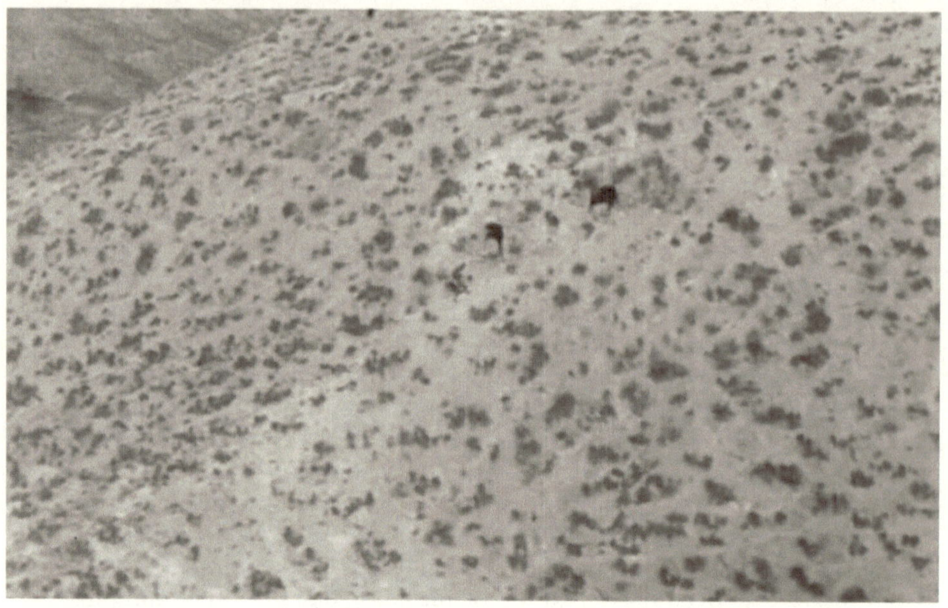

2.8 The pockmarked, extraterrestrial land seen from above. *La caza* (1965).

resonates, in part, in the many long shots that slowly pan the vastness of the campsite, bringing into view the abstract, measled appearance of the terrain, against which backdrop the men seem like tiny insects. The poetics of the visual shifts between extreme magnification and exaggerated long shots are fundamental – the land is lent corporeal contours and markings, while the men become mere abstractions, dehumanized and lost, as it were, either against the grain of the hillside or in becoming landscapes themselves through revealing close-up shots that trace the details of their flesh. In short, these geographical/bodily transformations mirror each other. As the campsite becomes more humanized (for Sally Faulkner, "personified"), the men become first animalized and then converted into geographies as the camera, in the same steady pan (left to right, diagonally) reveals the mountainous textures of their skin and clothing to emulate the land (in her language, "reified"). The fabric of Paco's corduroy pants seems to undulate in the same manner as the hills in the background (2006, 169).

But perhaps the biggest abstraction throughout the film is not the land or the male body but the completely absent figure of Arturo – the "open secret" that binds the men not only to their past friendship but also to the taboo subject of death – in this particular case, suicide. It is no coincidence that the question of Arturo's identity and whereabouts arises in a scene that is spatially separated yet temporally synchronous with José's unconcealing of his well-kept and selectively shared "secret." Less as a warning, and more in the spirit of sharing a gift, José says to Paco: "Te voy a enseñar algo. Es un secreto que tengo en estos montes. Nadie lo sabe, ni siquiera Juan" (I'm going to show you something. It's a secret that I have in those hills. No one knows about it, not even Juan). Before lunch, the men pair off – Luis and Enrique drive to a nearby village for bread, while José and Paco remain at the campsite. In these respective scenes, each reflective of and continuous with the other – this is established through a series of cross-cuts – we witness parallel exchanges and eventually learn about the subtext for the hunt (another "open secret"): José's dire financial situation. Their gathering, masked as José's attempt to rekindle old friendships, is the pretext for him to ask Paco for a loan. But as his requests are presented, they are quickly denied. Parallel to José's plea, Enrique in an earlier scene asks, "¿Arturo fue él que murío, no?" (Arturo is the one who died, right?), to which Luis evasively responds, "Esto no es la Inquisición!?" (What is this, the Inquisition!?).

As José and Paco enter through the door to the cave where the "secret" cadaver awaits them – arguably the turning point of the film, the point at which the hidden object literally guarded under lock and key is now revealed – the other two men arrive just in time to see the killing of a lamb in the nearby village. Thus entering the cave occurs simultaneously with the witnessing of a sacrificial killing; the remains found within the former (the dead soldier) are paired with the event of the latter (bloodshed, death). Marsha Kinder has described the village episode as the "sacrificial slaughter of animals" that prefaces human combat (1993, 161). But perhaps more interesting for our purposes is that the return to the site of death – indeed, to the place where death is embodied and literally entombed – is visually synchronized with an unexpected arrival at a spectacle of killing in the present, which is portrayed as a collectively witnessed event. Nor should we forget that the entry into the cave-now-tomb marks the moment of initiation (for Paco) – that is, the moment of coming into knowledge of what José "has hidden in there" (Paco only half-jokingly asks before crossing the threshold, "What do you have hidden in there? It's not a bomb shelter, is it?"). This initiation is both the moment when the secret is shared

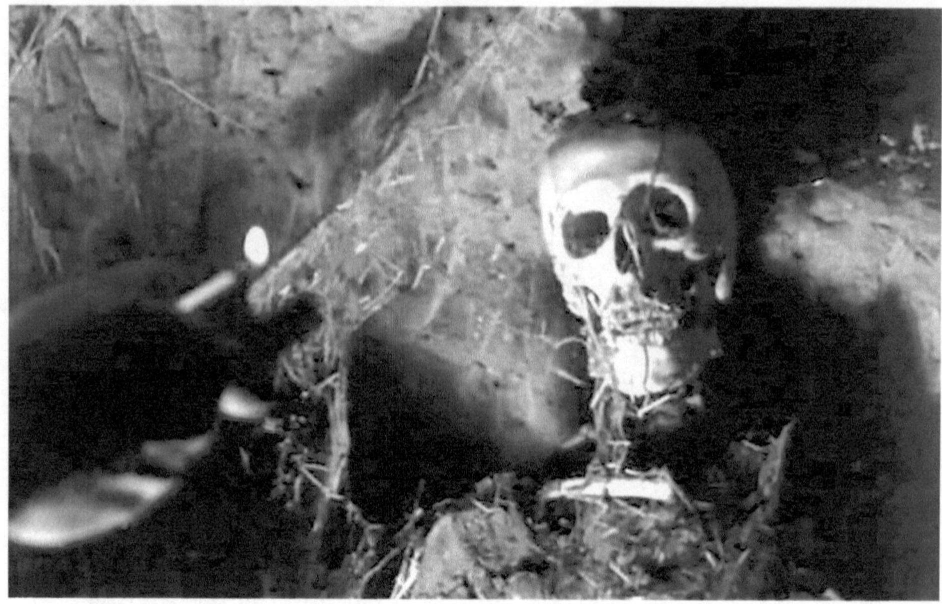

2.9 José's "secret" cadaver. *La caza* (1965).

("sacrificed" in the sense of "thrown" or "given up") and the moment of recognition when the uncannily hidden (and we might add, *lost* insofar as it has remained "unseen") object of history comes to light. This "coming to light" is visually reinforced in the cave scene as José lights a match and places it close to the dead soldier's "face" so that Paco, standing behind him in the dark, can now see. Of course, instead of an actual face, the starkly pale skeleton bears only two large eye sockets, which recall the hillside "holes" and Luis's earlier caution, which now registers as an eerie presentiment: "only the holes remain." Since the exchange in the cave scene is cross-cut with the village scene, on a visual level we are invited to connect them – the sacrifice and the sacred object – as experiences that both structure the bond between these men and at the same time cause their alienation and isolation. Seeing implies loss, "giving something up" – the secret knowledge of José's *muerto,* in one case, and the animal's life, in the other.

We quickly see that the once dark cave, now illuminated, is a place not of Platonic enlightenment but of denial. A far cry from a philosopher, José is more like a pirate who guards the buried treasure, and

Paco stands in not as prisoner but as an authoritative voice that expresses outrage at the sight of this "treasure," which he views as obscene and grotesque because it has not been properly buried. When Paco asks "¿Por qué no lo entierras como Dios manda?" (Why don't you bury it properly?), José's reply is straightforwardly rational and even callous – "De poco le va a servir que lo entierran ya" (Little good that would do now). I have suggested that we read the unveiling of the cadaver in the cave as the return to a site where the lost object (the remains of a body) marks the definitive moment (the open door, so to speak) for Saura's protagonists to bear witness to the horror of the past (the war and its aftermath) and to enter into knowledge of that past, a past that up until now, in the film's economy of silence, disease, and failed language, has been regarded to be as foreign and scorchingly uninhabitable as the land itself.[14] But this act of witnessing necessitates a kind of seeing in the dark – a seeing that harbours a kind of violence or force insofar as it counters simultaneously the logic of exposing and sharing with the logic of hiding and burying. If the secret/sacrifice is the object that binds these characters into a common knowledge, then it is also one that foreshadows their common fate – they will soon be subject to a similar tragedy in the exact same place. Like the soldier preserved in the hillside cave, the hunters will leave only traces of a violent past that is clearly yet invisibly tied to the land.

Bodies, Eyes, Traps

Nos estamos asando vivos aquí encerrados. Y este dolor.

Trapped in here, we're being roasted alive. And this pain.

¿Por qué cerrara los cepos?

Why would he close the traps?

La caza

The image of the body has been given considerable attention throughout scholarship on *La caza.* Besides the plagued rabbits and the dead soldier, which, as already discussed, are inextricably tied to the land, there are numerous references throughout the film to fetishized or "animalized" female bodies. There is repeated mention of José's girlfriend, Maribel, who is compared to the notably young, sexualized models of Paco's *Drag* magazine; there are Luis's off-hand remarks about the ferrets' physical similarities to women; there is the young body of Carmen (Juan's niece), who is portrayed as prepubescent, filthy, and sexualized. The connection between the landscape and the female body as an object of the dominant male gaze is subtly emphasized in Saura's camera work, which often brackets Carmen as a figure lodged "in between" – first, between the hunters as she helps them prepare for the day, then between the hillside holes as she dances to the radio, and, later on, framed by donkey legs as she bathes (a scene viewed from Enrique's perspective as he voyeuristically watches her through the viewfinder of his Yashica). Similarly, recall the scene where Enrique, after climbing the hillside, stops to survey the campsite below through his binoculars. As he swiftly grazes the landscape's profile, his eyes settle on the cover of the *Drag* magazine, slowly glossing the model's legs and torso until they finally rest on her eyes, which are "staring" back at him.

The evenly placed references to female subjectivity as an accessory to the hunt, as well as to male bonding and to interactions with the land itself, suggest an important link between the landscape and a feminine space. But it is perhaps more compelling to consider how the male body is bound to the land. Kovács and Faulkner equate the land's body with masculine bodies in that both suffer from battle wounds and are subject to extreme conditions of weathering as well as to undeniable signs of aging. Faulkner's thoughtful and engaging study "Ageing and Coming of Age" focuses on the notion of withering bodies no longer in their prime as a narrative point; she emphasizes how the spectator's awareness is drawn to the visible scars on the hunters' bodies. Her careful reading of the "siesta sequence" identifies the film's imagistic economy as one that captures the ephemerality of a weakened masculinity in order to allegorize Franco's by then waning dictatorship. In this sequence, the camera steadily traces the tired, sweating bodies of José and Paco in one continuous series of close-ups, paired with alternating voice-overs that reveal to the spectator the opaque content of their unfettered dreams.[15] Significantly, the "paralysis" with which the siesta sequence concludes (the camera is still, and the last words of José's dream are about the inability to move) is further intensified by the final image of José's open eye, now eerily returning the gaze by looking "back" at the camera and thus at the spectator. Thus, from the light of the blinding sun to the darkness of the cave, which is illuminated for a fleeting

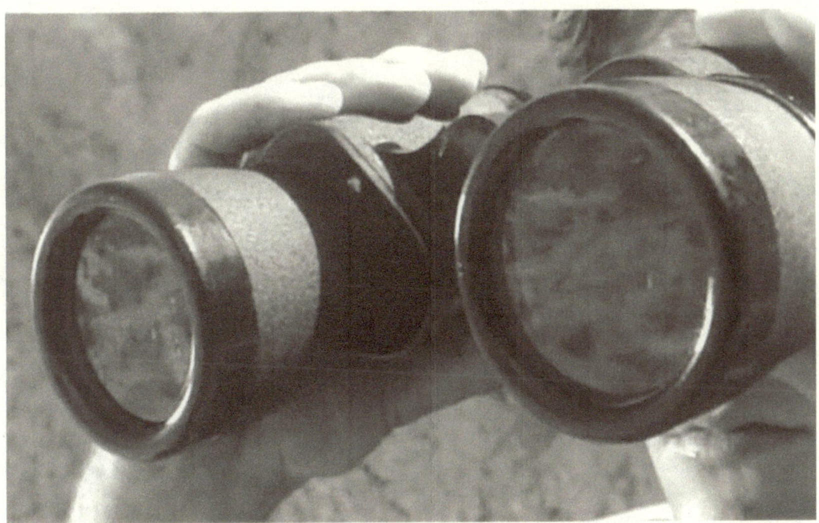

2.10 Enrique surveying the landscape. A new "binocular vision." *La caza* (1965).

moment, Saura's visual language now turns to frame the opening of the eye; this temporally marks an awakening from sleep and calls to mind the Yashica camera eye that formerly situated both protagonists and spectators between tenses, or as Nietzsche might say, "between the hedges of past and future" – that is, at the moment of anticipation of a future capture and during the time of imaging the "becoming" past. Here we are presented with a literal opening of the eye that reproduces and reaffirms the metaphorical opening of the cinematic apparatus (this also offers a remarkable visual echo of the final shot of *Los golfos,* where the half-slain bull's open eye signifies the moment of paralysis and imminent death). Here, significantly, the aperture that immobilizes now also sets into motion, lending movement to the confluence of time.

Like the hillside holes (in reality, bunkers) that can be entered but also are sealed off, the eye – here, mechanical *and* human – directs our attention to the film's oscillation between opening and closing, a gesture that brings us back to the land as a place of entrapment and enclosure. Earlier on, during the first phase of the hunt, José had avoided stepping in a rabbit trap; this had provoked him to set off the trap deliberately, while he thought to himself, "No me debo distraer. Olvídate de todo ahora. Si me coga el cepo, me pudiera haber roto el tobillo. Es

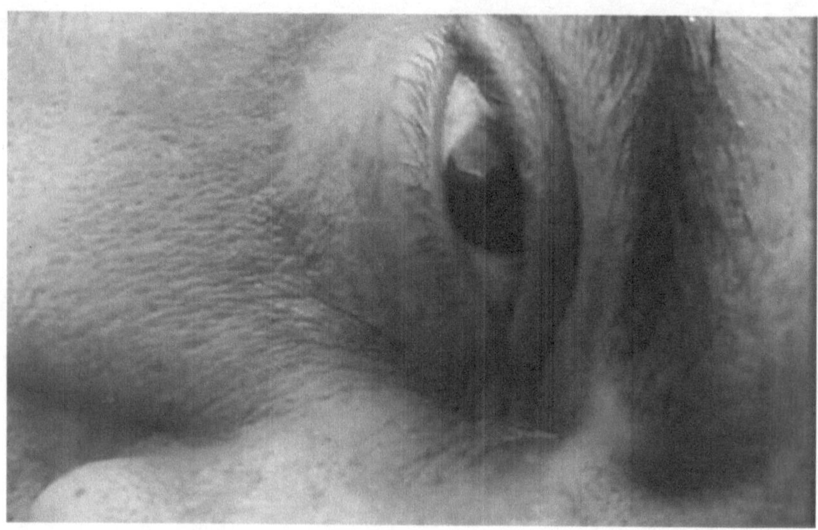

2.11 José returns the gaze to the camera/spectator. *La caza* (1965).

lo unico que me faltaba" (I shouldn't get distracted. Forget everything now. If I were to step in a trap, I could have broken an ankle. That's all I needed). The trap, like the camera/human eye, is initially open ("set" or "set up," at least), then closed by José so as to avoid injury. Ironically, though, in closing the trap, he is entering into the very logic of entrapment that will be his fate. Saura's choice to insert "openings" into his film – not just in shots of the land, but also as forces of narrative interruption or spaces of narrative perforation – is a vital one in that those openings suggest thinking in the subjunctive (i.e., in the realm of possibilities) rather than in the static logic of censorship, with all the connotations it bears – closure, coming to terms, arrest of movement. Note that the dream sequence is another form of narrative perforation, in that the spectator is "opened" to the characters' innermost desires and fears, those which we are led to believe have been sublimated into the masculine activities of hunting, financial control, and womanizing. Ultimately, though only a minor detail, "opening the eye" is a gentle but crucial reminder of what Saura is attempting to do with cinema. The opened eye is equated with spectatorial awareness, inviting us to ask both what the eye sees and what the nature of seeing in this context exacts. What do *we* see? What is *meant* to be seen?

Landscape, Preservation, and Survival

Vaya un día. Parece que arde la tierra.

What a day. It feels like the land is burning.

La caza

Up until now, I have been making a case for looking at apertures and cinematic openings as wounds, or ways of seeing the past emerge in the present, unsolicited and unsettling. For as much as Saura's camera glimpses the surface of this place, could we think of his film as an attempt to penetrate the landscape, a methodical exercise in excavating, "digging into" the land to discover what lies underneath? What are the narrative strategies that enact a feeling of burial and re-emergence? What are the cinematic strategies? As we have seen, the foregrounding cinematic strategy of *La caza* consists in using natural landscapes to construct unnatural or artificial modes of seeing. So it is indeed a remarkable feat that Saura achieves this sense of enclosure through the capture of vast, open, seemingly limitless spaces.

This has to do, in part, with Saura's visual interrogation of the landscape. We could ask, then, if Saura is interested in denaturalizing relations among a community of men in the postwar years? Is he perhaps equally invested in the tension between humanizing and dehumanizing the landscape? Plainly, the film draws on the authenticity of the landscape (its non-fictional "realness" is marked by the opening disclaimer on the authentic location of filming) in order to fictionalize the untimely emergence of the past in the present. For as monumental and natural as the landscape appears, it is also enigmatically extraterrestrial and shares striking similarities with the doomed "planeta negra" ("fifth planet") of Luis's science fiction novel – "Algo sobrevivió. Algo que ahora se ha olvidado por completo. Hubo lluvia, viento e hielo. Las cicatrices de la tierra se fueron borrando a través de milliones de años. No sabemos siquiera donde encontraban estas heridas y si para entonces existían seres humanos en la Tierra o sobre el quinto planeta" (Something survived. Something that now has been forgotten completely. There was rain, wind, and ice. The scars of the land were erased over millions of years. We don't even know where they found these wounds and if back then humans existed on the Earth or on the fifth planet). Though the land's scars "were erased" over the years, something, some indistinguishable *algo* survives. This survival, I suggest, is at odds with the cultivation and exposure of wounds, which up until now I have been arguing is the main thrust of Saura's film. Survival of the traumatic, according to Ross Chambers, is "trauma's failure to heal" and "takes the form in aftermath culture of 'surviving trauma,' a phrase that might be allowed to imply both the fact of one's having survived a traumatic event and the contrary fact of the pain's surviving into the present, the fact that one has not survived it so much as one is (still) surviving it" (2004, xxii). The fact that the land survives and endures through the persistence of wounds in the landscape as well as on the human body is never only a projection of a past traumatic occurrence but always testament to the fact that that trauma is *still* occurring.

After the afternoon siesta (which arguably breaks the film's narration into two parts), the men embark on the second phase of the rabbit hunt, which involves the use of *los hurones* – Juan's ferrets. The centrepiece of this episode, which has a notably quicker pace, is not the superficial mental musings of the hunters, as we saw previously, but now the underground shots that depict the ferret's ferocious attack on a rabbit, which shrieks in agony. The violence that takes place below ground is indeed continuous with the violent acts committed above ground by the hunters. The camera cuts to a shot of Paco as he shoots one of the ferrets. This killing, an act of deliberate and unchecked aggression that alienates each member of the group, is a catalyst for the film's final showdown – the tragic and grotesque human hunt with which the film ends.

This under/above ground continuum confirms the land's capacity to establish the conditions that dominate the hunt; it also mirrors the inadequacies that arise from and circumscribe the hunt. The land contains trauma and at the same time is inadequate to the task of that containing, all of which leads to an "outpouring" or outbreak. On a conceptual level, this outbreak of visible symptoms links the landscape back to contamination and disease and exemplifies how the land is not immune to the horrors it sustains and reproduces. On this point, Kovács's language is extraordinary. She notes that tensions among the men, like the environmental conditions, are "simmering," "bursting," "boiling over" (1991, 23–5).[16] This is true visually as well, from the scorching, blinding sun to the fire that sets the land ablaze, to the excruciating images and sounds of the underground animal attack, to the explosive shoot-out above ground. Saura stages a literal surfacing of violence, which manifests itself as a sudden, syncopated, and reciprocal eruption.

As the three older hunters-turned-enemies systematically execute one another, it is Enrique who is left to bear witness. As the only survivor of these incomprehensible and unbearably horrific events, he runs up the hillside in absolute panic, ascending out of the infernal *campo,* fleeing into the distant and unscreened barren landscape, into his unknown future. The film concludes with a freeze frame of the young Enrique's ghastly face, which leaves the spectator with an image of horror and trauma, one that is reinforced by the sound-over of his heavy panting – a strong indication that this member of Spain's younger generation is going nowhere fast. Here, the switchbacks between extreme magnification and extreme reduction offer a visual hyperbole that reveals a space of entrapment at once overdetermined and physically and visually ambivalent. At the end, of course, this ambivalence takes sides: no one leaves, or leaves unscarred. For as much as there is a sense of "confinement" and "quarantine," there is also an attempt to excavate (Kovács 1991, 24). Saura's language of entrapment here slides into a logic of penetration, excavation, and extraction, which is another way of saying that the film moves between a logic of wounds and wounding and one of surviving those wounds. Of course, the surviving subject (Enrique) is himself wounded, such that the film makes a strong argument for survival as something that can *only* occur (and that is destined to continually *recur*) through wounding.

Critics largely agree that the landscape in *La caza* both holds particular import, historically and culturally, and signals a kind of historical preservation (Leeder, 2009; Kovács, 1991; D'Lugo, 1991; Faulkner, 2006). But significantly, this preservation is indecipherable; its availability to the characters, all of whom have varying degrees of interest in "reading" the landscape's language, hinges on a paradox – namely, that its visibility precludes its legibility. In terms of both narrative coherence and the film's visual logic, what the land preserves only makes sense once an interrogation or intervention has taken place. Perhaps the most obvious moment of this "penetration" is when Saura's camera captures the subterranean scene of attack – when it literally enters one of the rabbit holes. Unlike for Alice in Wonderland, going down the rabbit hole does not imply entering a realm of fantasy and dream, but rather a strange confined space of torture, anguish, and nightmarish visions.

Landscape as Index

According to Faulkner's powerful reading of the film's "siesta sequence," the land's index of time coincides with the portrayal of bodies: "Just as the landscape reveals the strata of time in the first shot, so the body acts as an index of time in the second." Thus, as "the landscape is

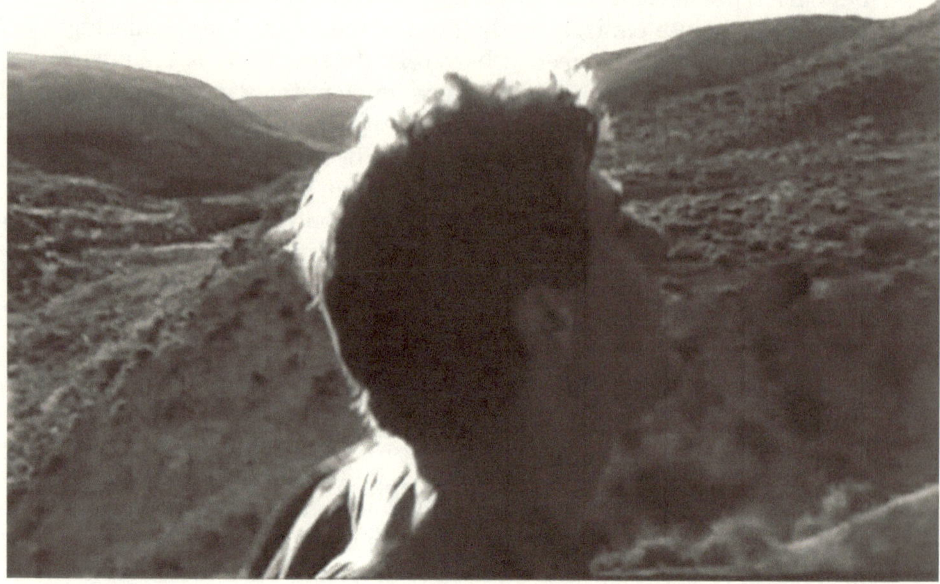

2.12 Final freeze-frame shot of Enrique's fleeing the scene of death. *La caza* (1965).

personified … the human body is, simultaneously, reified" (2006, 167; 169). She continues:

> The landscape takes on a hypnotic, static quality, which points to the timelessness of the physical environment, whose monumentality, compared to the man's ephemerality, seems overwhelming. On the other hand, that same shot contracts time, and the landscape becomes, in Santos Zunzuneguí's words, a "lugar de sedimentación del pasado" (place where the past is sedimented). (168)

I suggest something slightly different: it is not just a process of sedimentation that *La caza* so carefully and compellingly frames; it is also one of continual, persistent, and unwavering re-emergence. The film offers a simultaneous portrayal and interrogation of history's uncanny re-emergence in the present, not only in the way it settles in and unsettles, but strikingly in the way it "flashes" up and finds refuge in the land. On the one hand, it is accurate to think of the landscape becoming a sort of sanctuary where things fall into place and take up residence, so to speak. But as much as things settle in or "stick to" the land, they also loosen and become undone; resurfacing, they become unsettled in the sense of both "detached" and "haunted."

It is interesting to think about the notion of "indexing time," especially in a medium so indebted to time's passage or its slippage – time as something lost and therefore displaced and displaceable. Faulkner is interested in reading the land – like bodies – as places where time is located, static, fixed. But the potentially more compelling argument would be to think of these places as bodies, sites, terrains where the antinomies of time are mapped out, where time both originates and is lost, where history is awakened, indeed loosened from the bedrock of progressive, linear time, and reburied.

Here, one could argue that all land – which is to say all landscape – is an "index of time." What differentiates Saura's film, then, is that it is also an *index of trauma*. An index based on the axes of trauma and survival, on the one hand, and on aftermath and denial, on the other. In her superb study on the emergence of cinematic time, Mary Ann Doane notes that

> unlike icons and symbols, which rely upon association by resemblance or intellectual operations, the work of the index depends upon association by contiguity (the foot touches the ground and leaves a trace, the wind pushes the weathercock, the pointing finger indicates an adjoining site, the light rays reflected from the object 'touch' the film). (2008, 92)

The trace is key here and relates not only to cinematic vision but also to trauma. Aftermath is usually understood as a contiguous relationship with a past or present event. But denial and survival can deflate the temporality of this relationship; these are modes that "dedifferentiate" (Chambers's term) such that continuity and contiguity are not relevant factors in interpreting trauma and aftermath, but rather point towards the conditions of their un-interpretability.

Poetics of Displacement

> Todos hemos cambiado en estos años.
>
> We've all changed over these years.
>
> *La caza*

What does Saura propose with his incorporation of two different kinds of subjects who are equally incapable of accessing the very past that surrounds them? Perhaps it is this question, more than any other, that finds its answer in the idea of generation, which Faulkner has identified as the film's main narrative theme. While I agree with Faulkner's assessment that the film highlights the "clash between young and old," which "is intensified as it is one between a group that has fought in a war and a group that has not," I suggest here that Saura's portrayal of the clash of "age" is also understood – perhaps *best* understood – as a *shared problem* of gaining access to the past (2006, 152). This is also a shared problem of inheritance and return – indeed, a shared problem of being haunted by spectres. An alternative reading of *La caza* reveals that the problem facing Saura's four hunters is not necessarily the distance that separates them due to their age gap but rather the complicated space that *binds* them together in and through a poetics of displacement. For as much as they do not share first-hand experience of the war, or a mutual friendship with Arturo, it is the common place (a "plagued place," as we have noted) of non-articulation that unites the four men *in spite of* their generational differences. In the end, their common fate is explicitly linked to the politics and effects of censorship – to not being able to articulate the already unspeakable conditions and memories of the past that systematically govern their present reality.

Faulkner also notes that Enrique commands no visual interest for the spectator, yet his constant questioning of the others does. As a character he thus opens the gate to larger spectatorial questions about the group's relationship – past and present – and what this place *means* for them, or what value it holds. I argue that Enrique's inquisitiveness reinforces the notion that this new generation of Spaniards, like the audience, has been left in the proverbial dark, a point made all the more ironic if not paradoxical given the relentless and blinding glare of the sun. Not only is Enrique surrounded by evidence of a past that he sees but cannot comprehend fully, but the act or practice of seeing itself is at odds with this thirst for knowledge, for shared experience, entrance into the group, and a sense of belonging. At the same time that Enrique consistently probes into that which is unspoken and unknown, attempting to give it a new language, he performs the younger generation's need to *record* knowledge (while demonstrating its lack of interpretive strategies). His camera becomes that unsettling apparatus, a mechanical extension of his inquisitive mind, a machine that captures but also unsettles and divides.

Photography: Moving into Stillness

Era por llevarnos un recuerdo.

It was for us to have a souvenir.

La caza

As we have already noted, Enrique as both photographer and photographed subject is located both behind the camera and in front of it – an existence that simultaneously, and paradoxically, locates him outside the photograph's frame as well as within it. His double-placement finds its parallel in the film's narrative; he is both positioned inside the place of the past (the battlefield turned hunting ground) and displaced from its desert landscape, repeatedly cast out and denied access to its "secrets" (we learn that he is the only one in the group who hasn't entered the cave). We should not forget that Enrique's camera – the film's metacinematic device – is an instrument that he uses to emphatically capture, record, and preserve history. In fact, his constant photographing (he takes pictures of José, brings his camera to the village, and promises photos to Carmen), his documentation of "the now," sets him apart from the others as much as it disturbs them. In particular, José becomes annoyed and viciously tears up the portrait of himself that Enrique gifts him. The intrusive presence of the camera locates the young hunter as a subject who exists both *in* and *behind* the production of knowledge – he is producer of facts, artefacts, and testimony, yet his technology introduces stasis (from the Latin *staticus* and the Greek *statikos,* "causing to stand") into the landscape, it *captures and arrests.*

In this way, photography functions as Enrique's mode of collecting and documenting reality and as a means to generate a new history – something material that can be seen and read, exposed and reproduced. Besides photography, the spectator is offered the subtle suggestion that Enrique's perspective, like our own, is consistently framed in specific ways – ways that are sometimes not readily available or recognizable to us. When the four men first arrive at the campsite, Enrique views the landscape through the crosshairs of the gun he is holding. Here, the landscape not only is brought into focus for him, as for us, but also doubles as a target. (We could even say, without too much exaggeration, that it is the "target" of the entire film.) When he is not taking photographs or shooting a gun, his way of seeing and experiencing the landscape is always mediated by something else – music, magazines, mirrors, mannequins. Moreover, the control of his gaze through the camera, binoculars, and crosshairs establishes him as "a spectator-in-the-text" (Kinder 1993, 161; D'Lugo 1991, 62–5). He watches, observes, and surveys; his constant looking is precedent to his constant questioning.

Indeed, Enrique's way of seeing, like the images he captures with his instant camera, is always framed and offers the spectator an implicit understanding that his experience of the present is likewise framed, implying that what he sees is always contingent on what he does not see or what is excluded from the frame. Photography offers a kind of answer to the questions he poses. It testifies to the event, the singular moment, the "once was," and leaves a trace. In essence, it materializes that which the landscape produces but which subsequently drifts, disappears, and vanishes. What photography and landscape share, then, is the ability to *inscribe* "what would otherwise be an ephemeral instant, unarchivable" (Doane 2008, 102). Photography underscores the problem of aftermath by reinforcing the problem of temporal discontinuity that co-emerges with physical and material contiguity, or the trace. The crucial link here is that photography, like Saura's film itself, acts as a form of witnessing and as a mode of what Chambers calls "testimonial affirmation."

Also, there is implicit in both media a strong desire to "archive" or catalogue the present. Whereas in cinema that archival logic becomes one of movement, presentness, and ongoing accumulation, in photography it becomes one of stillness, arrest, and death. Indeed, the photographic affirms the "pastness" of the past, or as Roland Barthes would have it, the "that-has-been." Barthes's discussion of photography as a conjunction of the "here" and the "then" means that the photographic image carries within it the trace of the past or the temporality of the "once was," as we will see in the next chapter. We could say then that the very presence of photography within the film calls attention to the "brute facticity of the past," as Barthes suggests, while offering a counterpart to the projective, fluid, and fictional qualities of the film medium (Barthes 1981, 75; Doane 2008, 103). While Saura's film offers the spectator an impression of the real, photography – both the idea and the practice of it on screen – disrupts that impression, countering it with actual, tangible evidence of the immediate past. It engages us with the fact of discontinuity and rupture, *not* least of all by interrupting the film's fluidity, not so much to still or embalm time as to still the representation of movement and to "frame itself," if only for a moment.

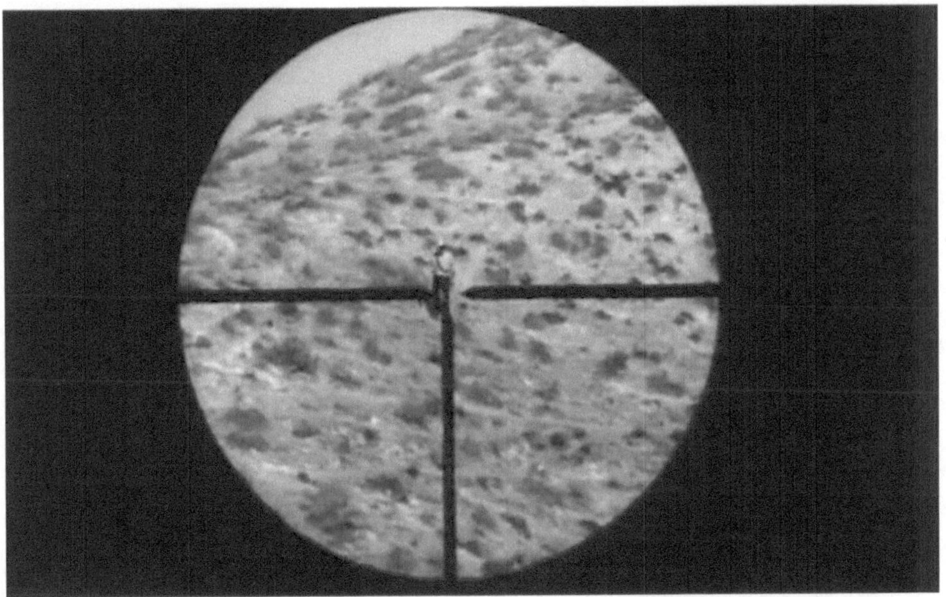

2.13 Enrique's view of the landscape through his rifle. *La caza* (1965).

As a subject who sits in between the present and the past, who straddles both sides of the proverbial fence of history – as creator who makes photographs and as participant who is subject in his own framing and being framed – Enrique bears another important role in the film. He is what Marianne Hirsch would call a "post-memory" subject, one who inherits the memory and trauma of an event uncannily familiar to him yet ultimately distant and strange (Hirsch, 1997). Enrique, unlike the other three hunters, as he runs out of the desert, will carry into the future the memories of a past that he cannot directly experience; nor, in any practical way, can he come to terms with that past in the present (we remember that the last image is a freeze frame of Enrique with the voice-over of his heavy panting – he lives and breathes yet is "stuck" in time and space). Ultimately it is the figure of Enrique in the film's final scene that, like his own photographs and like the failure of Spain's political, economic, and social *apertura*, calls attention to the tension between, on the one hand, recording and preserving history, and on the other, erasing and forgetting it. Enrique, as censored subject, post-memory subject, and subject *in between*, is

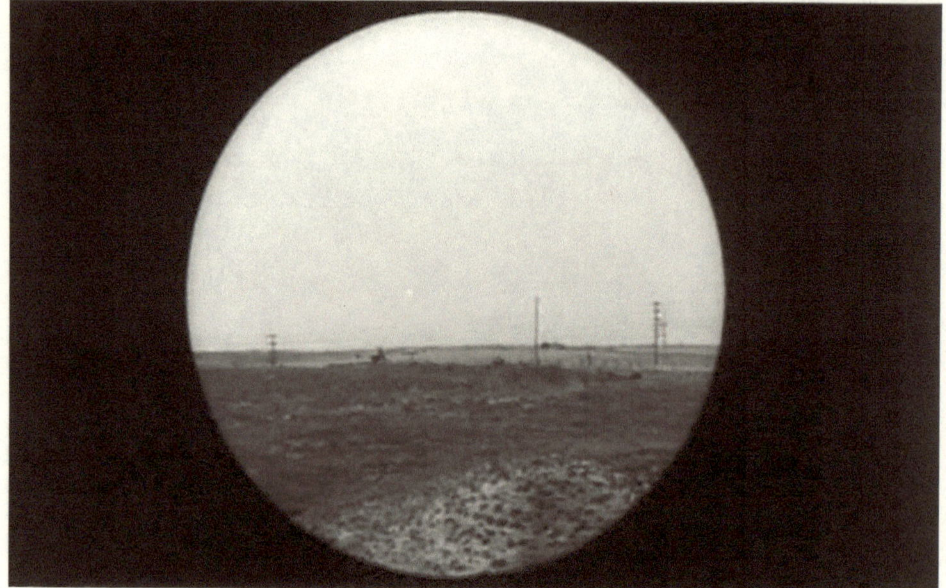

2.14 The landscape captured. Shots such as this one consciously call attention to specific framing mechanisms and subjective perspective. *La caza* (1965).

frozen on the screen, which is also to say frozen *in time*. In this way, the film's final scene serves as a tacit reminder that Enrique, who previously stood both behind and in front of the camera, is now trapped within the frame of the camera and the symptomatic landscape of the *campo* – he is inscribed into and affected by a history to which he simultaneously does and does not belong.

Landscapes of Untimeliness

I have argued that *La caza,* often read as an allegory for postwar Spain, is principally interested in using landscape to theorize new ways of seeing and relating to history – that is, in reading history *as* cinema, which is another way of looking at history as an *assemblage* of images and fictions. In *La caza,* as with his previous work, *Los golfos,* Saura presents his audience with specific images of modern Spain as doubly blinded – as unable to see the present reality of an alienating, failing, and untimely modernity, and at the same time incapable of articulating a traumatic past, the signs of which roam and haunt the landscape. The film ultimately reveals symptoms of an infected and contagious but also shared and inherited cultural forgetting; in doing so, it exposes the double-bind of a desire to access an inaccessible past. History stands at odds with this desire to know, communicate, and remember. It is not buried, nor does it remain out of sight; rather, it slowly creeps into the time and place of the present, wounding it repeatedly and violently. Saura's four hunters thus portray subjects caught in the strange yet illuminating paradox of impossible exchanges – that is, the desire to know yet the need to forget, the unconjured return of phantoms from their past met with their subsequent conjuring and eventual suppression and reburial. Of course, the fact that so much of the film hinges on the constraints of knowledge – whether desired or undesired, whether collective or individual – is curiously and I would add not insignificantly visualized through the vastness of the open and immediate yet barren and inhospitable landscape that literally engulfs the hunting grounds, where most of the film's action takes place.

I believe that ultimately, Saura's text is primarily invested in rethinking the residue of historical trauma – how place retains and stratifies traumatic events, how it archives them, how the land acts as a catalogue of catastrophic experience and container of memory. *La caza* also exhibits a deep desire to discover how historical trauma impacts both personal lives and collective violence, how it emerges in the present in the form of an extreme, unwavering spectrality – open wounds, undeniable signs of illness, and the oppressive heat and light of the sun, at once illuminating and blinding, elucidating and bewildering. As a response to the burden of inheriting a silenced past that continues to survive and wound the present, *La caza,* in its relentless desire to read and know the landscape, creates a responsible seeing of history's ghosts that visualizes what cannot be said.

Chapter Three

Photographic Interventions: Two Meditations on Landscape and Loss

Perhaps we have an invincible resistance to believing in the past, in History, except in the form of myth. The Photograph, for the first time, puts an end to this resistance: henceforth the past is as certain as the present, what we see on paper is as certain as what we touch. It is the advent of the Photograph – and not, as has been said, of the cinema – which divides the history of the world.

Camera Lucida (Barthes 1981, 88)

The important thing is that the photograph possesses an evidential force, and that its testimony bears not on the object but on time.

Camera Lucida (Barthes 1981, 88–9)

Photography is, first of all, a way of seeing.

"Photography: A Little Summa" (Sontag 2007, 124)

Photography's Reach

Nearly three decades before Susan Sontag would write her "little summa" photography treatise – a small but compelling contribution to what would be her last collection of essays – she made the political value of photography in the modern world matter in a way that it never quite had before. The text that placed politics in dialogue with the cultural appropriation and cult status of photography in its various roles ranging from persuasion to fact (the photograph as document, as art object, as journalistic evidence, etc.) was her polemical and unapologetically passionate 1977 work *On Photography.* Among that essay's compendium of fragments and reflections on the nature and action of photography (what Vilém Flusser would later call the "gesture" of photography), one idea in particular has always stood out for me, an idea to which I repeatedly return and, to be sure, one that remains simple yet central to the main arguments of her text.[1] Photographs, Sontag insists, are not so much representations as they are pieces of the world, fragments that enable our perception of holding and thus possessing the world. From this claim she also contends that photography is a means by which the world's wholeness becomes fractured. The power of photographs as objects lies in their ability to resize the visible and illuminate the invisible; they particularize and obscure, they reduce and amplify, they "fiddle with the scale of the world," bringing it in and out of reach (Sontag 2010, 4). As interpretive processes, photographs extend across time, offering us the "look of the past" as well as the "reach of the future" (4). They are images as much as gestures and events. For Sontag, and others, whom I will discuss throughout this chapter, photography is not merely one of the pinnacle achievements of modernity, but a fundamentally crucial way of engaging with – by which she means *living in* – the modern world. This is why, as Tom Gunning maintains, photography is "anything but a neutral medium" – in radically altering the history of modern technological vision, it has likewise "transformed our sense of perception and [here's that remarkable verb again] *reached* beyond the boundaries of the visible" (2008, 55). With photography – "light writing" as it has often been called – life is no longer limited to those things that only the eye can see; rather, in effect, it can enter into spectral territory, into the place of the ghost, by making previously unseen or unseeable aspects of life (cells, microorganisms, to name only two examples) come into view. Photographs offer portals not only into time but also into fields of vision. They change the scope of our sight and in so doing change the manner (and matter) of seeing. But it is through the study of photography as a practice and mode of seeing and not as seeing itself that we gain critical insight into how – and perhaps more importantly, *why* – we look at things. That is, how and why certain things *become* seen or, conversely, *remain* unseen.

In the previous section, I made the claim that cinema, and specifically Carlos Saura's cinematic apertures, open us to the world through fractures not only understood as the splicing of time or the entanglement of multiple temporalities, but also screened through landscapes in which place becomes both an imagistic metaphor for a violently wounded past and a continued site of affliction. Without wishing to reverse or undo those claims, here I want to shift gears and discuss how this notion of fracture operates not in the moving image but in the still one. Specifically, I want to explore two cases from the context of contemporary Spanish photography in light of what Sontag calls the medium's "grammar" and its "ethics of seeing" (2010, 3). If chapter 1's discussion of totalitarian optics drew on the science of sight to link the production of spectacles to the creation of a haunted subjectivity and spectatorship, and chapter 2's analysis of "new wave" apertures connected cinema to the symptomatic exhibition of temporal and historical ruptures or the cultural condition of untimeliness, then the present chapter considers the primary force of photography as one of contemplation and intervention. Such a force, as it were, evokes both action (intervening) and a sense of passivity (thought). Thus, in this trajectory from seeing to opening to instigating, the following pages take up as a point of departure the denotative meaning of the word "intervene" as a "coming between" and aim to rethink the place of photography, from capture to exposure, as one that beholds and reveals loss. As such, these readings situate photography as a poetic process that mediates our experience of knowing and understanding the world as it relates to our coming into and losing sight of it.

Returning briefly to Sontag, the present chapter also reconsiders the contention that the act of photographing, while constituting an event and a form of participation, runs counter to the act of intervening. In an intriguing passage at the beginning of *On Photography*, Sontag argues:

> *Photographing is essentially an act of non-intervention.* Part of the horror of such memorable coups of contemporary photojournalism as the pictures of a Vietnamese bonze reaching for the gasoline can, of a Bengali guerrilla in the act of bayoneting a trussed-up collaborator, comes from the awareness of how plausible it has become, in situations where the photographer has the choice between a photograph and a life, to choose the photograph. *The person who intervenes cannot record; the person who is recording cannot intervene.* (2010, 11–12 my emphasis)

Whereas recording implies a "stepping back," a distancing or moving away from the targeted object to be captured on film (the camera, in that scenario, would act as the physical device positioned between photographer and photographed subject), to intervene conversely suggests a "stepping forward" directly into the event or situation at hand. It is fairly easy, in fact, to understand that in any given moment of taking a photograph, one must make a decision to stand either behind the lens or in front of it (self-portraits inevitably complicate such a division of labour by placing the same subject on both sides at once). Yet it seems that removal or non-inclusion could also function as a form of intervention – not the physical kind, of course, but as a symbolic move. Certainly, the medium has been credited for its interventions into the fields of vision and history, into the mechanics and technology of the image, into formations and representations of the subject. As Jeannine Przyblyski writes, "photography is a defining modern mode of representation intervening in the construction of the self" (1998, 4) – which recalls the images of any number of artists working in photography today (Cindy Sherman, Nan Goldin, Nikki Lee, Robert Mapplethorpe, Alberto García Alix, to name only a few). With that in mind, I want to pose a related but slightly different question: What kinds of interventions can certain landscape photographs, understood as objects that fracture and, as Barthes suggests, *divide the history of the world*, bear? How might the act of reading such photographs facilitate an interventionary mode of looking – a seeing but also a seeing *into* and *in between*?

This chapter considers, as a counterpart to the non-intervening act of taking photographs, the interventionary possibilities that arise from the act of reading and interpreting photographic images. To do so, it turns to the works of two contemporary Spanish photographers: Manuel Sendón, a Galician-based artist and photography professor in the Facultad de Bellas Artes in Pontevedra (Vigo); and Bleda y Rosa, the Valencian-based artistic team known by their combined surnames. The former tends to show concrete artefacts of the past in his images; the latter veer away from concreteness in favour of framing the absence of such artefacts. Nevertheless, these works are brought into dialogue by a common interest not in direct intervention (into things or places) but rather a kind of indirect intervention (into modes of seeing) in that they capture place as something always in a state of transformation, using the camera to witness the ephemerality and mutability of place. With Sendón, "capturing change" takes the form of the ruin – places once inhabited and full of life now stand in decay and disrepair, verging on death. In Bleda y Rosa's works, which could be viewed as the "anti-ruin" to many of Sendón's projects, such change takes the form of vacancies and open spaces situated between geographic specificity and an abstract, vast ghostly void. In attending to the spatial and temporal textures of places in transition, all of these images meditate on the visibility – and we could even say, the landscape – of time. In doing so, they also meditate on time's entropy and its loss. Though this thread of capturing time in place (in some ways, the contemporary equivalent of

Marey's chronophotograph) figures through distinct styles and methods, the works discussed in the following pages have another element in common: they are interested in *things* – houses, buildings, monuments, memorials, memories, traces – *that remain*. The readings presented here draw on this concept of "remains" as a double-reference to materiality (remnants, residue) and temporality (duration, lasting, permanence, afterlife). That which remains is thus taken as that which stays, even if it does not stay the same. Among the things the camera finds in its view, these photographs compel us to ask: what remains unseen? What goes unnoticed, undetected? What gets lost?

If, as Foucault noted, the discipline of history makes documents into monuments, then these artists take the medium of photography and make monuments into poetry, into objects of the camera's gaze but also objects for our viewing, contemplation, and interpretation. Indeed, as will become evident, monuments figure prominently in these images, which are as deeply invested in framing and imaging places as they are in reframing and imagining those places. In fact, it is not only the temporal and structural elements of place that these works "view," but also the fictionality and memory of their sites. In a different way, these photographs work to aid our reconsideration of how landscapes, like screens or masks, reveal as much as they conceal. In short, what primarily occupies these images is precisely what drives the entire problematic of the photographic medium – that every photograph paradoxically frames both the referent and its absence. In calling attention to this paradox, these images bring to the fore what Janet Malcolm identifies as the "the camera's perverse noticingness" to think more deeply about the consciousness of the camera – not what it happens to "catch" unknowingly but what it searches for actively and willingly (quoted in Horstkotte and Pedri 2008, 14). Here, another paradox: What happens, then, when the object the camera looks for is nothing but loss itself?

One final commonality among these works lies in the question of surface. The following readings in many ways explore these photographic images *as* surfaces, but they also treat surfaces – whether exterior walls of houses or interior walls of rooms, whether doors or gates or fences, whether tombs, memorials, or open fields – *as landscapes*. Jean-Luc Nancy reminds us that "the landscape is the contrary of a ground: the 'land' in it must be entirely surface" (2005, 58). One possible understanding of Nancy's idea, I propose, is that landscapes constitute a plane in which the shifts between appearance and disappearance are played out, though not always neatly. This would inevitably mean conceptualizing the landscape-as-surface idea as a line or relation between the visible and the invisible, between a concrete materiality and an ambiguous spectrality. While the term "surface" suggests a zone of non-intervention, staying above the ground or "on the face of things," the readings here reflect on that relationship and explore the ways in which surfaces excavate – that is, the way they are situated between burial and revelation and thus not only stand between but also mediate and potentiate loss and sight. The following two meditations contemplate surfaces – ghostly landscapes, in a sense – as pathways to visibility, as ways of bringing the spectral world to light.

I. THE MODERNITY OF RUINS: MANUEL SENDÓN'S ARCHITECTURE OF PHOTOGRAPHY

In the ruin, history has merged sensuously with the setting. And so configured, history finds expression not as a process of eternal life, but rather as one of unstoppable decline.

"The Ruin" (Benjamin 2008, 180)

Photography, Barthes reminds us, is the technology of ruin. In it, one makes a commitment to destruction's eventuality, to future memory. It promises, in some far-off time, to permit the viewer to experience the impossible temporal duality in which the one pictured can be seen to be both dead and anticipating death.

In Place of Origins (Morris 2000, 280)

The Ruined Landscape

In an article published in *Las Apariencias*, Antonio Muñoz Molina, evoking José Ortega y Gasset, writes:

> El paisaje español, escribía Ortega, está poblado de proyectos en ruinas … Están sucediendo siempre, ahora mismo, infatigablemente modificados y usados, solicitándonos con la premura de un presente que no se termina nunca y que nos ofrece la posibilidad continua de volver. Aun desde lejos los vemos alzarse en medio de una desolación de novedades en ruinas.

> The Spanish landscape is populated with projects in ruins ... They are always happening, right now, tirelessly modified and used, attracting us with the pressure of a present moment [or time] that does not ever end and that offers us the continual possibility of return. Even from far away we see them rise up in the middle of a desolation of novelties in ruins. (20 November 1990, *El País*)

It is perhaps a difficult point to contest. Spanish modernity since the nineteenth century seems undeniably tethered to – if not outright defined by – its various "projects in ruins." Indeed, some of the most powerful visual associations with Spain's entrance into modernity are those images centred not on the spectacle of technology or economic and industrial progress common to other European nations, but rather the freighted and all too unforgettable images of decadence, decay, and deformation; loss and failure; grotesque and sickly states of being, the spineless and withering body.[2] Interestingly, this passage tells us that ruins allow "the continual possibility of return" – a spectral return that marks the "pressure of the present moment." What kind of history might this state – the state of ruin, one conditioned by the process of ongoing discovery and repeated return – suggest? More pressing still, what kind of future might it behold? That such ruins should be not only spatially but also temporally ubiquitous, "always happening, right now," "rising up," suggests a permanence or temporal mode that locates any notion of futurity both within the logic of the continuous and the always occurring ("a present moment that does not ever end") *and* within the historical, or that which has already been yet is destined to re-emerge. In thinking about these questions, I turn to photography and specifically, in this first meditation, the photography of architecture. How might the medium of "light writing," a medium predicated not only on capture and arrest but also on the return of the dead, as the early writings of Benjamin and Kracauer claim, and as the later musings of Barthes and others follow, open up a space – a visual plane, or an aesthetic experience – in which we might begin to conceptualize ruins and their relationship to temporality and existence, on the one hand, and to historicity and modernity, on the other? How might photography approach not only a philosophy but also a poetics of ruins? Put simply, what might the photograph and the ruin hold in common? Can an image of ruins intervene in our seeing and understanding of history? Whereas a precondition for ruins is, as Muñoz Molina asserts, the "pressure of the present moment," the photograph, in contrast, has a somewhat different relationship to the present. In the words of Eduardo Cadava, "the photograph asks us to think the remains of what *cannot* come under a present" (1997, 128). In the pages that follow, I turn to photographic images of ruins to consider this tension between remaining and becoming.

Arguably one of the best visual representations of this problematic can be found in the work of the contemporary Galician photographer Manuel Sendón. Though he is certainly not the only or first photographer to capture ruins, Sendón's photography capitalizes on a particular aesthetic of loss that directs attention to the abandonment of and return to uninhabitable structures. In large part, his work gravitates towards a contemplation and visualization of the temporality of ruins. While early projects such as *Paisaxes* (1989–91) and *Cuspindo a barlovento* (2003) demonstrate his notable interest in the landscape question as it relates to Galicia, the periphery, disaster, destruction and ruination, it is his more recent work that deals specifically with structures that embody loss.[3] In this embodiment, I argue, loss becomes a way of seeing place and constructing landscape. Perhaps Sendon here is most aesthetically similar to contemporary artists working in the American urban context – Andrew Moore (*Detroit Disassembled*, 2010), Yves Marchand and Romain Meffre (*Ruins of Detroit*, 2011), and Richard Misrach's series of ruined houses in the aftermath of Hurricane Katrina, *Destroy This Memory* (2010). We might say that Sendón's works can be defined by their compulsion to capture and repeat variations on one theme: structures, whether found or made, in the process of dying. This attention to the "becoming ruin" – capturing a site or structure in the process of extinction – is perhaps most evocatively displayed in *Casas doentes* (*Ailing Houses*, 2007), an extraordinary documentation of rural houses in his native Galicia, a place widely considered "pre-modern." The project as a whole formally stylizes an impressive serialization – what Alejandro Castellote has called an archive of "pathological index" – of different structures awaiting their eventual and foreseeable "deaths" (2007, 15). But the houses are not the objects of Sendón's camera eye as much as they are the measure of modernity's sweep and time's destruction. Capturing these houses in the moments of their deaths, I will argue, works less to prolong and sustain their lives than it does, following Benjamin, to offer a visual theory of "history decayed into images."

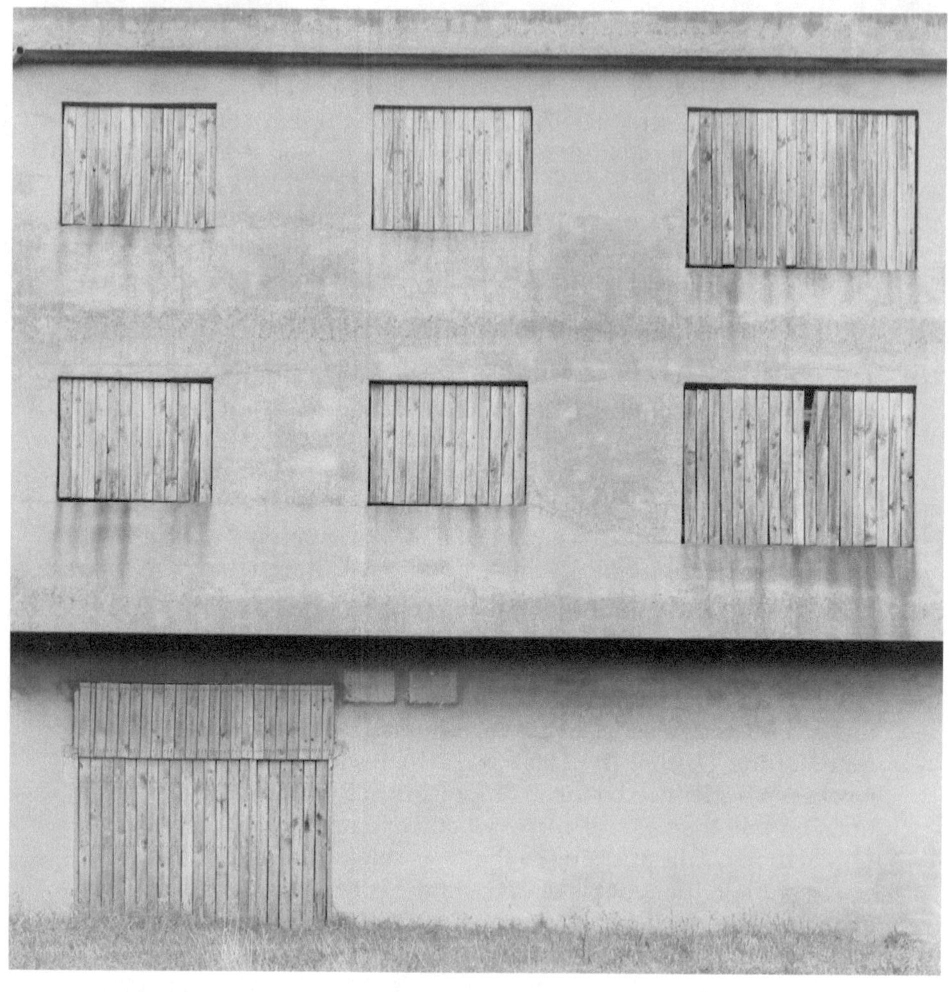

3.1 *Casas doentes* (2007). Copyright Manuel Sendón.

Dead Matter: The Stuff of Frontispiece

Photography is the medium in which we unconsciously encounter the dead.
Light in the Dark Room (Prosser 2005, 1)

Manuel Sendon's architectural photographs participate in a kind of imaging of the ruin. Careful not to transform the reality of these structures in their various states of decay, Sendón's tactic is made all the more visible when one notices this pattern repeated throughout the project: the camera never crosses the threshold. It remains outside. Occupying this exterior space, the camera's slow, methodical observance at first appears to be one of non-intervention; it neither rebuilds nor demolishes, it neither accesses nor ignores; it neither restores nor erases. It simply presents us with an image of a structure's current state of being.

Encountering these once-inhabited dwellings now in ruins, Sendón turns his attention to specific details and connects what remains of the houses through an imagistic play of their facades. Drawing on the serial power of repeating and differentiating their so-called "faces," his photographs transform the buildings into a kaleidoscopic pattern of symmetrically reflected surfaces, frames, and thresholds – first singular, then plural, accumulating and sequencing their sameness and difference. The compositional layout of *Casas doentes*, described by social anthropologist Marcial Gondar Portasany as "monothematic and diverse at the same time," establishes a seriality that oscillates between distinct photographic scales and perspectives (2007, 90). On the one hand, there is a difference in size ranging from individual large format photographs (1 × 1 m) to multiple images assembled together in smaller isometric mosaics (0.4 × 0.4 m; 0.5 × 0.5 m, groups of 3, 4, and 6). On the other hand, there are subtle shifts in content and visibility – viewers stand before images of facades, but at times those facades stand naked and bare, while other times they are veiled or boarded up. In effect, what emerges is a dialogue between images of weathered and exposed structures undergoing intense erasure and natural foreclosure and images of buildings subject to restoration and enclosure, ones in the midst of being "saved."

Despite these minor differences, a consistency in perspective unites the entire series; this is especially notable when we look through the photographs in succession, as organized in the catalogue or in the exhibition space: the images always face the front. In fact, there is a theatrics to this "front matter" as well both in terms of staging the images of

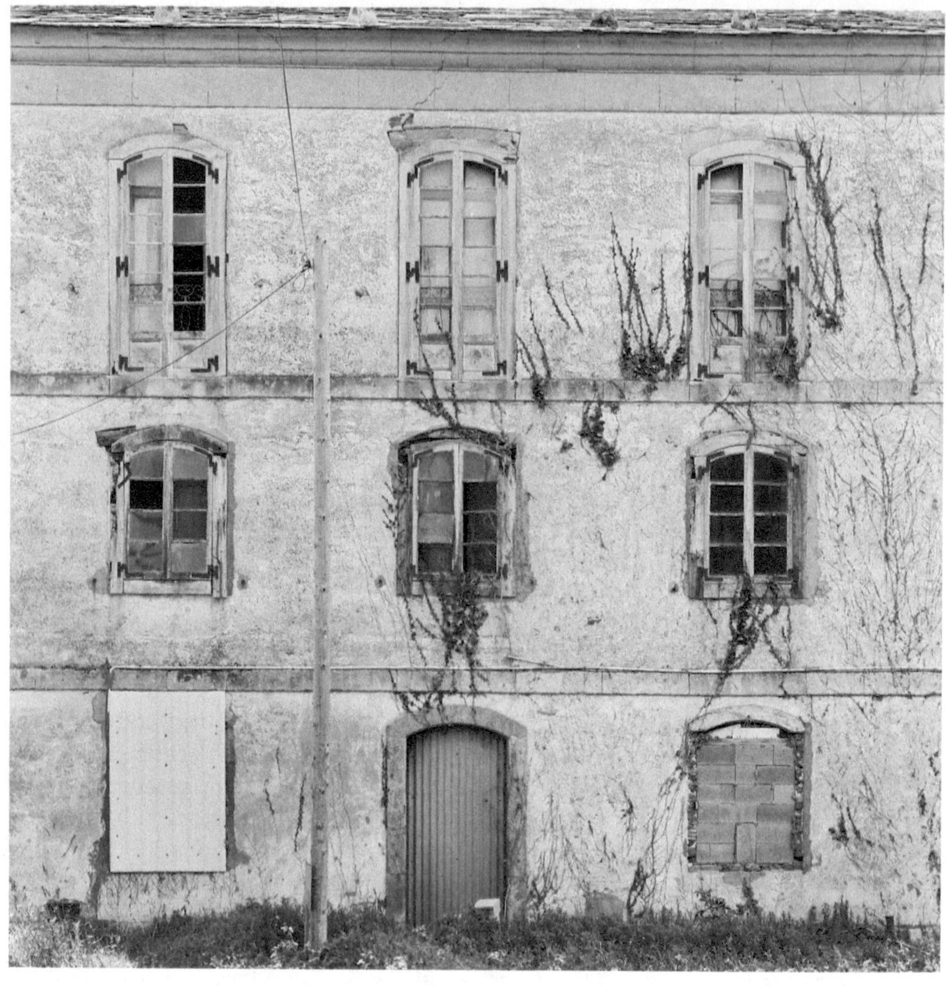

3.2 *Casas doentes* (2007). Copyright Manuel Sendón.

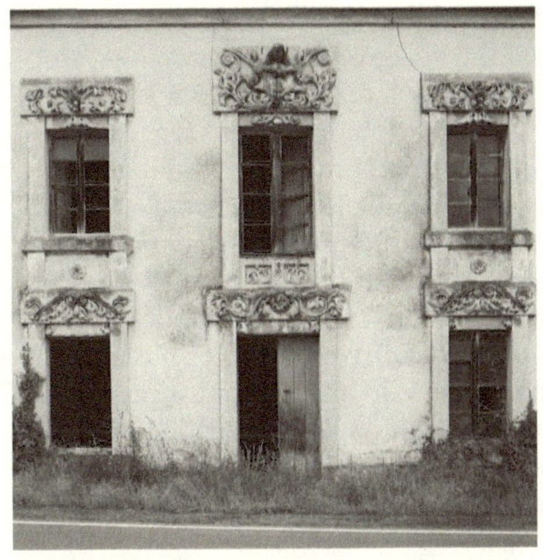
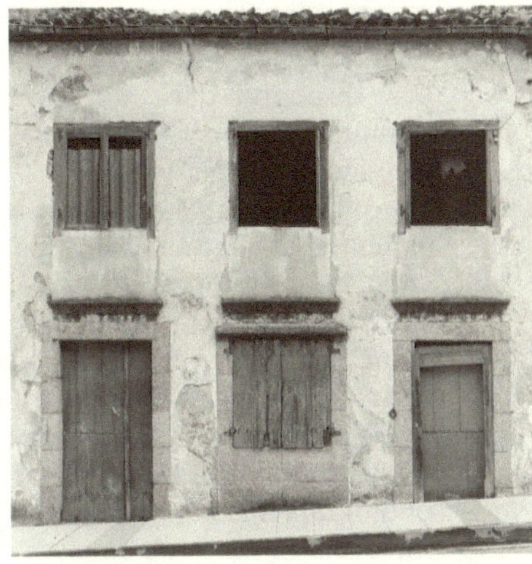
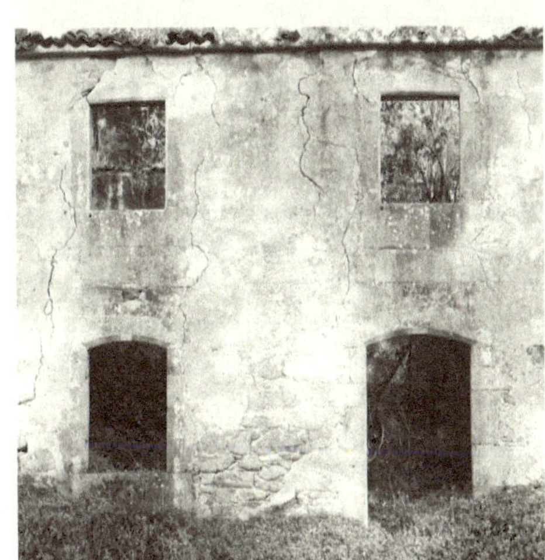
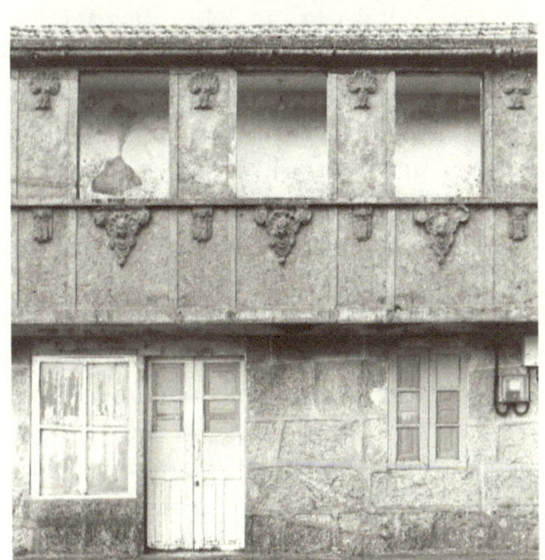

3.3 *Casas doentes* (2007). Copyright Manuel Sendón.

facades and in positioning the viewer in front of them. Upon entering the Fundación Barrié (A Coruña) exhibit space of *Casas doentes*, viewers pass through a darkened foyer where four large screens (3.5 × 3.5 m) illuminate the space through a random rotation of images.[4] Combined, the screens display over three hundred photographs of facades from the collection. As the entranceway – the frontispiece, as it were – to the exhibit, the video slideshow choreographs an interesting play between stillness and motion. As the viewer pauses to take in the cascade of still images being projected, their rapid flow creates cinematic movement, the quality of which generates a repetitive rhythm of the imminent destruction of the houses, a narrative told always from a moment in the present. In a certain sense, the four-sided video projection, which recalls the four sides of the house, sides that are never shown in the photographs, both forestalls and ensures their deaths; it recalls what is there and at the same time what is *not*.

It is perhaps obvious that Sendón uses the image as a means to *return* to ruins, to confront and quite literally stand before them. Perhaps less obvious, however, is what standing in front of these ruins amounts to. Do the photographs participate in a nostalgic return, a kind of romantic vision of ruins? Or are they visionary, enacting a kind of fantasy or future imagining that would contemplate not the houses as they once were intact in the past, but their spectral remains as they appear in the present? What kind of capture is at stake? What kind of intervention? The camera is careful not to enter these structures; instead, it faces them as they, in turn, face death. By never crossing the threshold, the *Casas doentes* images stay on the surface, where they index and crystallize time's passage. As photographs of facades, we might read these images then as the frontispieces to a larger visual narrative about the "face value" of indexicality, as well as about building and dwelling, about architecture and photography, and last but not least about the practice of framing and tracing loss.

Mask, Unmask: Facades, Frames, Screens

It seems that beyond the barrier, there are only more barriers.

"Entropy and the New Monuments" (Smithson 1996, 15)

Why only the facades? Some critics have equated the "facial" component of the *Casas doentes* photographs to a humanized aesthetic in

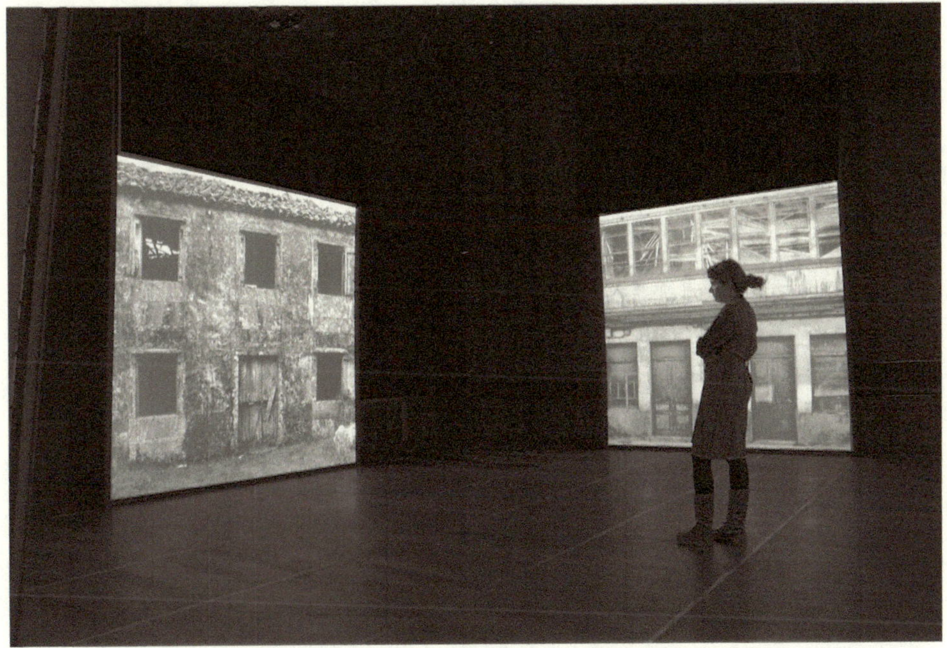

3.4 Installation of *Casas doentes* (2007). Copyright Manuel Sendón.

which the houses are exposed as frail, wounded, and at times "bandaged up" skeletal frames of architectural "bodies" (figure 3.5).[5] As facades, Sendón's images are exemplary of Barthes's claim that the photograph cannot signify "except by assuming a mask" (1981, 34).[6] Behind such a disguise lies a certain depth (the interior space, the subject housed within, perhaps even stored memories) that the photographs do not necessarily make accessible, though they may bring their concealment to light. Like the mask, these facades obscure the interiority of these dwelling spaces. And it is precisely because we never gain access to the home, because the viewer, like the photographer, does not enter the image's reality "inside," as it were, that the facades become at once the subject of and the obstacle to our viewing. This obstacle comes into sharper focus with the last segment of the series, which features various facades behind canvases – a double-imaging of the simultaneous poetics of concealment and exposure staged in each photograph. Any number of interpretations can be given to the

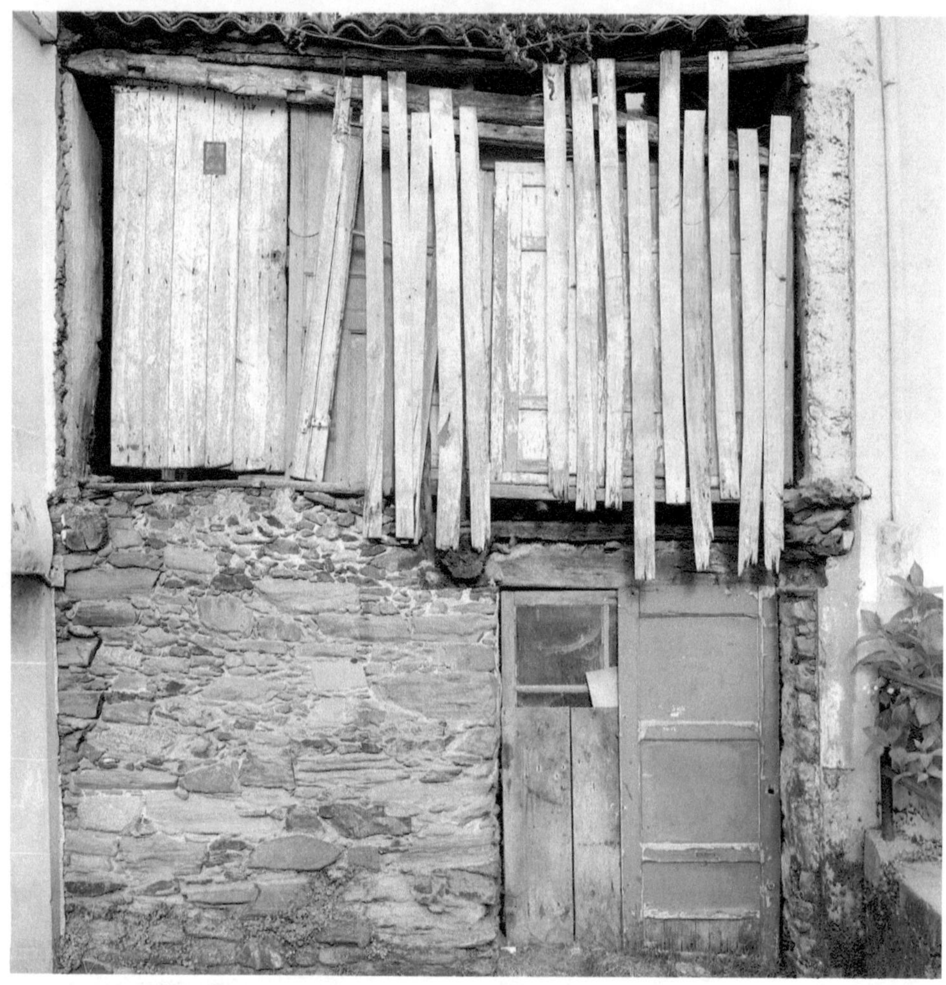

3.5 *Casas doentes* (2007). Copyright Manuel Sendón.

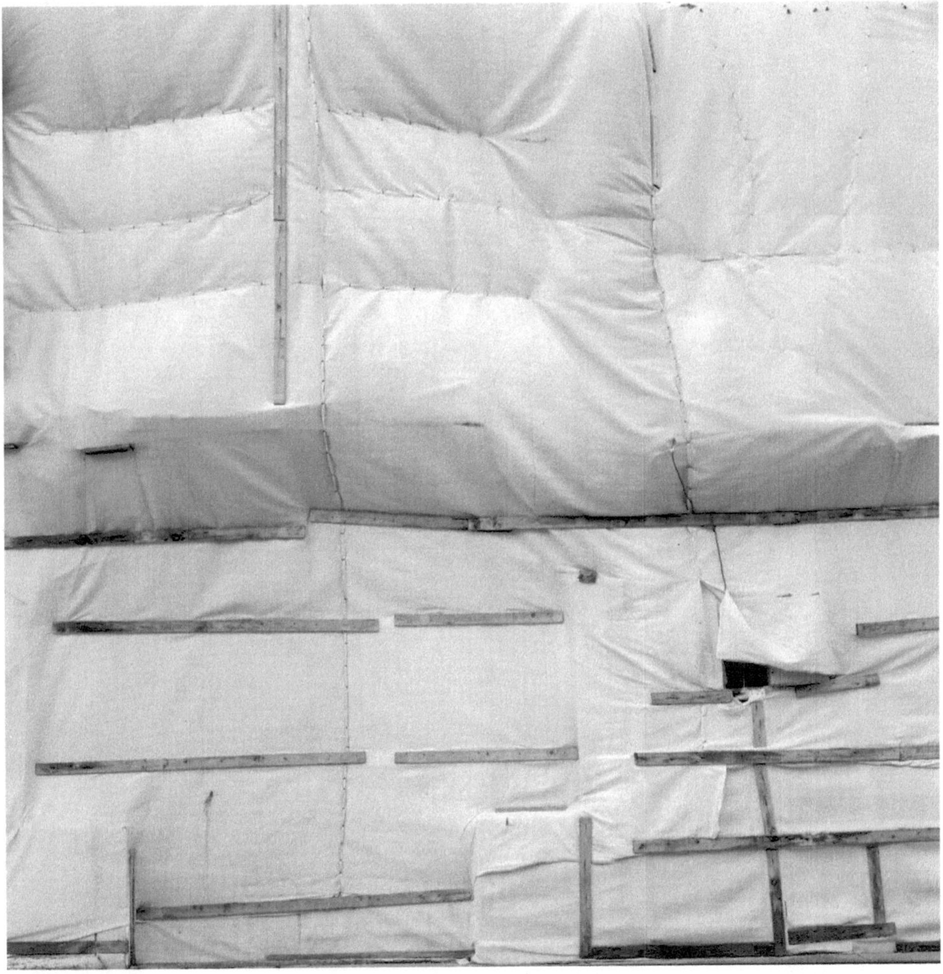

3.6 *Casas doentes* (2007). Copyright Manuel Sendón

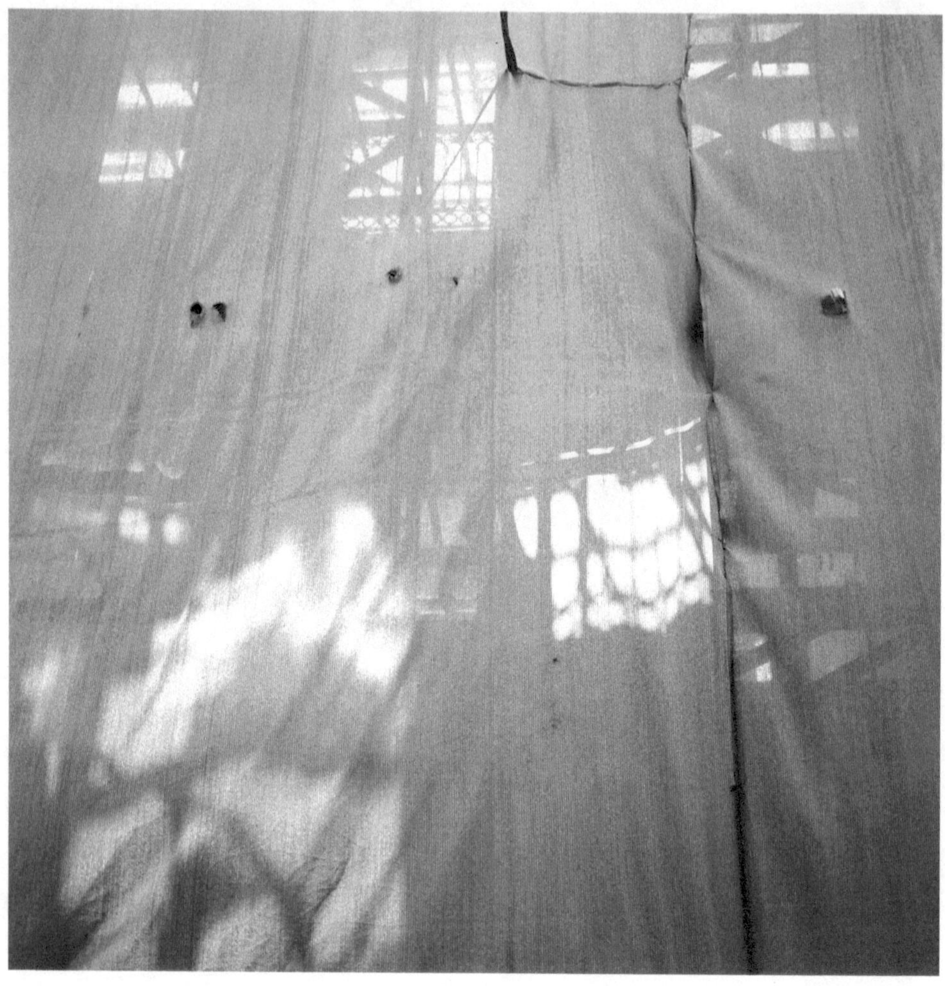

3.7 *Casas doentes* (2007). Copyright Manuel Sendón

canvases – a materiality that in covering the houses brings into view their invisibility, the epitome of death masks, funereal shrouds, or simply "allegories for illness" already alluded to in the title "doentes," which translates into "ailing" (Castellote and Cao 2007, 20).

The comparison between the canvas coverings and death is not too far-fetched. The project is invested in the mortality of Galician houses – that is, in the life of their deaths; photographs such as the one in figure 3.6, masks of masks, make it possible to see not only the death of these houses but the vitality produced through their death. They are, in a sense, being brought back to life. The image in figure 3.7 exemplifies such a vitality as well: a slightly transparent veneer on which shadows are cast and light is reflected. The camera deconstructs these ailing houses as much as it exhumes them, resurrecting them by "filling the sight by force," drawing on Barthes's language, with the visualization and demarcation – that is, the transparent veiling – of their ghostly presence (1981, 91).

Dwellings, Remains, Traces

As things decay they bring their equivalents into being

Dillon DeWaters[7]

Real ruins of different kinds function as projective screens for modernity's articulation of asynchronous temporalities and for its fear of and obsession with the passing of time.

"Nostalgia for Ruins" (Huyssen 2006, 11)

If photography creates planes of possibilities on which viewers can interpret the language of the image, then Sendón's work not only situates those planes in the ruin itself but also resurrects the ruin as a potential space for bringing the invisibility of loss to light. This is a space of plurality. Ruins, like photographs, are thus not only objects that signify a loss, but also a vital process by which visualizing and interpreting loss becomes possible. In this way too, images of ruins doubly reinforce the spectral temporality of loss tied to every photograph, or what Jeannine Przyblyski calls photography's "ambiguous status as both an image suspended in an ever-present and a concrete artifact of the past" (1998, 3). In a compelling analysis of photography and loss, Jay Prosser similarly tells us that "photography is the medium in which we unconsciously encounter the dead" (2005, 1). Yet in such an encounter lies a "hidden truth" – "photographs are not signs of presence but evidence of absence … Photographs contain a realization of loss" (Prosser 2005, 1). Photographs, in this sense, are ghostly. They perform spectrality. In Sendón, this realization crystallizes in the figure of the ruined house – that anti-sublime structure that, recalling Freud, becomes uncanny the more it remains, the more it decays into unfamiliarity and, in this case, into abstraction. Gondar Portasany argues that the realization of loss, absence, and death in Sendón's work operates "not from explicitness of the image but from suggestion" (2007, 90). Articulating this point further, he writes:

> The compromise assumed by Sendón is not to tell us what to think and feel about that segment of life (or rather, non-life) that he photographs but something deeper and more humanizing, to make us think and feel (but only if we are willing to) in such a way that things don't pass by our side without questioning our lives. The result is that his messages, rather than conveying some content, create fields, rather than build specific thoughts they build the conditions for any possible thought in the fields of living and dwelling. (2007, 90)[8]

This creation of fields of dwelling and living to which Gondar Portasany turns, but which he ultimately fails to develop, is a key point. Sendón's project frames loss not as antithetical to but as the condition for living and thinking, and thus for dwelling and being. It is not only the once-inhabitable structure of the house but also the now-uninhabitable structure of the ruin that shapes existence and opens a space for thought.[9] Of course, in Sendón's work we do not just have houses in ruins but *photographs* of houses in ruins. Photographs that, of course, capture these houses in their "being-towards-death." I suggest here that the capture of a structure in decay is not simply a gesture of taking but importantly one of holding and holding on to. What might be at stake in preserving the mortal remains of these houses is an ontological question. It is not only an architectural concern or photographic study related to modes of construction and reproduction; at the intersection of the two there lies a question of being. Heidegger, in his well-known 1951 essay "Building, Dwelling, Thinking," links the question of being to the notion of building and distinguishes between two kinds of building (*bauen*): the first means constructing, as in the raising up of an edifice; the second recalls a means of living and dwelling. The first, largely spatial definition leaves little or no room for a concept of habitation, life, or lived experience; the second does in that it invokes a sense of cherishing, protecting, preserving, caring for, and/or nurturing. To think of building in the second sense, in terms of dwelling, means then to think about it in terms of *being*, a way of living that is present to itself because it can access the time of an experienced past and at the same time can imagine an unknown future. Though in the modern world, according to Heidegger, this notion of building has been stripped of its original sense of *dwelling*, it is nonetheless in dwelling that we find the root of existence, the essence of our "being-in-the-world." Dwelling bears important implications for being because it is rooted in thinking, and thinking, for Heidegger, is tethered to memory, which itself is a structure of loss that relies on a system of mental imaging to return the past to the space of the present moment: "thinking holds to the coming of what has been, and is remembrance" (1971, 10). Heidegger so beautifully notes in another passage of the "Building" essay that "dwelling itself is always a staying with things" and is related to the logic of preservation as well as (though he does not use the word) *remaining* (2008, 353).

Casas doentes maintains a persistence of vision tethered equally to loss and the time of destruction on the one hand, and remains and the time of remaining on the other. Do Sendón's images turn houses into objects that intentionally anticipate and thus stand for death? Or is the project more about stalling their foreseeable deaths by preserving their remaining time, indeed by holding on to the memory of their frail, final moments of life? Whether or not the photographs are conscious attempts to preserve these houses in ruins or create the conditions for their survival and thus afterlife, we can ask what they achieve in forcing our engagement with the problematic of their death – the *pastness* of their withering away into oblivion, but also their futurity. What is at stake in such a photographic posterity, in the capture, and thus the future memory, of these isolate moments of dying?

Though one could hardly say that Sendón's houses are habitable structures and thus suitable for dwelling in the sense of living in or occupying, they do invite us to contemplate the poetics of structural foundations in decay through the photography of architectural forms. They likewise allow us to ponder the architecture of photography. In this case, that translates into an architecture of loss – but also and importantly an architecture that brings into equivalence life and death, building and decaying, imaging, imagining, and losing sight of things. It is a visual concept of architecture that brings to the surface absence, decay, death, and the time of destruction. It seeks to think about the way we look at and approach, the way we see and mediate, once inhabited structures now rendered uninhabitable. Insofar as they build a loss into their larger visual framework, these images also invite us to think about the way we engage with something that defies entrance. Or, to put it somewhat differently, the way we encounter and understand something in a perpetual state of decomposition, of undoing and unthinking. According to curator Joel Smith, the key conceptual difference between architecture and buildings is that while the former is constituted by an "immaterial kingdom," or network of ideas, commerce, materials, and trade that has a traceable historical unity, the latter is something that can be photographed and whose narrative exists as one of physical continuity (2011, 18–19). Of course, images of buildings in ruination blur this distinction by drawing on the visual language of traces. These images, in essence, fail to capture the physical continuity of buildings, since that very continuity is threatened already by decay. Instead, they opt to frame the "traceable." Such traces, as Benjamin reminds us, are signs of dwelling – indeed, they are signs of life for Benjamin – and thus speak to both the materiality of existence and the historical non-materiality of their becoming visible even as they deteriorate and threaten to disappear (2008, 104).[10]

Traces are often understood as things left behind rather than things made. But the photographs in *Casas doentes* seem to invite a slightly different interpretation, or at the very least they seem to complicate that view. In what ways could we say that Sendón's images trace traces? And in this process of tracing, how might they build and what might they suggest about dwelling and thinking? I have been suggesting that Sendón's images are best read for their poetics of loss, which is to say for the way they render ruins – as spectral traces that populate the Galician landscape – as sites of possibility for thought and habitation. For thinking historical time not, as Benjamin poignantly reminds us in "Theses on the Philosophy of History," as homogeneous and empty time, but as "time filled with the presence of the now" (1968, 261).

Crossing the Threshold: Losing Sight, Seeing Inside

> As its own grave, the photograph is what exceeds the photograph within the photograph. It is what remains of what passes into history. It turns in on itself in order to survive, in order to withdraw into a space in which it might defer its decay, into an interior – the closed-off space of writing itself.
>
> *Words of Light* (Cadava, 1997, 10)

The *Casas doentes* photographs, in suggesting a tension between permanence and imminent destruction, between restoration and erasure, also mark a tension between the moment of danger and the image's potential poetic transcendence from such a threat. By virtue of capturing and freezing, arresting and, as André Bazin famously theorized in "The Ontology of the Photographic Image," "embalming the dead," these images hold each ailing house in a fixed moment of decline (1960, 4).[11] Cadava reinforces this claim when he suggests that the power of photography lies in its creation of sudden death: "the camera's click suspends life" (1997, 8). Sendón's photography draws on the static image to reproduce the layers of a world imbued with multiple temporalities, but as we have seen, he also is careful to oscillate between the exposure of crumbling, ramshackle exteriors and the veiling of those exteriors through a calculated zooming technique as well as by alternating between single images and multiple images or collages. This is perhaps, first and foremost, a way of calling to mind how images also and inevitably blind us to what they ostensibly show by never *only* revealing what lies within the frame, but also and always revealing something *beyond* it. This paradox of Sendón's images – that they hide *and* seek – echoes Barthes's claim once again: the photograph, as an object of the visible, produces invisibility (1981, 5–6). In this case, we never *only* see the houses, in their singularity or multiplicity, but importantly are invited to see the way in which they *become* images – the way their exteriors are exposed and then concealed, the way their interiors are hidden and then revealed. In turn, we see how images trace not only the ghostly presence of an object but also the absence of a presence – always adjacent, waiting in the shadows. This trajectory – from structure to image to absence, loss, and death – culminates in one particular photograph from the series in which the camera uncharacteristically, though only metaphorically, "crosses" the threshold.

As the only photograph in the exhibit that shows the inside of a building, the image in figure 3.8 is somewhat of an anomaly and certainly stands apart from the other photos due to its style, colour, and manner. It shows a different "face" – as if the inside contours of a mask or a reverse facade. Marked by the faint outline of stairwells and door and window frames swallowed in a flood of bright orange, this image effectively collapses the distinction between interiority and exteriority, between structure and surface. In fact, in capturing a structure whose ghostly interior is literally missing yet remains insofar as its traces are visible, Sendón converts the emptiness of this house into a luminous

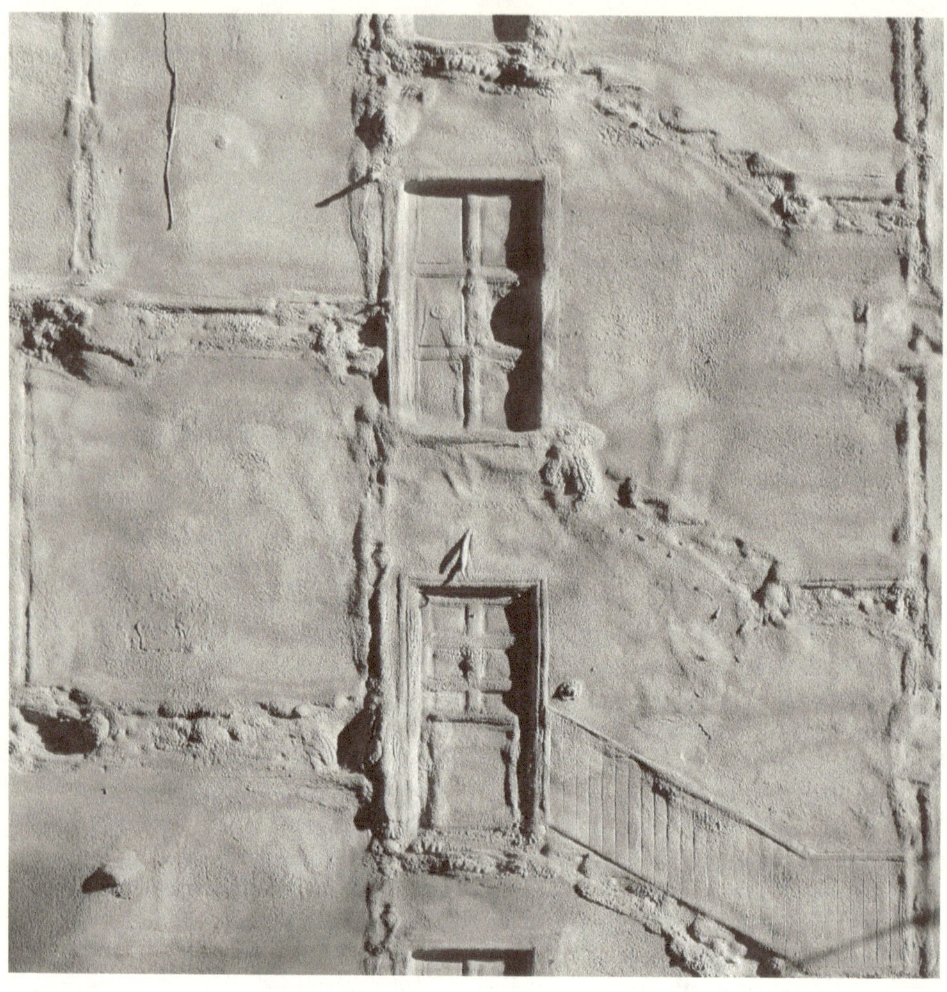

3.8 *Casas doentes* (2007). Copyright Manuel Sendón.

spectrality of things.[12] What no longer exists is nonetheless still present; the traces, in signalling an absence, bring an otherwise invisible death to light – or, we might say, into a state of afterlife. This particular image frames emptiness as a form of evidence. Here the residue of a multi-tiered, three-dimensional structure now appears as a one-dimensional plane, outlining a space that exists in the threshold, uncannily positioned between two different times, in two distinct dimensions. The ghostly traces of the inside of a house are traced, in turn, by the camera lens, producing a kind of eternal return. As a trace of a trace, the photograph undoubtedly explores the interior textures and the anatomy of a house. But does the photograph of the inside still function as a facade? The mask that formerly covered the symptoms of a diseased or ailing edifice here is turned inside out, exposing the inside as pure exterior. In a sense, we could read this image as the conscious uncovering of such symptoms – that is, as a view of the way such symptoms have been internalized but also of the way in which, as images, they bring into view a *remaining past* that persists in and haunts Galicia's social imaginary.

Mapping, the Topography of the Photographic Image

Beyond the architecture of loss and the potential memory of what Christian Caujolle has described as "a long-gone world from which only images remain," the *Casas doentes* photographs could also be read as the self-conscious production of the surface of the image, one that turns each facade into a detailed topography from which emanates lines, layers, textures, and holes – all points of interest for the eye to observe and ponder. In short, Sendón's photographs exceed merely documenting or representing buildings; they build ideas as much as they layer, contrast, and highlight textures and traces. Similarly, we could think of the images as palimpsestic maps that trace, perhaps only and quite literally, the superficial life and death of a place, bringing into equivalence an interplay between the materiality of these structures (and of the photographs) and immateriality of their transformation and death, the intangible immateriality of their time left, which, as I have been suggesting, is a *remaining* time.

Just as interior and exterior appear interchangeable in the previous image, in this next image the surface of a facade illustrates its very depth. Somewhat similar to the traces left by a door or staircase, this photograph depicts the front wall of a house as a kind of palimpsest, where various materials, colours, textures, and patterns converge and

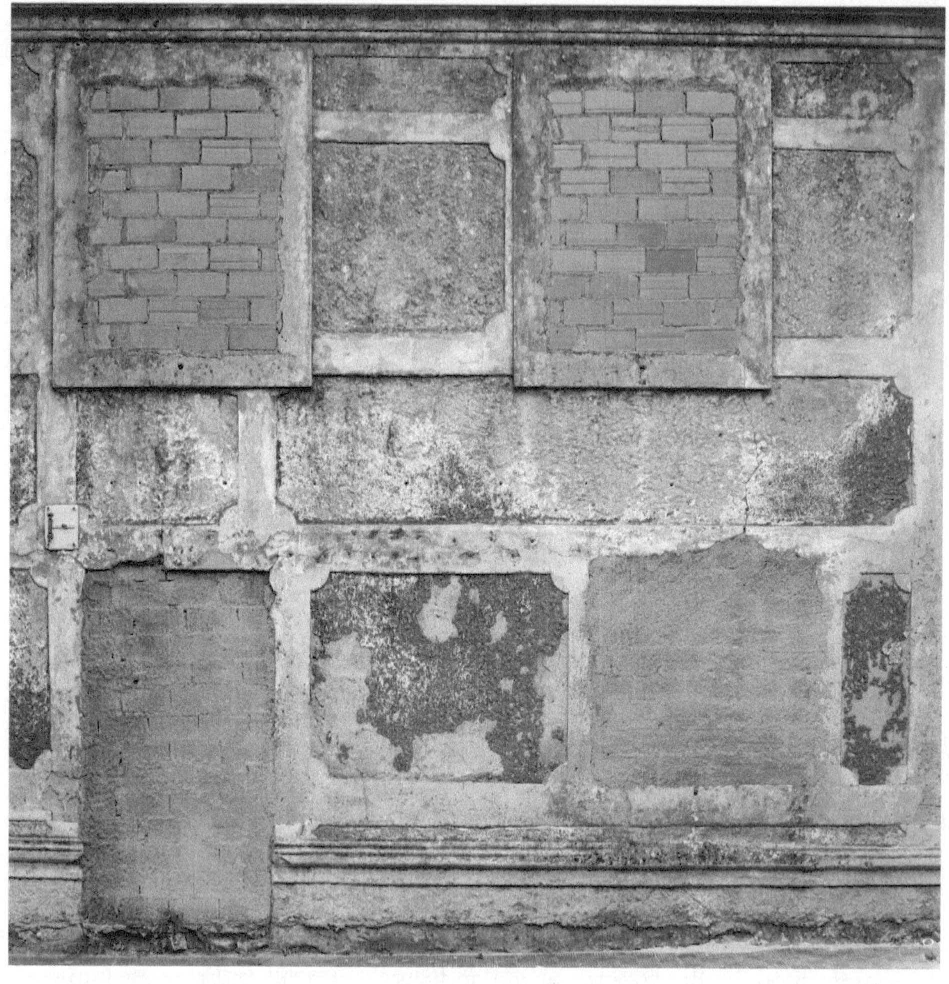

3.9 *Casas doentes* (2007). Copyright Manuel Sendón.

intermingle. Almost like an abstract painting or sculpture, this house is portrayed not only as a collage of coexisting surfaces that border one another but also as distinct textures sewn together within the frame. In fact, one could even see how Sendón uses this photograph to frame the framing of textures – offering the viewer no single point of entry into the image but rather a dishevelled, non-linear sequence of different, indeed dynamic geometric shapes, each constituting a self-contained canvas with a frame around it. Textures become the main focus, or subject of the image. In effect, we read what lies within the frame as the detailed evidence of its illness, its symptomatic traces. Sendón captures the surface of this facade – a wounded and scarred wall – as a way to illuminate the very materiality of discontinuities, ruptures, punctures, and spaces of "breaking out"; this in turn yields a visual theory, a framing of harmonious discontinuity. A quite exceptional and evocative result, given that the image's very containment and closure also opens up new possibilities for thinking about these structures as surfaces upon which history and time are measured and imprinted.

Sendón's detailed, ornate, and intricate surfaces, weathered over the years, perhaps over centuries, transform into cacophonous cartographies – walls that obstruct our seeing but through which various textures emerge and careen out. They shift from topography, or a surveying of the surface, to cartography, or a mapping of time and place. Consider for a moment the photograph in figure 3.10, which strikingly resembles an antique map. The contrasts are numerous: between the perfectly rectangular window frames and the jagged, swerving, almost oceanic patterns, between the clean edges of the windows and the unevenness of the two-toned wall, between the vertical lines on the door and the horizontal layers of the stones, between the smooth surface of the white and the peeling away of the muted browns and oranges. The "territory" of each distinct texture is outlined as if drawn onto the facade itself, bringing potentially variant dimensions all onto the same plane. In slightly different terms, this facade-as-map presents us with a visual record of time – it surveys not a spatial geography (e.g., land and sea), but rather a temporal one. The past pushes forth through the barrier of the present. And like any map, this facade is a representation – it offers only a small fragment of the real house to which it belongs. Also like a map, the image allows us to read the charting of lines and figures throughout, directing our sight towards the discovery of places that exist beyond the horizon, new landscapes and new terrains that we know are there but must imagine nonetheless.

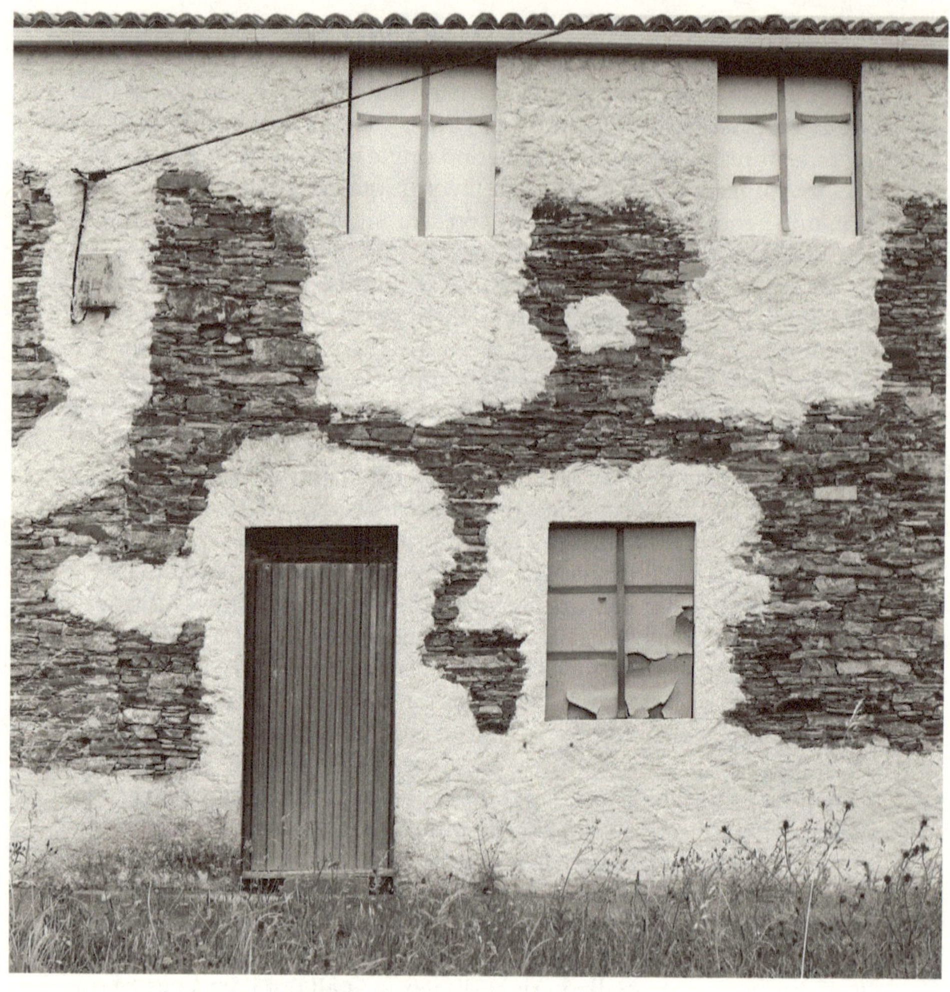

3.10 *Casas doentes* (2007). Copyright Manuel Sendón.

Surfaces as Landscapes: A New Intervention

If a house, a building, or a city is not palpably haunted in its architectural features – if the earth's historicity and containment of the dead do not pervade its articulated forms and constitutive matter – then that house, building, or city is dead to the world.

The Dominion of the Dead (Harrison 2003, 36)

In many ways, it is perhaps obvious that Sendón's project is less concerned with representational forms and more invested in a poetics of the surface, on which he maps tensions between exposure and concealment and frames spectral asymmetries located between materiality and immateriality, life and death, past and future. In a beautiful essay to the exhibit, "The Life and Death of Buildings: On Photography and Time," Joel Smith contends that "through discrete, mechanical choices, the photographer of a building can make a point of singling it out or lay stress on the relationships that define it as a place in the world" (2011, 23). For Smith, whereas the landscape view offers a density of "interconnected details" that "set the eye in motion and stir the narrative and historical imagination to life," the close-up directs the eye into "an engagement with form, structure, and surface" (23).[13] This is an interesting distinction between surface and landscape – the former understood as something enclosed but largely lost or unseen in the latter. Interestingly, in Sendón's work, the surface emerges as a kind of landscape insofar as it constructs a way of seeing and reading the life and death of ruins. That is, the larger narrative and historical life comes into focus through the lens of death, which the camera both suspends and perpetuates, both halts and calls forth. We should remember that it is not only buildings *in* decay that comprise the heart and soul of *Casas doentes,* but also the building *of* decay and death. Importantly, in gesturing towards a time that is long gone, these images also constitute the building of a remaining time.

The surface, as a place where both the embeddedness and the emergence of traces is visualized, suggests both a density and a porousness of the image. But it also suggests a spectral economy, not only of the house or the ruin but also of the act of photography itself – as something that captures, destroys, and returns. In this way, Sendón's camera functions as a kind of "portable tomb" – "as if to suggest that its function is to capture the subject so that its future is buried in the destiny of the image" (Merewether 1997, 31). If the camera is a tomb, an apparatus that "writes and harbors its own death," then we might think of the photograph as a glass coffin, a container the surface of which brings the transparency of death to light (Cadava 1997, 10). Though the connections to landscape and loss may be clear, what might this discussion of the surface, death, and the photography of ruins have to do with the politics of intervention? While these photographs make no attempt to rescue the objects of their gaze – and indeed, to the contrary, *enable* their deaths through a kind of photographic burial – they do complicate and disrupt the way we see and read the image of time in its infinite and at times contradictory permutations. In short, Sendón's photographs make no intervention into the physical landscape, but they do intervene in our sight by suggesting that our viewing is bound to the surface yet constitutes a seeing beyond it.

Thinking Past Future Time

> When the camera's subject is an enduring structure, the photograph accomplishes a kind of tunneling-through of space-time.
>
> *The Life and Death of Buildings* (Smith 2011, 23)

> The photograph is always related to something other than itself. Sealing the traces of the past within its space-crossed image, it also lets itself be (re)touched by its relation to the future. Related to both the future and the past, the photograph constitutes the present by means of this relation to what is not. If a space must separate the present from what it is not in order for the present to be itself, this space must at the same time divide the present. In constituting itself, in dividing itself, this interval is what Benjamin calls "*space-crossed* time" – time-becoming-space and space-becoming-time.
>
> *Words of Light* (Cadava 1997, 63)

The gist of my analysis up until now has been this: whereas ruins measure history and time, the photography of ruins visualizes loss. In Sendón's photographs, these two measurements – the historical and the temporal – come into equivalence. In reading the aesthetic evidence of ghostliness – which is to say, a remaining, returning, or haunted time – through the various frames, masks, traces, and surfaces of these images, I have repeatedly turned to a larger question about what these photographs say about ruins and the lives (and eventual deaths) of ruins. But how might we think of these images as suggesting something *beyond* the ruin? Are Sendón's houses memorials to the non-contemporaneity of modern (and here, peripheral) Spain? Are they fragments of time and time's passage? And, in this way, could they be thought of as ephemeral sculptures? Are they monuments to the architecture of photography – the way photography builds and dwells, the ways it frames these places of habitation and the way it *inhabits*? Are they monumental remains that testify to what Robert Smithson called the "entropic landscape" – death in an accelerated modernity? Do the images constitute monuments to a future time? Are they memorials not of the past but of an imagined future event?

The *Casas doentes* photographs maintain a persistence of vision tethered equally to loss and the time of destruction, on the one hand, and on the other, to remains and the time of remaining. Sendón's images turn houses into objects that intentionally anticipate and thus stand for death. But the project also and importantly stalls their foreseeable deaths by preserving their remaining time, indeed by holding on to the memory of each house's frail, final moments of life. Whether or not the photographs are a conscious attempt to preserve these houses in ruins or to create the conditions for their survival and thus afterlife, we might ask what they achieve in forcing our engagement with the problematic of their death – the *pastness* of their withering away into oblivion, but also their futurity (the fact that they have not yet completely passed). What is at stake in such a photographic posterity, in the capture – and thus future memory – of these isolate moments of dying?

In his well-known 1966 essay "Entropy and the New Monuments," Robert Smithson claimed that time, if it is not decay, is "an infinity of surfaces or structures" (1996, 11). Accordingly, then, time is not loss but a means of visualization, a way of mapping loss. It is notable that the decay – the "ruin factor" – of each house is aestheticized in a way that both frames and overshadows the visibility of its various states of material decline. Thus far, I have been reading these photographs as images that reclaim ruins as objects of inquiry, ones that attest to time's passage but also to its resistance, to the fact that it remains. This question of remaining is also a question of futurity, as Charles Merewether notes: "In remaining, they [ruins] are always already of the past, yet given to the future. Ruins collapse temporalities" (1997, 25). In their gravitation towards past and future, photographs of ruins imply a finitude that has already happened and is yet to come, a finitude that is, in Merewether's words, "both disruption and continuity" (1997, 25).

Walter Benjamin tells us that ruins are both objects and processes. In fact, and all the more pertinent to this study, in Benjamin's thought ruins are a landscape of possibilities for thought and for historical materialism.[14] If ruins are the end result of a shattered continuum of history, if fragmentation and decay offer productive spaces for thought, then our embrace of ruins, our contemplation of ruination – indeed the *photography* of ruins – with all of the transience and discontinuity that ruins bear, provides a critically reflexive tool for understanding the condition of our times. A time of brokenness, unevenness, and visible disrepair. As if he had copied a page from Benjamin's notebook, Sendón crafts his images so that ruins reveal as much as they conceal, so that they visualize absence even as they obscure and at times void the loss they ultimately come to signify. In an anti-romantic aesthetic gesture – and we could say even a post-totalitarian and post-fascist vein – Sendón's visual concept of the ruin exposes, borrowing Naomi Stead's rephrasing of Benjamin, "a means of laying bare a truth buried beneath layers of false romantic aesthetics" (2003, 10). But to what truth does this refer? Perhaps the truth *is* the surface, which Sendón shows us repeatedly and compellingly. Perhaps it is never only a facade, but more intriguing always the *opening* to history and time, a scratch on the doorway.

Doors and Doorways, Open and Ours

Whenever we are before the image, we are before time.

Compelling Visuality (Didi-Huberman 2003, 31)

The ruin is not the triumph of nature, but an intermediate moment, a fragile equilibrium between persistence and decay.

"Fragments from a History of Ruin" (Dillon 2005, 7)

In the end, as much as Sendón's facades conceal or reveal the state of peril in which these houses exist, as much as they mask and unmask traces of history that bleed through their walls, and as much as they illustrate the disjuncture between presence and absence, they offer us something else too. Each facade, like each image, is itself a threshold – that grey area, or as Brian Dillon suggests, "an intermediate moment," between us and the edges of a meaningful foundation that (as Heidegger stresses) we must bridge so that it may be contemplated (2005, 8).[15] In most cases, we cannot see through the walls, or through

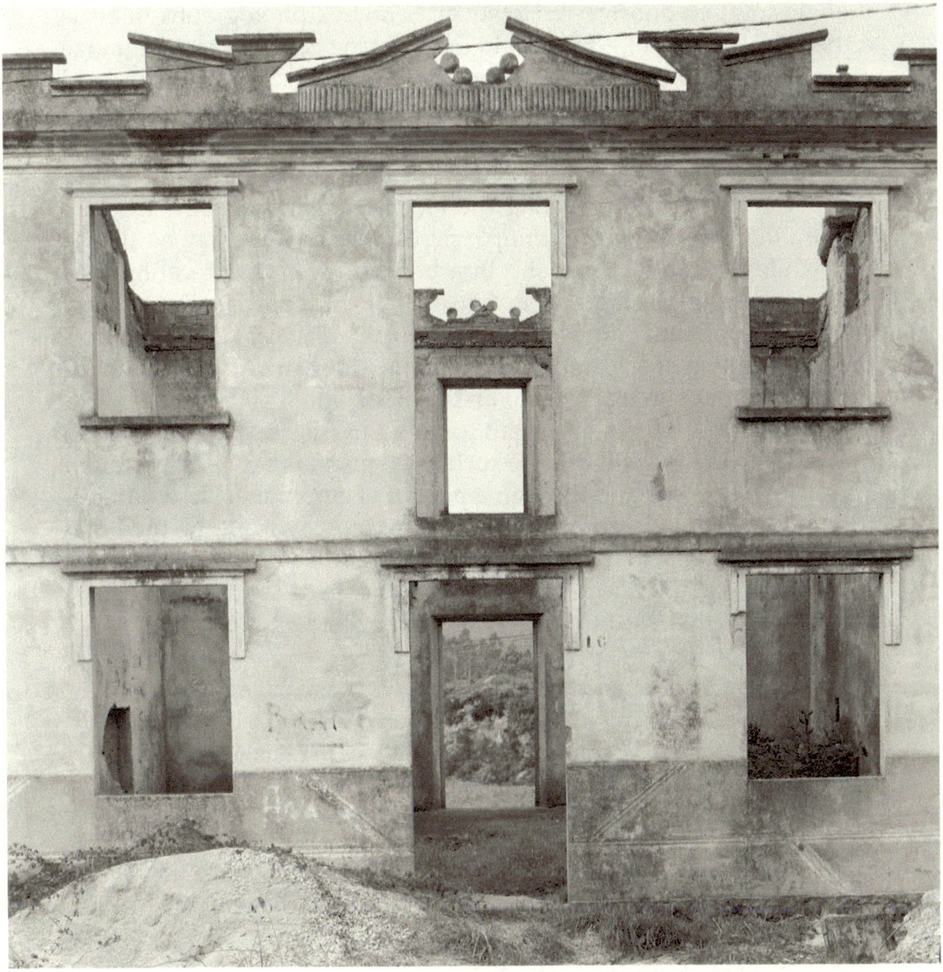

3.11 *Casas doentes* (2007). Copyright Manuel Sendón.

the windows or doorways. However, Sendón's photographs offer us a rhetorical question: Why should our viewing cease where the image stops? Why should what we see be determined by where the threshold ends rather than the place from which it might begin? Why should we not extend our sight to look, as I have been attempting to do, into the very depth of surfaces, into the very time of textures, and into the very complications of deconstructing and reconstructing a ghostly structure that frailly exists between multiple times? The answer may be simple yet: while we cannot cross the threshold, even in that rare instance when, as in the photograph in figure 3.11, the door is open, we *can* contemplate what the threshold frames even in its bleak state – we can imagine another space and time *beyond* the doorway, another path luminous and open to us, the field on the other side.

Where ruins stand as testament to time's passage in Sendón's work, for the next artists I will discuss such a testament is expressed through vacancies and voids and through a poetics of emptiness. Here, a trajectory of ghostly landscapes begins to form, moving from the time that remains to the space that remains. In closing this first meditation, and as a way of opening the next, I will leave the reader with a quote from Chris Merewether's captivating essay "Traces of Loss":

> Ruins remain. They persist, whether beneath the ground or above. In remaining, they are always already of the past, yet given to the future. Ruins collapse temporalities. Landscapes and buildings in ruination, reduced to abandoned sites, are traces that embody a sense of loss … They remind us of finitude as both disruption and continuity, of the necessity of living on among ruins. (1997, 25)

II. THE SPACE THAT REMAINS: BLEDA Y ROSA'S MONUMENTAL PHOTOGRAPHY

> A photograph therefore speaks as death, as the trace of what passes into history. I, the photograph, the spaced out limit between life and death, am death. Yet, speaking as death, the photograph can be neither death nor itself. At once dead and alive, it opens the possibility of our being in time … This is why the event of photography is necessarily anterior to any history of photography – *photography does not belong to history; if offers history.* It delivers history to its destiny. It tells us that the truth of history is to this day nothing but photography. Nevertheless, *the photograph* – as what is never itself and therefore always

passing into history – *asks us to think the remains* of what cannot come under the present. *How can an event that appears only in its disappearance leave something behind that opens history?*

Words of Light (Cadava 1997, 128 my emphasis)

Placing Photographs

What does it mean to capture a place? This is arguably the driving question behind all photographic images. "Capture," theorized by the founding fathers of the discipline of photography (Benjamin, Bazin, Kracauer, and, much later, Barthes and Berger), was often understood conceptually as a form of seizing, embalming, or arrest, and later was reconfigured in terms of wounding, holding, and believing. Indeed, from its inception, photography, a medium aligned with truth, objectivity, and authenticity, used technology to "capture" reality as it was and in so doing to present facts to any viewer willing to see the uncontested and (at one point in time) uncontestable certainty of such facts, which in turn were believed to be truths. To capture something – truthfully, objectively, or in what Barthes would have called its "facticity" – meant in ordinary language to "take" from reality.[16] On the one hand, this notion of taking implied not so much the action of copying or duplicating reality as quoting from it, as Susan Sontag and others have suggested; on the other, photographic action understood in terms of taking rather than, say, giving lent a certain currency to early theories of the medium's ghostly qualities – that is, its direct relationship to the dead, since it was regarded as a suspension of life and, in that suspending, denoted a literal taking from reality, a kind of death. Though to materialize this death – or what Eduardo Cadava has called "the trace of what passes into history" – photographs in fact aided the belief in the camera's ability to literally suck the life out of reality (1997, 128). This meant, more importantly, that photographs were equated not with likeness to death but with death itself. And, in this way, according to Benjamin's formulation, photography spoke as the "corpse of experience" (Cadava 1997, 128).[17]

Of course, there is a second and no less ambiguous term in the question with which I began this section, one that is arguably the foundation of all photography. That term is "place." It is perhaps an all too obvious point that while not all photographs are "of places" in the geographical or site-specific sense of the word (one can think of any number of self-portraits or images of specific objects that provoke less of a "where?" and more of a "what?" or "who?" line of inquiry), all photographs *are* inextricably linked to place in another sense – the place of objects (or subjects) within the frame, the place in time when the photograph was taken, and the place the image itself holds in relation to both the person who took the photograph and the viewer. In light of this second consideration of my initial rhetorical question – What does it mean to capture place? – there is necessarily then a threefold way of addressing "place": (1) as a positioning of objectivity or subjectivity, (2) as a temporal phenomenon, and (3) as a relational device or structure of relationality.

Devoted entirely to this question of how to capture place in its multidimensionality – as position (positionality), as time (temporality), and as structure or relation (relationality) – is the creative work of the Spanish artistic team María Bleda and José María Rosa, otherwise known as Bleda y Rosa. Throughout their photographic corpus, dating from the early 1990s to the present, one finds not only an impressive range of variations on the common theme of placing place, so to speak, but also intricate and at times elaborately unorthodox patterns of difference and repetition that play on the always interrelated notions of "image," "landscape," "visibility," and "memory." In fact, one could argue that at the very heart of their projects (and as I hope to show) is a compulsive drive to capture the uncapturability of place, or what critic Alberto Martín has called "la captación de lo intangible" (2010, 134). Put somewhat differently, the drive to make visible the intangible or untraceable that, for Bleda y Rosa at least, comes to define all places means using photography – itself the trace of what passes into history – as a way to encounter traces of the past that may linger, dwell in, or define the spectral textures of a prehistoric city now in ruins, a memorial site now uninhabited, or a vast country field now desolate and overgrown. Encountering traces of the past also comes with its logical counterpart – discovering that the past at times *remains* invisible, lost, or absent in a place. In other words, discovering what we might call the tracelessness of a place.

In addition to Bleda y Rosa's process of seeking out traces and non-traces, a process of photographic differentiation of place, which I am suggesting hinges on a reconceptualization of the notion of "capture," is perhaps the key and often unvarying component of the photography duo's series. I am referring here to their straightforward, objective, documentary-style approach, one that emerged with the post-expressionist movement of the 1920s known as the New Objectivity (*Neue Sachlichkeit*) and that was later reappropriated into the now renowned photographic works of Bernd and Hilla Becher, whose classically composed typological studies of industrial architectural structures and their soon to be obsolete functions effectively inaugurated a new school of documentary photography.[18]

Very much influenced by the Bechers' photography, Bleda y Rosa's landscape photography features places on the verge of extinction, ones that are threatening to disappear, whatever their claims or allusions to historical significance. However, Bleda y Rosa's work does not display images of industrial obsolescence such as those in the Bechers' famous water towers series. Rather, their works tend to give exposure to natural sites that have become as deserted as they are remote, often highlighting the eerie, serene stillness of places less travelled to, ones forgotten or buried in the archives of history or in the latest travel guides.

Visiting select locations within Spain and more recently travelling around the globe, Bleda y Rosa's work gravitates towards a slow process of documentation that involves the search for these abandoned, lost places – a kind of staged re-encounter with sites whose history is unknown but always potentially legible. Their work involves less a transformation or intervention in the landscape and more a contemplative experience of *being* in the landscape, which in turn produces the photographic image and which they describe in one interview in the following way: "porque no transformamos el espacio, no intentamos generar un cambio, o sea, nuestro hecho artístico no es producir una transformación del paisaje, sino más bien estar en el lugar y tener una experiencia que posteriormente trasladamos a una imagen" (because we do not transform space, but try to generate a change, that is, our artistic stamp is not to produce a transformation of landscape, but rather to establish a being in place and an experience that later we translate into an image) (2010, 145).[19] Producing the image from the experience of encountering something on the verge of death is an all too important aspect of their work and one that should not be overlooked. As the past is simultaneously lost and rediscovered in these places, the image itself, the product of that experiential knowledge of being in a particular place at a particular time, becomes the "flash" of the historical – that instant, not so much the one caught as the one that emerges at the moment of a threatened disappearance. This is one of the ways in which we might see their projects as creating movement in otherwise static places – a point to which I will return later.

Capturing Fields, Vanishing Cities

Every photograph presents us with two messages: a message concerning the event photographed and another concerning a shock of discontinuity.

Another Way of Telling (Berger 1995, 86)

Bleda y Rosa's 1992–5 series *Campos de fútbol* (*Football Fields*) offers a good example of their formalist, documentary approach to capturing places that, despite bearing a strong – and in this case, visible – connection to the past, now appear as little more than vacant spaces waiting to be filled. While the shared formal attributes of tonal range, scale, land-to-sky ratio, depth of field, and camera position could characterize each photograph in the series as a uniform, quasi-scientific document of each playing field, the collection as a whole might best be read as a kind of lament, each image a different stanza in the poignantly composed, three-year-long elegy to these places once full of energy, movement, and life. Curiously but not coincidentally, all of the images in the series testify to the paradoxical specificity and at the same time non-specificity of location, which we could think about in terms of the distance between word and image. Yet the images do not necessarily record the changes in these places either; there are, for instance, no before and after shots. Rather, these images are manifestly interested in recognizing and making visible that which has remained. Though representing different locations, the photographs enact a repeated reading, as if in a book, of the now unused though perhaps not entirely useless goalposts, which are usually positioned on the left, with the remaining landscape or *campo* opening to the right. Of course, there is the occasional exception to this rule – which the artists deliberately label either as "typological accidents," as with their photograph of a dilapidated basketball court, or as a "diptych," as with the images "Cañete I" and "Cañete II," which together neatly bracket the landscape for us, giving it some semblance of unity and continuity. These few moments of rupture in the series are not entirely out of place, however. Or at the very least, they are no more out of place than the observer who casually stumbles upon these places of solitude, alone in the midst of nothingness, these open doors with nothing (and no one) to enter through them. Such calculated ruptures or breaks in an otherwise hermetic and seamlessly patterned "documentary" series are themselves an interesting way of creating a visual discontinuity that parallels the temporal

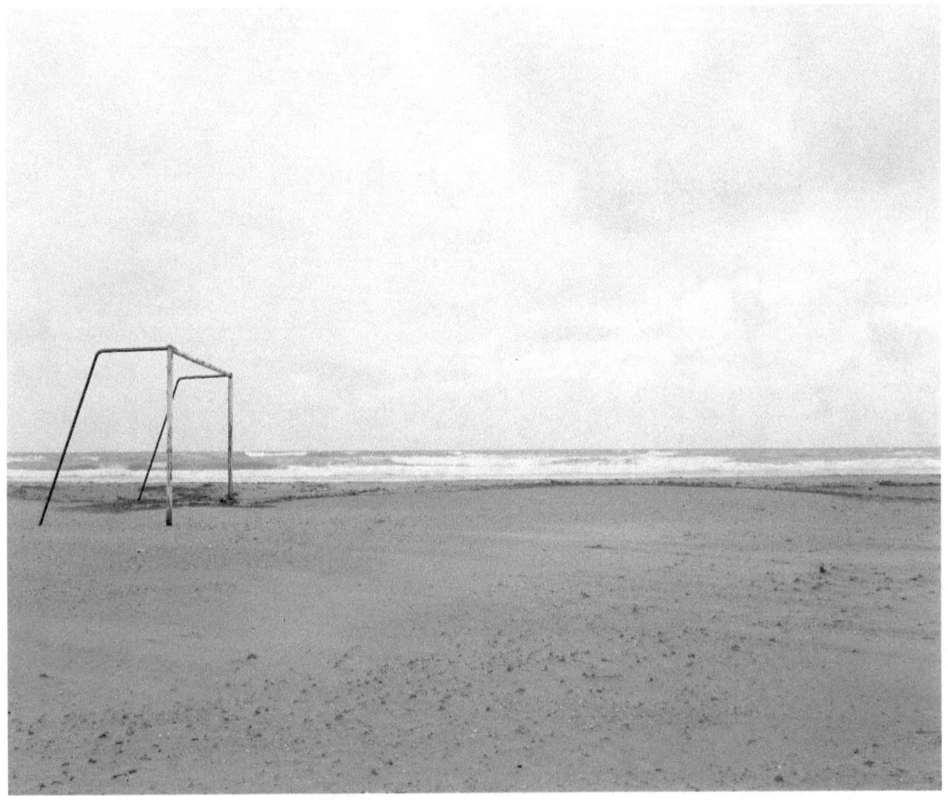

3.12 Bleda y Rosa, "Grao de Castellón" (1993). © 2014 Artists Rights Society (ARS), New York / VEGAP, Madrid.

disjuncture of the *campos* or fields themselves. While the images show the fields as now vacant, weathered, or in decay, and the goalposts as skeletal remnants of the games they once demarcated, they also recall events that once took place there, the games once played as well as the players and possibly spectators who would have occupied this space.

With this in mind, then, I suggest that the *Campos de fútbol* photographs do not document the uselessness of these vacant places so much as give their vacancy meaning through the photographic image, which here ascribes to each *campo* a specific time (1993, 1995, and 1994 respectively) and place (Grao de Castellón, Paterna, Albacete, and Cañete).[20] Put somewhat differently, the series as a whole captures – which is to

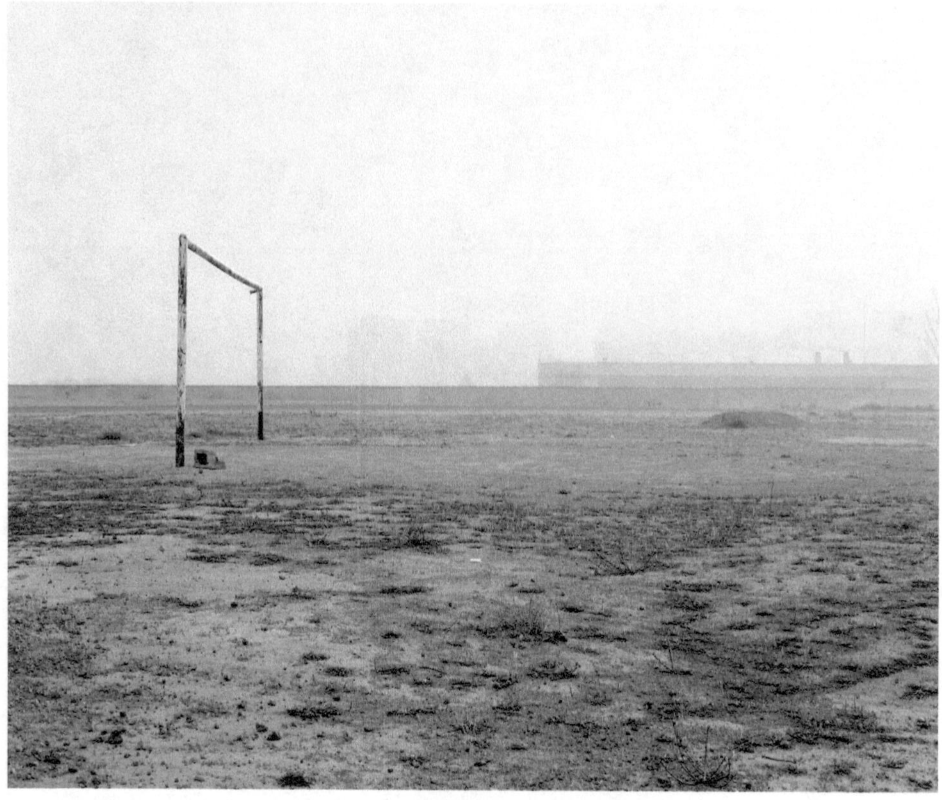

3.13 Bleda y Rosa, "Paterna" (1993). © 2014 Artists Rights Society (ARS), New York / VEGAP, Madrid.

say, takes – these empty, abandoned places at the very moment of their potentially being forgotten or lost and reinvests them – the football fields but also the cities that give each image its name – with meaning. They reinvest emptiness with fullness. Capture, in this sense, could be understood as a kind of rescue from oblivion, a lending of time, or a kind of "bringing back" to sight or life. Of course, if we take Bleda y Rosa's self-description at face value, this act of converting lost into found, empty into full, potentially forgotten into actually remembered, is less about the transfigurative or transformative power of photography. Recalling their claim that "we do not transform space but experience it," they carefully place the burden not on the photographic apparatus or image, not on the place temporarily inhabited by the

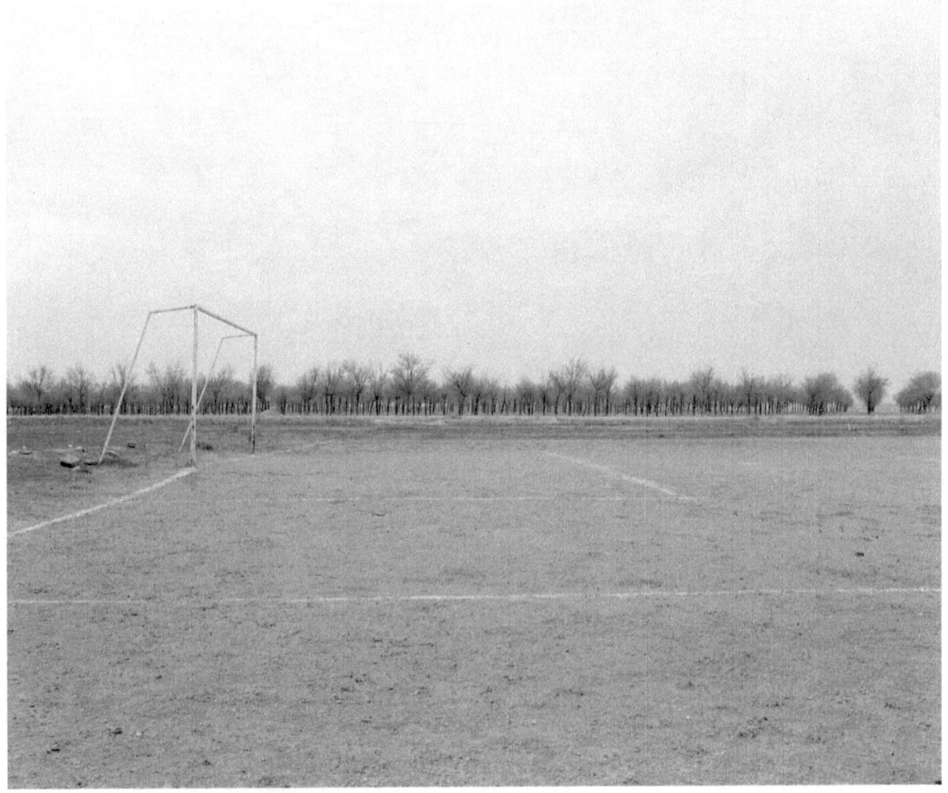

3.14 Bleda y Rosa, "Albacete" (1994). © 2014 Artists Rights Society (ARS), New York / VEGAP, Madrid.

artists, but on the viewer, on the eyes – those "organs of asking," recalling John Berger and David Levi Strauss's beautiful reminder (2005, vii). These moments of capture, of capturing place, of collecting and framing, of taking but also giving, neither change the landscape nor "illustrate the recognition of the original"; rather, they constitute, in the words of Siegfried Kracauer, "the spatial reconfiguration of a moment" (1993, 13); in not telling us how these *campos* once were, Bleda y Rosa's images invite us to remember them as we see them now.

Like the football fields series that preceded it, Bleda y Rosa's next project, *Ciudades* (*Cities*), uses textual cues to indicate the location of each image. The titles of these photographs have a double function – to both define and suggest. In naming specific sites, the titles answer the

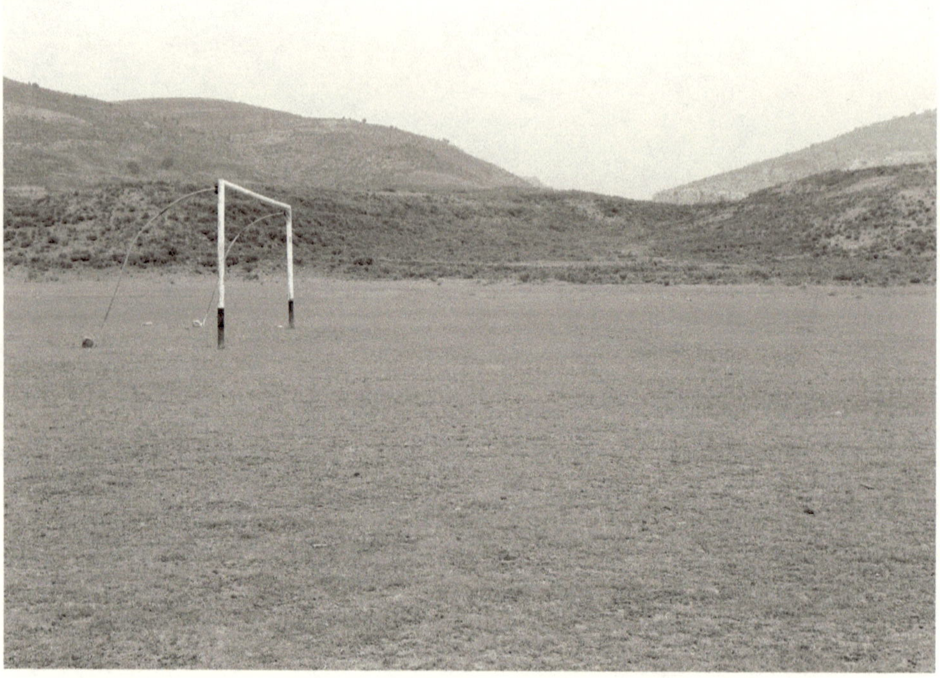

3.15 Bleda y Rosa, "Cañete I" (1994). © 2014 Artists Rights Society (ARS), New York / VEGAP, Madrid.

question of place (i.e., "Where is this?") but only allude to what we see represented, which oftentimes appears as mysterious as it is vague. In the example "Hacia Valeria, Segóbriga" (1999), both image and title unequally reference the historic site of the pre-Roman Celto-Iberian "victorious city" (from "sego" and "briga") considered to be the most important urban centre on Iberia's southern *meseta* (plateau), dating back to the first century BC, the ruins of which have been conserved as part of an archaeological park outside Cuenca. This image does not show any of the ancient ruins of Segóbriga, the ones that might typically be found in a history book or tourist brochure or on a cultural website; instead, it frames the absence of such ruins, inviting the gaze

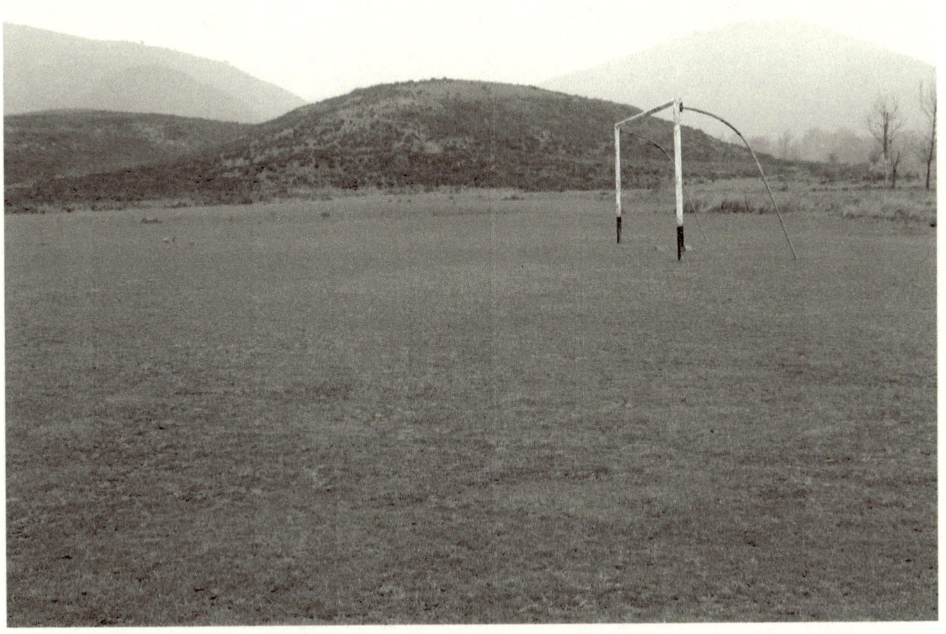

3.16 Bleda y Rosa, "Cañete II" (1994). © 2014 Artists Rights Society (ARS), New York / VEGAP, Madrid.

to rest on the edge of the visible. The particular photograph in figure 3.17 of a nondescript overcast landscape is representative of the entire series, given what it enacts on the viewer's sight: we expect to see a place that visually matches or parallels the historical significance associated with its name, but the surface reveals, through abstraction and monotony, only a kind of paradoxical non-place.[21] We do not see the site of history, as if from afar; instead, we are placed in the middle of it, which means that effectively the referential quality of the title (like all the individual titles in the series) has been remapped. The name of each location, supposedly added to each image in order to make legible and accessible the historical specificity of what we are

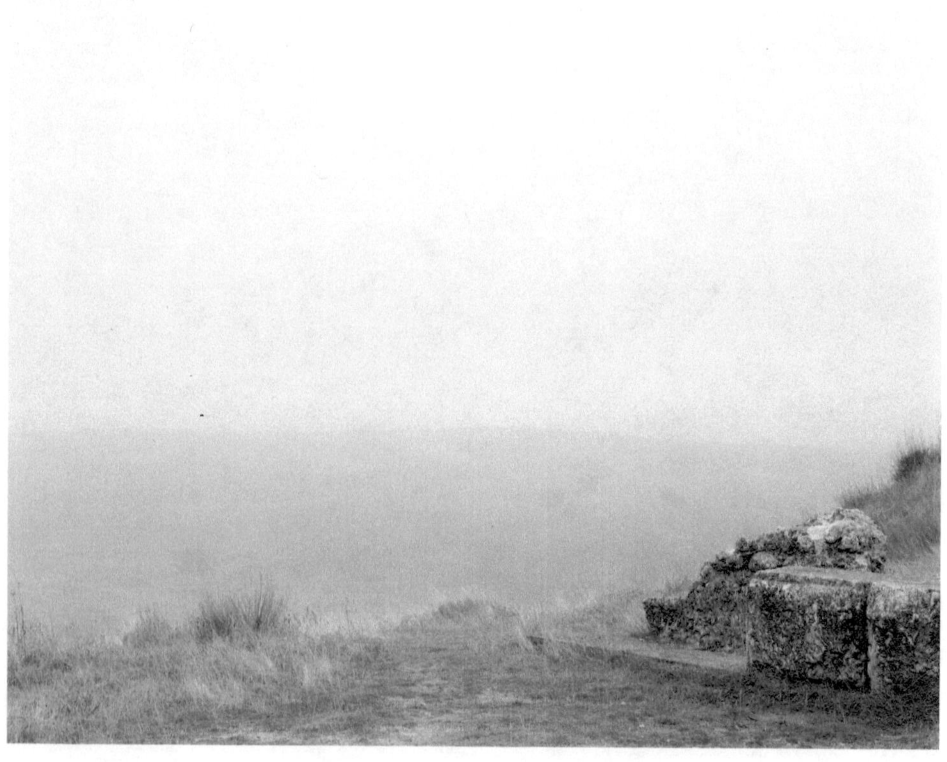

3.17 Bleda y Rosa, "Hacia Valeria, Segóbriga" (1999). © 2014 Artists Rights Society (ARS), New York / VEGAP, Madrid.

viewing, now constitutes a mere allusion to those places and their history – a delicate play between situating the viewer within a historical narrative and removing or distancing him from it. Here, the elusive "hacia" ("towards") Valeria suggests only an approximation, not an arrival at the destination of Segóbriga – a way of reminding us that we never reach or arrive at history through sites (or through photographs, for that matter); it is a way of reminding us that we do not necessarily *know* history simply because we see a site that *recalls* history. What these images tell us, if they tell us anything, is that we do not always enter into knowledge of the historical by viewing or encountering a site where a historical event took place. In capturing neither remnants of this once great city, nor any material clues that might define its quasi-mystical surroundings as unique or historically significant, the photographs of the *Ciudades* project question not only the physical limits of cities but also the conceptual limits of place and of placing history. Equally important, these images, in situating us in the middle of nowhere (*in medias nusquam*), invite questions not only about the location of history but also about the boundary between visualizing place and making it visible to others. All the while we are left to wonder what, if anything, remains.

Origins Emerge

All photographs are ambiguous. All photographs have been taken out of a continuity. If the event is a public event, this continuity is history; if it is personal, the continuity, which has been broken, is a life story. Even a pure landscape breaks a continuity: that of the light and the weather. Discontinuity always produces ambiguity. Yet often this ambiguity is not obvious, for as soon as photographs are used with words, they produce together an effect of certainty, even a dogmatic assertion.

Another Way of Telling (Berger, in Berger and Mohr 1995, 91)

There is an analogy between the photographic approach and scientific investigation: both probe into an inexhaustible universe whose entirety forever eludes them.

"Photography" (Kracauer 1993, 264)

Following the *Cities* project, and perhaps more ambitious in the way it visualizes, references, and mediates historical knowledge, is Bleda y Rosa's next series, called *Origen* (*Origin*, now in the singular, in contrast to the plural *Ciudades*). This project is centred exclusively on questions of culture and the roots of human civilization. In picking up where *Cities* left off with its interrogation of the conceptual limits of place, the *Origen* project marks a notable shift away from the fringes of ancient urban centres, in favour of going further back in geological time, digging deeper into the prehistorical layers of place as a way of questioning the conceptual limits of photography. Consider for a moment the image in figure 3.18 titled "Homo habilis," which features a panoramic view of the landscape at Olduvai Gorge in Tanzania, one of the most important archaeological sites for the study of human evolution. The title suggests this importance somewhat indirectly by referencing an object discovered there but not shown in the photo. For the avid reader

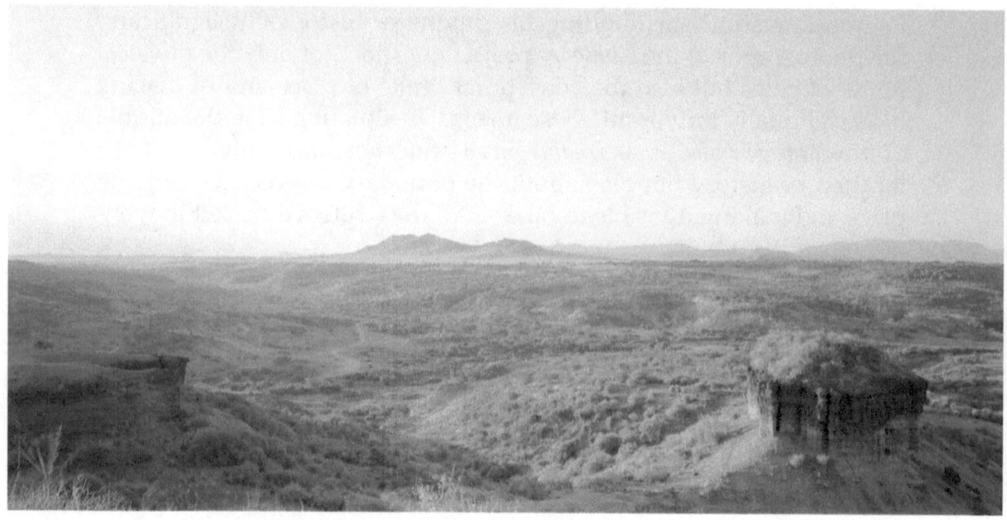

3.18 Bleda y Rosa, "Homo habilis. Garganta de Olvudai" (2008). © 2014 Artists Rights Society (ARS), New York / VEGAP, Madrid.

of archaeological discoveries or for those (myself included) who may have to undertake a bit of research, we may know (or learn) that *Homo habilis* refers to a species of the *Homo* genus that is believed to have lived 1.5 to 2 million years ago, the fossils of which were found in this region by the British archaeologists Louis and Mary Leakey in the early 1960s. As with the other photographs in the series, which reference artefacts by their scientific or pseudoscientific names – "Paranthropus boisei," "OH 9," "Mrs. Ples," or "Sangiran 17," to give only a few examples – the text-in-image component, always neatly centred underneath the image, is as much a way of measuring place through scientific classification as a way of locating history beneath the surface of each image.[22] In the process of defamiliarizing the landscape through language, there is an attempt to link each place directly to its history by placing the origin of that history "in frame." In this regard, the words in each title are not merely supplementary, but become the primary focal point, the crux and at the same time the invisible content of each image. Moreover, in evoking something unseen, the text of each photograph acquires a certain power that is contingent upon and also reinforces the "inadequacy of the image [context] in which they are placed" (Smithson

1996, 61).[23] In an important way, the titles – centred *and* central to each photograph's meaning – are as much about the places captured and represented as they are about what remains *outside* the frame, located or lost in the archives of history or annals of archaeology. Thus, situated between locating history and losing sight of place (or perhaps the other way around), the written component of each image migrates meaning in the same way it shifts the gaze: bidirectionally – first outward, then back inward.

Bleda y Rosa's photographic representations of landscape thus repeatedly, serially activate the same tracing mechanism throughout. In linking title to what is absent from the image, the viewer is prompted to connect specific evidence of human origins back to those places featured in the twenty-six photographs comprising the series. In the end, interestingly enough, the question of what remains is tied to the origins themselves, which we recall are consolidated under a broad, singular heading: *Origen*. Such remains, in terms of ancestral "remnants" or "residue" from the past, are, we are led to believe, the sole starting point. The process of reading these photographs is akin to pulling a loose thread only to discover that we are suddenly unravelling the entire piece; of course, in that unravelling, we discover we are gravitating back to the beginning. However, the source is not the object referenced or the event represented but the process of doing and undoing – that is, hinging and unhinging the image from the text. This starting point, the point of origin (not to be confused with the source of knowledge or history) that Bleda y Rosa draw on, is a way of reconceptualizing photography in terms of the knowledge it renders available through the dismantling and subsequent remapping of appearances.[24] In other words, the appearance of each landscape neither completely reveals nor completely conceals. Whether objects, images, or language, the origins that remain in effect generate a process of centring that displaces and excludes; the textual key (here, the trace of writing) becomes a supplement that suggests a subtraction. As such, *Origen* is ultimately less invested in making lost objects appear or reappear and, I would argue, much more inclined to notice their absence by decidedly *not* reappearing or revealing them. The photographs of the *Origen* series depict each landscape as an appearance that may reference but not reveal certain objects. Working from experience and phenomena and not from facts and the "truth" of appearances, the concept of origin is not the source of a place's essence (whether Tanzania, Pekin, or Sitges); nor is it the source of landscape; rather, it constitutes the displacement of such an

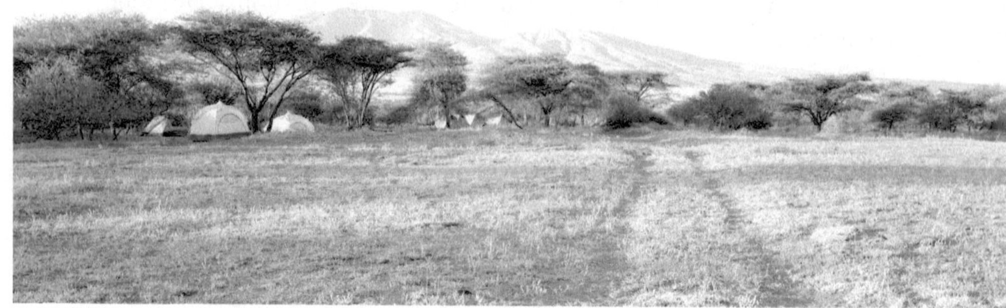

3.19 Bleda y Rosa, "OH 9. Garganta de Olvudai" (2008). © 2014 Artists Rights Society (ARS), New York / VEGAP, Madrid.

essence in favour of experiencing and gaining knowledge of a place by other means, through the delicate interchange of seeing and not seeing – and, by extension, through being and not being there.

In a second image from the same series, "Mandíbula de Sitges," we see only a fragment of a seascape, whose title refers to the fossilized jaw of a prehistoric Neanderthal. That jaw, discovered in the 1950s, then catalogued, shelved, and subsequently forgotten in the Archivo Histórico de Sitges, was rediscovered in 2005 by the archaeological team of Montserrat Sanz and Joan Daura and is now thought to be the most "modern" of the Neanderthal fossils discovered on the Iberian Peninsula to date. In his review of this series, David Torres argues that *Origen* "triggers a penetration into time" by merging the concepts of recollection, signification, and the insignificant in a way that allows for their mutual interrogation. At first glance we may see only, as Torres puts it, "a rugged Mediterranean coastline," one that is virtually meaningless "other than [as] a hypothetically sublime beauty applied to the landscape," so it is noteworthy that Bleda y Rosa pair such sweeping vistas with names of found objects that direct our gaze away from the vastness or beauty of the image, thus calling attention to the often overlooked fact that what we see (and without too much exaggeration, what we *desire* to see) is not within the frame at all.[25] It is not the photograph we see, or the place, but something else entirely.[26] In a similar way, these images do not establish meaning but displace and unsettle any meaning we might attach to each place. In orienting our attention both inward towards the landscape and outward towards the writing of history based on the unseen material traces that are linked to these places but that are never made visible for the viewer, these photographs raise questions about not only the always tenuous, always fragile relationship between knowledge and sight, but also the nature and desire of the archive and the objects housed within archives.[27] The sites documented (but, as we will see, also carefully composed) throughout *Origen* are not singular but all single-handedly hold information that may be accessible though not immediately visible. They break down the interdependence between word and image, reconfiguring it as displacement. They connect scientific discovery with a poetics of the invisible that counters nineteenth-century advances in photography. In the nineteenth century, photography was employed into the technological realm to render visible elements of the invisible world (the microscope allowed one to see cells, the telescope allowed one to see stars); here, Bleda y Rosa reverse the order and scale of vision – they use a highly advanced visual technology to call attention to what remains invisible despite the photograph's attempt to touch upon it, to scratch and even pierce through the surface.

In fact, when read as a whole, the series replicates an archival logic. The images individually reference specific objects (craniums, jaws, and other material traces of different genera of prehistoric men) through words and names; together, though, those same images accumulate origins from different locations and in doing so assemble various theories into one larger narrative. Such narrative itself remains linked inextricably to the image but also distinctly removed from it. These remains are, in a sense, "registered," but they can only be recalled in absence of the event that each photograph actually captures. That is not the event of prehistoric man's existence or of archaeological discovery; rather, each photograph reveals the event of encountering these places from posterity. In this sense, they are doubly past – the images show us places from the present (now, by virtue of time's passage, past) and at the same time locate a more remote, distant past within a larger historical and geological timeline. The photographs all perform, as it were, the temporal distance (and distancing) inherent in all photographs – that

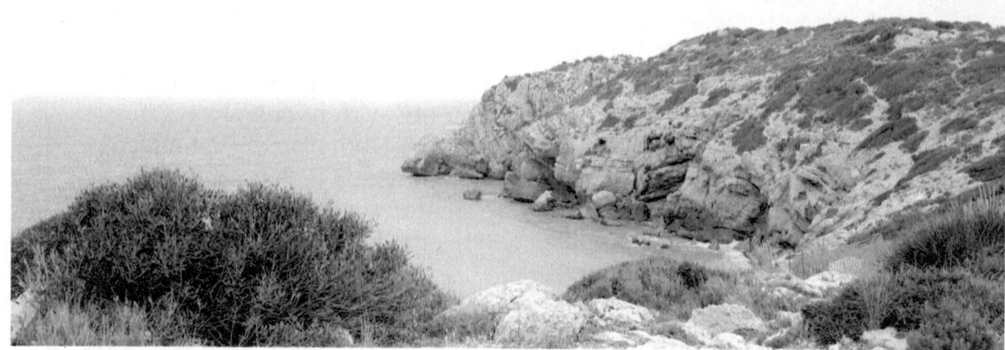

3.20 Bleda y Rosa, "Mandíbula de Sitges. Sitges" (2005). © 2014 Artists Rights Society (ARS), New York / VEGAP, Madrid.

is, the time between the event of viewing (the present and future time of the viewer), the event of "capture" in terms of taking the photograph (the present time of the artist), and the moment of discovery in each place (the past time of the archaeologists). In the end, Bleda y Rosa take instants and make them *processes,* duration; they make references that in turn stage events by hinging and unhinging our gaze from what is both present within and absent from the photograph.

Finally, the titles do not recover a lost history or historical object, just as the images do not reveal to us a landscape that "once was." Instead, the twenty-six titles and accompanying images only gesture towards a unified (and again, singular) theory of the origin of man through a profound absence. Of course, such an absence is in fact a repeated process of *absencing* – one almost opposite of the manoeuvre that I suggested took place in the *Football Fields* series. Here, meaning develops slowly over time. Just as the images in *Origen* are appearances that, contrary to the action of appearing, never show what lies beneath their surfaces, Bleda y Rosa *re*surface that history through language – the word stands in, becoming the presence of the unseen object, the same one buried over time and refound through a persistent process of unearthing and encountering the land. The discovery is the invention, the event is the trace: just as these photographs turn appearances into interpretative processes, they also turn human remains – material origins – into artefacts, articles for our imagination and attention.

In taking the scientific approach of documentary and recalibrating it, these artists shift away from positivist thinking in favour of investigating metaphysical questions of presence and absence, temporality and being, existence and experience. In this investigation, they create what I call a "nomadic photography" – one that both emerges from their own travels to remote and distant places and captures place in a sort of "drift," in a fleeting or ephemeral mode. The *Origen* photographs, like all those that preceded them, neither testify to the permanence of the landscape nor document the land's changeability over time. The landscapes as Bleda y Rosa construct them make places appear in a moment of their respective states of transition and evolution. Thus, the *Origen* images, by evoking temporally separate events and physically different remains, all enact a visual and mental wandering that subtly invites us to look both at the photograph *and* elsewhere, calling us simultaneously to look at what we see and to recognize what we do *not* see. In sustaining this line of inquiry with each image, an inquiry that I suggest is predicated on wandering and drifting, on encounters and traces, and on constantly though delicately shifting meaning and perspective, Bleda y Rosa show more than places and their respective present or absent remains. They also capture the place of photography, exposing not simply what photography represents but what it *reveals*. In between representation and revelation, they develop and trace an origin of seeing.

So far, I have been reading the trajectory of Bleda y Rosa's work as moving backwards through time and gradually expanding both spatially and temporally outside the image, which in some cases means outside the frame as well as outside of "place," understood both as a site and as a concept. The different series, when read in tandem, transition from the everyday, personal, local, and recent places of experience to larger questions of the historical and what it means not only to document or to remember the past, but also to read and to be in a place. Ultimately, whether representing places of leisure, city centres, prehistoric dwellings, or sites of scientific discovery, these images are all in one way or another about *inscription* – that is, about how traces of the past leave their mark, how they become inscribed indelibly in the landscape, and conversely how those traces and inscriptions, despite being present, may go undetected because they are unseen or invisible to the eye. But we should remember too that Bleda y Rosa's projects are equally concerned with how things once inscribed in a place become, however slowly or quickly, *removed*, because they have been either physically excavated or culturally or historically displaced. Besides raising the basic question of capture, which in these works relates directly to the problematic of documenting, organizing, cataloging, and archiving, Bleda y Rosa's images raise questions about the nature and substance of experience and knowledge, history and memory.

An Architecture That Remembers

Photographs have the merit of rendering, and thus preserving, all those transient things which are entitled to a place in "the archives of our memory."

"Photography" (Kracauer 1993, 266)

Photography tends to suggest endlessness. This follows from its emphasis on fortuitous complexes which represent fragments rather than wholes. A photograph, whether a portrait or action picture, is in character only if it precludes the notion of completeness. Its frame marks a provisional limit; its content refers to other contents outside of that frame; and its structure denotes something that cannot be encompassed – physical existence.

(Ibid., 264)

On that note, and on the question of visualizing the work of memory in a place – specifically the work of historical memory – I now turn to Bleda y Rosa's *Arquitectura/Memoriales* (*Architecture/Memorials*) series, arguably their most politically determined and aesthetically abstract project to date. The project spanned five years (2005–10), traversed three distinct locations (Jerusalem, Berlin, and Washington DC), and resulted in twenty-three colour photographs (approximately 3 × 3.5 feet).[28] What binds the collection's three cities together is not their architecture, which is radically dissimilar, but the space of memory inscribed on their urban fabrics and the spatial practices of remembrance and commemoration that in one way or another have come to define each capital. According to Alberto Martín, here the artists advance a dedicated reflection on "the categories of memorialisation as well as on the conditions of monumentalisation of memory," never failing to "allude to and evoke any of the complex questions associated with … the materialization of memory, the condition of the places being recalled, the imprint of trauma, the progressive loss of the function of memorials, and the abuse of memory" (2010, 217). Though the project more or less straightforwardly addresses both the place of memorials and the way they place memory in our social and cultural imaginary, the images in the series do not represent memorial sites in any recognizable or uncomplicated way. On the contrary, they offer us only fragments, opting instead to demand from the viewer a minimum level of curiosity and attention to detail that would allow her to follow along an unspoken line of inquiry into the way conventional memorials may open or close memory, the ways in which they construct and inhibit the act of remembrance, and last but not least, the ways they may divorce the past from or tether it to the present.

The Surface is the Image

> A monument can be nothing more than a rough stone, a fragment of ruined wall as at Jerusalem, a tree, or a cross. Its sanctity is not a matter of beauty or of use or of age; it is venerated not as a work of art or as an antique, but as an echo from the remote past suddenly become present and actual.
>
> *Ruins* (Jackson 1980, 91)

For those of us who have been to Jerusalem, or have seen pictures of the Wailing Wall or Zion's Gate, these photographic fragments – in reality, corners of each site – may seem familiar. Almost as if to counter-document the daily relevance of these real sites of remembrance, the images here expose common gathering places (sacred places of worship, for instance) as uninhabited and virtually devoid of human presence, save for the small traces of paper prayers wedged into the cracks of the wall or the traffic sign indicating "no entrance." The photographs miniaturize otherwise historically, politically, and culturally monumental places by bringing into sharp focus small, seemingly insignificant details – textures of stones and foliage, corners and lines where two or more surfaces meet, cracks and holes that may from a distance or certain angle go unnoticed. Though these details act like keys that unlock the mysteries of each photograph, it is important to note that there is no "zooming in" on them. Rather, there is a manner of framing that allows minor elements of each site, those that I am suggesting would otherwise recede into the background, to float to the surface.

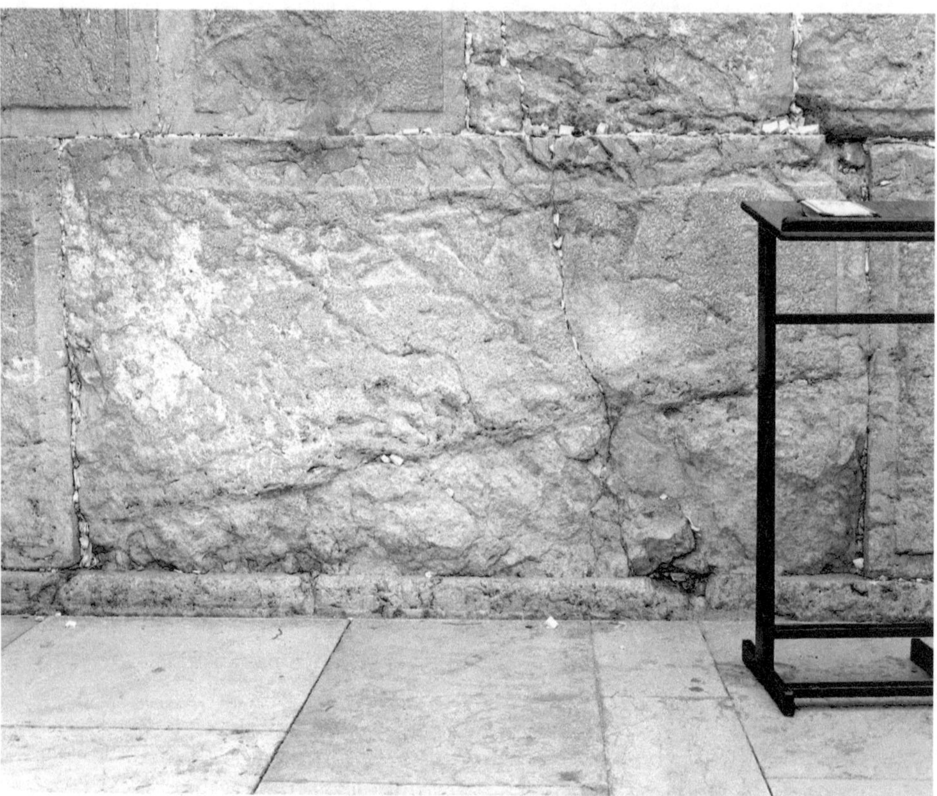

3.21 Bleda y Rosa "Muro de las Lamentaciones Monte del Templo. Jerusalén" 2010. © 2014 Artists Rights Society (ARS), New York / VEGAP, Madrid.

At times, this surfacing produces supplements or clues that allow the viewer to access the meaning of the image; other times, it creates obstacles to seeing the very sites ostensibly depicted. In fact, at times the barrier to seeing the memorial has as much to do with the artists' conscious fragmenting, framing, and surfacing techniques as it does with the representational balance between uneven textures and surfaces that exist in reality and the calculated evenness of the photographic image in terms of colour, proportion, placement, size of objects in the frame, transparence or opacity. In these two examples – the wall and the gate in figures 3.21 and 3.22 – it is interesting that both entrance to the city and accessibility to the image are predicated neither on seeing the totality of

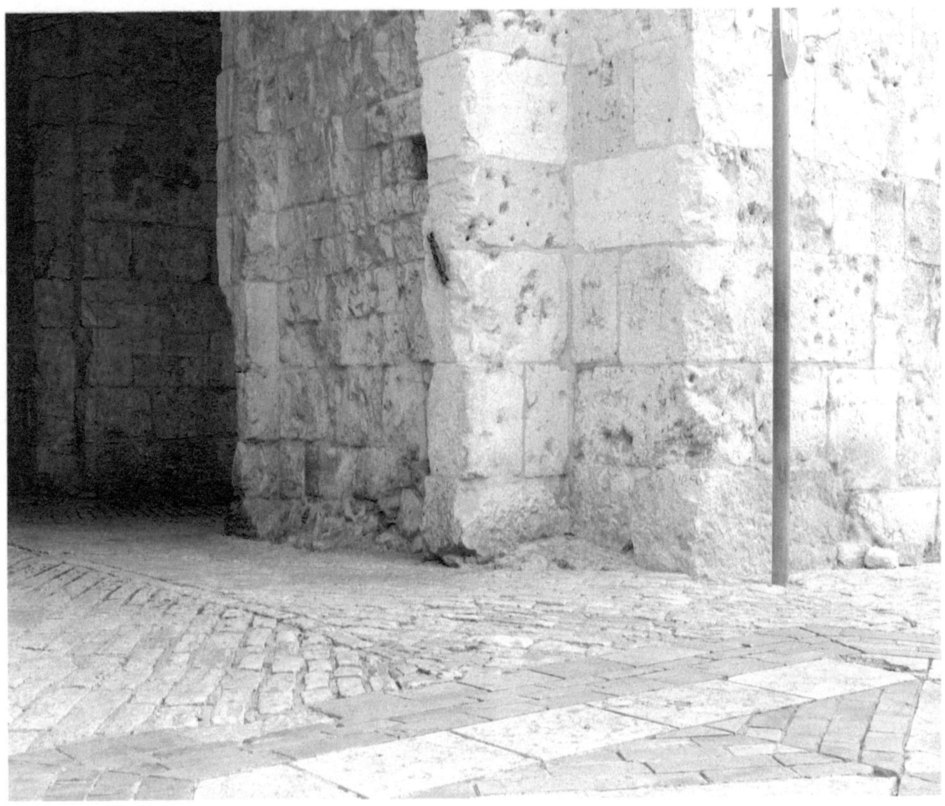

3.22 Bleda y Rosa "Puerta de Sión Barrio Judío. Jerusalén" 2010. © 2014 Artists Rights Society (ARS), New York / VEGAP, Madrid.

either structure nor on passing over the threshold but rather on reading the traces of writing (the paper trail of prayers but also the language of violence) that become legible as they emerge over time – the time it takes not just to look at the image but to see truly the web of objects and concepts it places before our eyes, the time it takes to figure out *what the photograph sees and also wants us to see*. Positioning these fragments of memorials as the centrepiece allows the image to approach the memorial while staying safely at the edge of each site. But why capture the monumental as the minor or mundane? What is at stake in bringing the materiality of these places to light? What do we understand from the photograph that makes the traces of a site's history visible?

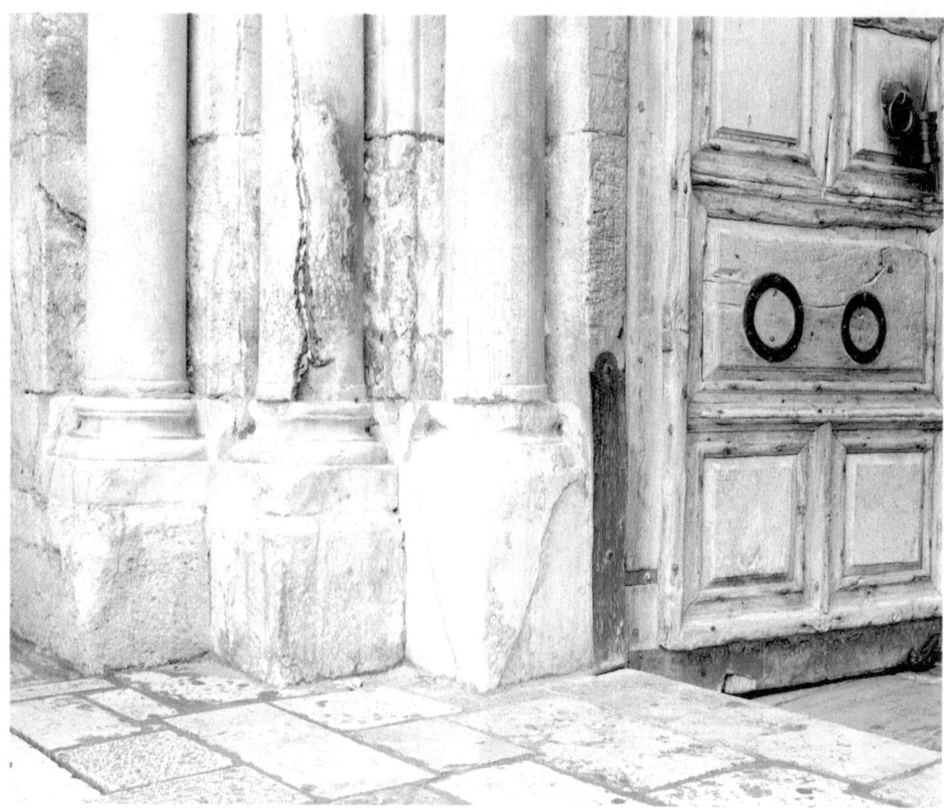

3.23 "Santo Sepulcro Monte Gólgota. Jerusalén." Bleda y Rosa (2010). © 2014 Artists Rights Society (ARS), New York / VEGAP, Madrid.

Consider, for a moment, another photograph from the "Jerusalem" section of the *Memorials* series, titled "Santo Sepulcro (Monte Gólgota)." Textures of wood, stone, and marble and the folded-up paper on the ground – which perhaps has just fallen from the sinusoidal crack in the pillar above it – reveal traces of writing. As with so many of Bleda y Rosa's photographs, here we encounter another allusion to the image as a place of inscription and the writing of history. While it may be the various crevices and seams that first grab our attention, or even the geometry of the image with its two-dimensional rectangles, squares, cubes, circles, and cylinders, I would argue that it is the tiny palimpsestic inscriptions of crosses – Christian etchings in the edifice, marking it as the threefold site of crucifixion, burial, and resurrection – that emerge, becoming visible over time and filling our sight with force. These written inscriptions are ingrained in the material structure of the holy tomb, yet they are not immediately legible. That legibility rests on the image's power to make the presence of such traces surface and thus be perceived but only after the fact, after we have studied the image for some time. A *presencing afterwards*.

Memory's Time, After Image

What real monument of stone or glass, people's names or lofty literary quotation, can compete with invisibility?

Walter Benjamin's Grave (Taussig 2006, 19)

Critics have commented that the *Architectures* collection in general marks a notable shift in Bleda y Rosa's oeuvre, from an aesthetics of documentation deeper into the realm of composition and abstraction.[29] *Memoriales* is no exception to this in that it essentially unifies specific sites not through a homogeneous process of measuring, capturing, and framing, as with the previously discussed series, but through heterogeneous responses to individual sites of memory. Moving from macro to micro perspectives, the photographs discussed in the following pages gather places in ways that both connect them through a shared burden of memory and juxtapose their differential treatment of memory's weight and density – or as Bleda y Rosa put it, the distinct ways in which each city reveals the remnants of history and "the mark of time" (2010, 10).

Moreover, this shift from documentary to compository style suggests a kind of writing (here, of course, "light writing," as we recall photography has been called since its conception) based on an arrangement and instrumentation that hones in on minute particularities of place, ranging from fragments and scraps to surfaces and edges. These details, at first seemingly unimportant, ultimately come to highlight Bleda y Rosa's primary interest in the multiple textures of place as well as – borrowing James Young's evocative term – the "texture of memory." In an essay introducing the series, the artists liken their methodology to the Benjaminian notion of reading the past by "brushing history against the grain" (2010, 10–11). Rather than approach the memorials as places where memory is distilled or disseminated, solidified or liquidized, seared into the surface or erased from it, they draw on the power of the image to "establish a reflection ... on the function of memorials as a depository of memory" (10). In short, their project is not one of looking at memorials as much as *looking at the image of memory* in places that ostensibly memorialize the past, ones that claim to "hold" memory in place. In looking at history not as "then and there," but instead as "here and now," *Memoriales* turns subtly towards the trace, what remains in history's wake. Looking at the image, then, implies observing (we could also say *tracing*) how memory is "built into" the urban scenery, whether collectively or individually, and how it might be "deposited," or, drawing on the word's etymology (*deponere*), "laid aside." At the same time, this looking implies a process of *imaging* in which instants of memory are created to call into question not only the textures and surfaces but also the *time* of memory, its duration and will to permanence, along with its fugitive nature.

Through the emergence of these traces, the project poses crucial questions: How do images anchor or unanchor memory? How is memory simultaneously the centre of each memorial – and by extension each photograph – and its periphery? In what ways does the image illuminate or imitate how memorial sites paradoxically hold memory in place and at the same time lay it aside or discard it altogether? Confronting all of these concerns, *Memoriales* refocuses the viewer's line of sight to perceive what the camera reveals rather than what it represents. Embedded in this revelation, we should remember, is not only what Bleda y Rosa call "la imagen latente" (the latent image) but also, and significantly, a testament to the ways in which the mysteries, enigmas, traces, and affects of place gradually seep into our sight (132).[30] How does the image – here, the *after image* – remain, and in that remaining produce, affect, or distort memory?

Memory Here? Tracing History's Ghosts

Not only is the Photograph never, in essence, a memory (whose grammatical expression would be the perfect tense, whereas the tense of the Photograph is the aorist), but it actually blocks memory, quickly becomes a counter-memory.

Camera lucida (Barthes 1981, 91)

The ghostly photographic remains are sapped memories, a mock reality of decomposition.

"Incidents of Mirror-Travel in the Yucatan" (Smithson 1996, 127)

The *Origen* series situated the viewer within the landscape and at the same time oriented the gaze outward, to a point located out of frame. The *Memoriales* project undertakes a similar task of modifying placement and perspective in order to invite our contemplation on the placement, or on the twofold sight/site of memory. Unlike *Origen*, however, the series moves in the opposite direction, drawing us *into* the memorial sites by showing us only pieces of them. Like the Jerusalem photographs, the following two sections – Berlin and Washington DC – carefully position the camera at the edge or threshold of select memorials, thus keeping the viewer somewhat at a distance. The images in figures 3.24, 3.25, and 3.26 from the Berlin portion of the series reveal traces of a traumatic past in three distinct forms: wounds, walls, and barriers.[31] In "Grosse Hamburger Strasse," the partial scaffolding that frames – not shields – the bullet-riddled exterior wall of what seems to be a building undergoing renovation reveals virtually nothing to us of the numerous memorial sites that now define Berlin's largest historic Jewish neighbourhood of the same name, sites such as the nearby (and notably colossal) Monument to the Murdered Jews of Europe" and, on a smaller but equally powerful scale, the *Stolperstein*, which are individual pavement memorials (literally "stumbling blocks" or "obstacles") embedded in the road, on which are inscribed the names of Jews who lived there before being deported to concentration camps and killed.[32]

The fact that these photographs all concentrate on the memory of everyday spaces – that is, on how architectural structures "hold" memory or how traces of history are carved into ordinary textures of places – reflects a compositional choice that highlights another fact: that memory in these places may go unseen or undetected precisely in its *not* being announced as anything other than quotidian. To say the very least, this is a bold move on Bleda y Rosa's part. They situate our perspective on memorials neither at the point of oversight nor at the moment of monumentalization.[33] In *not* photographing memorial sites explicitly, the photographs themselves become both the obstacle to seeing those sites *and* the space that makes possible the very imagining, tracing, and reframing of memory's always shifting, always unsettled, and therefore always spectral place.[34]

But what does it mean to photograph places of memory *as obstacles*? At what point does the photograph itself become an obstacle too? Consider the image in figure 3.25. It is notable that in "Jüdische Friedhof Schönhauser Allee," the impenetrable block of concrete cast in half-light (in Spanish we would say "penumbra," in half-shadow) frames

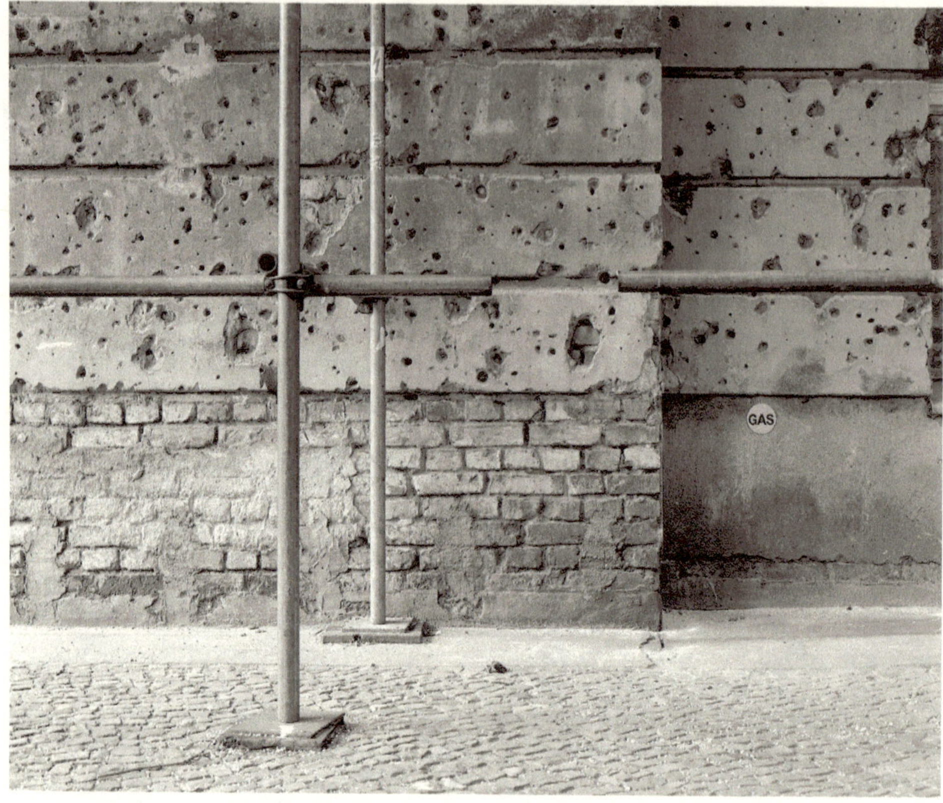

3.24 "Große Hamburger Straße Scheunenviertel. Berlín." Bleda y Rosa (2005). © 2014 Artists Rights Society (ARS), New York / VEGAP, Madrid.

for us neither the cemetery's interior, which is referenced in the title, nor other memorial sites such as the sculptures that now stand in place of the neighbourhood's former Jewish cemetery (which was used as a round-up point for soon to be deported Jews and later destroyed by the Gestapo in 1943, during the war). Instead, and distinct from the previous image of a wall on which the tactile traces of violence committed against the city are made visible, we are presented with traces of light, texture, and shadows. What does this image of the wall achieve if not an enclosure of memory, "walling" it in and in so doing shutting it out, thus placing it out of sight?

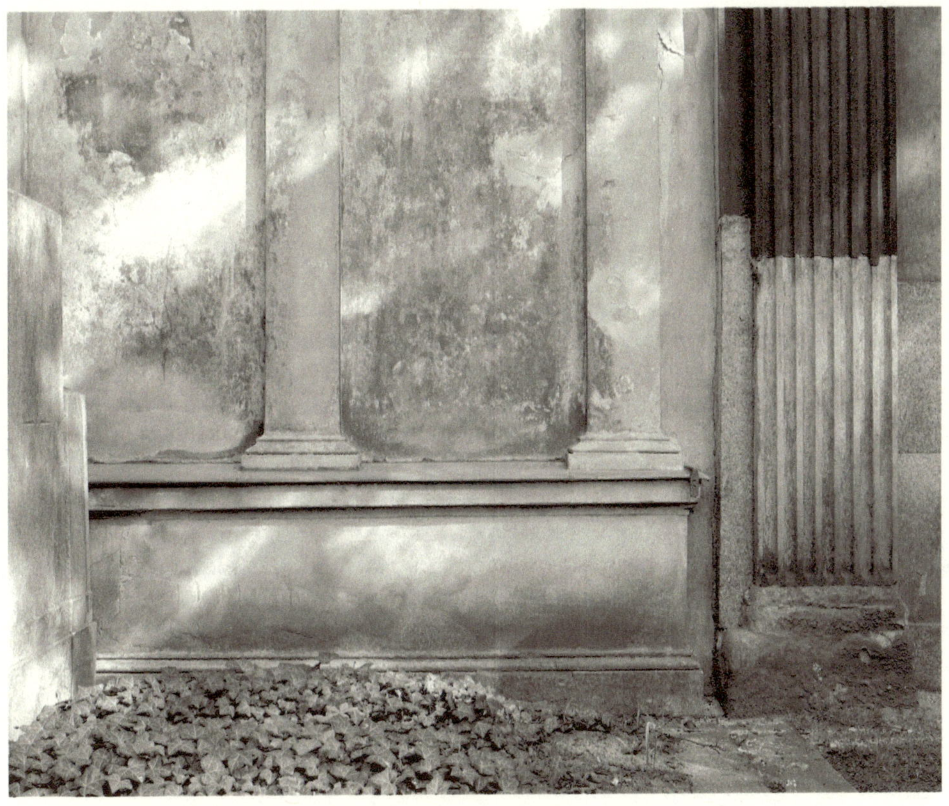

3.25 "Jüdische Friedhof Schönhauser Allee. Berlín." Bleda y Rosa (2005). © 2014 Artists Rights Society (ARS), New York / VEGAP, Madrid.

In making visible traces of the past that are present (e.g., bullet holes) *and* calling on the viewer to imagine sites *not shown*, Bleda y Rosa's photography performs a repositing (a "placing back") of memory that lifts the past out of – and, I would argue, counteracts – the dangerous "depository" (the "laying aside," if we recall) of memory so common to conventional memorials. The photographs, when read together, present to us what remains and at the same time re-present or stage for us how those remains go unseen. If our sight is unsettled by looking at these images, it is precisely because what we expect to see is absent yet undeniably referenced. In other words, these photographic images re-enact the problem of the memorial – namely, that "in contrast to memory …

it seems more interested in being seen than in making seen [revealing] that which it represents" (Bleda y Rosa, 2010, 11). Just as certain memorials become obstacles to the very remembrance they were designed to invoke and perpetuate, so too does the series presents us with a string of visual barriers that incite us to ask: What do we see here? What memory is *here*? In *this* place? It is perhaps in placing such barriers before us that we are led back to the practice of remembering itself.

It is significant that Bleda y Rosa make a point of visiting structures that not only memorialize a historic event or serve as monuments commemorating a traumatic past – a sacred place of prayer, another of mourning, and so on – but also seek out architectural places that are substantial, even monumental, in size, physically and historically speaking. It is certainly true that in these places monumental events have occurred. Setting the monumental aside, however, at times they quite literally raise an important question for us all: Does the logic of the monument contradict the work of commemoration and memorializing? Does it deny the act of mourning? And if so, does the series attempt to reaffirm memory by forcing us, through these images, to remember after we have repeatedly, systematically lost sight not only of the memorials but also of the objects to be remembered in and through those sites? Or does it, conversely, enable us to mourn that which cannot be remembered, by bringing us into closer contact with the very moment of its being lost?

From traces that remain to barriers that block, from the barely visible to the inescapable, we could say that all of the images in *Memoriales* share a "repudiation of monumental forms" – that they negate, fragment, or make absent such forms, such totalities, in order to call attention to "minor details" (Young 1993, 22). Such details are illuminating in the ways they displace or centre memory and in the ways they expand, condense, or void memory's legacy. Furthermore, the photographs in *Memoriales* carry out a "performative" function so that when read together, the images present us time and time again not only with traces but also with non-traces, things lost, out of sight, invisible, or inaccessible. In light of this second function, I have also alluded to another component of Bleda y Rosa's project: the construction of a narrative of loss. I suggest here that such a narrative is better understood when we consider first, the notion of thresholds, and second, the sequence of the photographs.

Thresholds play an important role in the series. At times, they are partly open, as with "Santo Sepulcro"; at other times, they are completely closed, as with the image in figure 3.26, "Gedenkstätte Plötzensee Hüttigpfad," which represents a former Nazi prison and execution site in Berlin, now an interactive memory museum. This photograph brings together three surfaces – concrete, brick, and iron – but crops their respective places – the outside pavement, the building walls, and an entranceway. The threshold in this particular example (the closed gate and barred window) presents an interesting case of a physical barrier that at the same time may not obstruct sight – at least not completely. There are, after all, openings in the structure of closure represented here. Sérgio Mah has written that the "apparent neutrality" of the *Memoriales* photographs is indicative not of abstention or critical renunciation but rather of their ability to potentiate "una percepción dialéctica de la imagen, es decir, poner al espectador ante la posibilidad de una experiencia de confrontación y de duda que desautoriza una lectura simplemente identificativa de lo que se hace visible, de lo que se documenta en la imagen" (a dialectical perception of the image, in other words, to put the spectator before the possibility of an experience of confrontation and doubt that deauthorizes a simple identificatory reading of what is made visible, of what is documented in the image) (2010, 7). This "experience of confrontation and doubt" is key, and the threshold presents it directly to us. We might ask: Confrontation with what precisely? To which we should recall that the threshold – in Spanish *umbral*, from the Latin *umbra* – means "shadow" or "darkness" but also (more relevant to the present study) signifies the ghost. In light of this, I suggest that in images that purport to visualize memorials, to *remember by other means*, the figure of the threshold is not a means to cross over or through, nor is it about remaining exclusively outside the bounds of memory; rather, it is a way to grasp memory from an in-between space as it gets buried and settles, as it re-emerges and unsettles. In short, thinking from the threshold constitutes a way of reading the ghostliness of memory and place. We could take this logic one step further: each image, in turn, becomes a threshold too – a physical dividing line as in a doorway or gateway, and also a temporal in-betweenness and connecting point. On the one hand, the image as threshold is an obstacle to sight that presents us with a way of seeing how we lose sight of memory; on the other, such a threshold may connote an opportunity to confront and engage with those obstacles, which is a way of confronting and engaging with ghosts as well.

Beyond standing at the doorway in and *of* the photograph through which we confront loss as a process, a figure of representation, and an

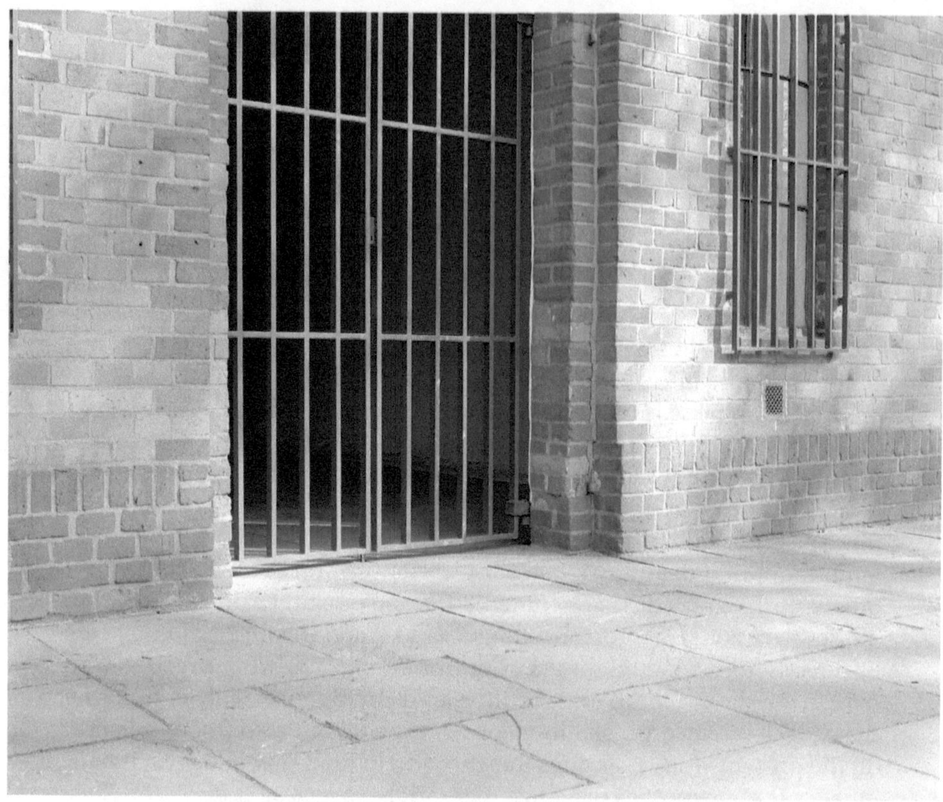

3.26 "Gedenkstätte Plötzensee Hüttigpfad. Berlín." Bleda y Rosa (2005). © 2014 Artists Rights Society (ARS), New York / VEGAP, Madrid.

image, it is important for us to consider not only the content of each work (image and text) but also its place in the sequence. From Jerusalem to Berlin to Washington DC, the artists map different configurations of memory's work – both works of memory, understood as sites, and the work of memory, understood as an act that requires participation, be it voluntary or involuntary. As we look at the photographs in a catalogue or in a gallery space, we move from holy places that are also contested territories of past and present religious violence and political occupation to places that embody or entomb terror, imprisonment, and death.[35] The Berlin photographs are unique in that they expand on the language of violence and occupation that is set forth in the Jerusalem section; they also reclaim memory through loss and by placing within the frame images of living traces of the past that recall sites of former terror and death. The leap from Berlin to Washington DC may be striking to say the least. Besides being national capitals, what do these cities have in common historically? What do they share with regard to their contemporary practices of memorializing? The narrative told by the photographs changes tone and demeanour as we quickly realize that the series does not exclusively recount moments from Jewish history per se; at stake, rather, is the larger issue of truth, justice, and the freedom of memory – we could even say the *democracy* of memory.

Memory's Democracy: At the Front Door

There is nothing in this world as invisible as a monument.

"Monuments" (Musil 1995, 61)[36]

A framed staircase. We may be tempted to identify these as ordinary steps until we research what the title "Petersen House, 10th Street" signifies. The steps suddenly take on a certain vibrancy, a different magnitude and intensity, when we learn that this is the house where President Lincoln was taken on the night he was shot in the back of head by John Wilkes Booth at the Ford Theater, and where he died the next day, 15 April 1865. Like the steps in the "Petersen House" photograph, the distinctive red gate and adjacent alleyway in "Surratt Boarding House, Chinatown" may say nothing to us. Potentially less compelling might be the Chinese takeout restaurant Wok and Roll, whose sign overshadowing the memorial plaque on the wall (situated in the upper right of the frame) tells us nothing about the house where Mary Surratt is believed to have conspired to assassinate Lincoln (a crime for which she became the first woman executed by the US government). The details in both images, as if on silent tour, lead us literally to the memorial site's front door, which in the latter image is engulfed in the noise of advertisements announcing lunch specials and happy hour deals. Similarly, the other photographs of Washington DC often depict memorials as secondary characters standing in the background to whatever now – at the moment of encounter and capture – has become the main show. Whether bloodstains or a textual inscription marking a place of conspiracy and treason, these images, monumental in their seeming indifference to documenting the totality of such sites and their respective

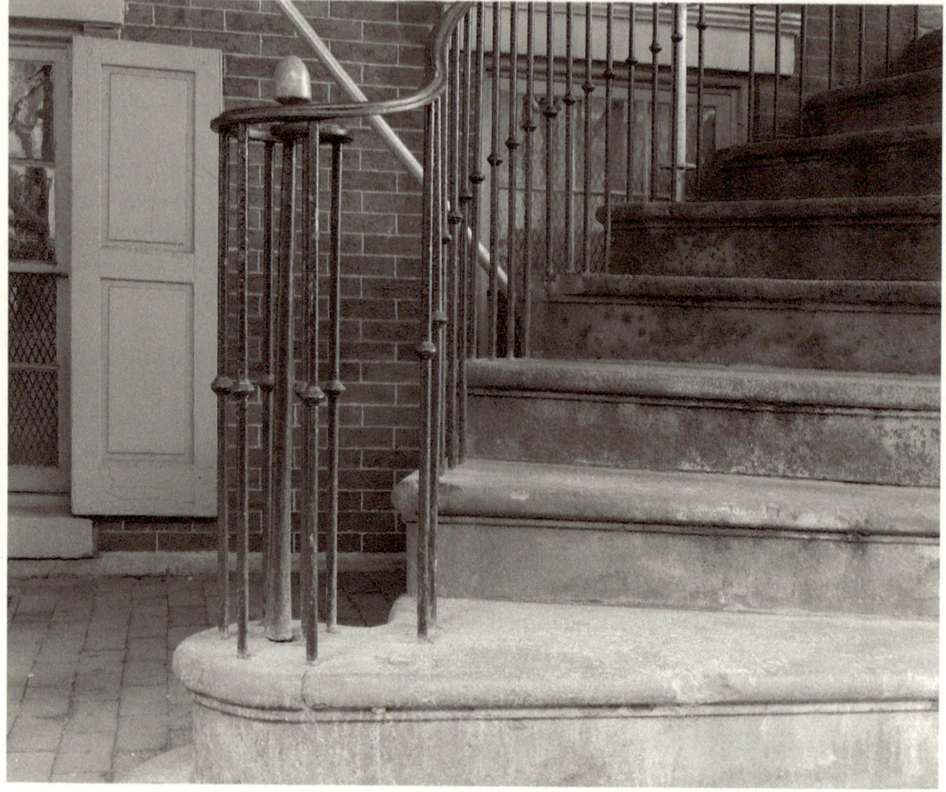

3.27 "Petersen House, 10th Street, Washington." Bleda y Rosa (2010). © 2014 Artists Rights Society (ARS), New York / VEGAP, Madrid.

and complete histories, offer testimony to time's passage and to the different spaces of conversion that have placed traces of the past between visibility and invisibility.

The Washington DC photographs are unique in that they are the only ones in the series to break the logic of exteriority in which the camera and subsequently the viewer remain on the outside or at the threshold of a memorial site. Including doorways, alleyways, fences, and gates in this third and final section, Bleda y Rosa are careful not to rupture threads of continuity within the series as a whole. But here they also present us with interiors, a detail that curiously sets the DC photographs apart from the rest. The photograph "Ford's Theater 10th Street"

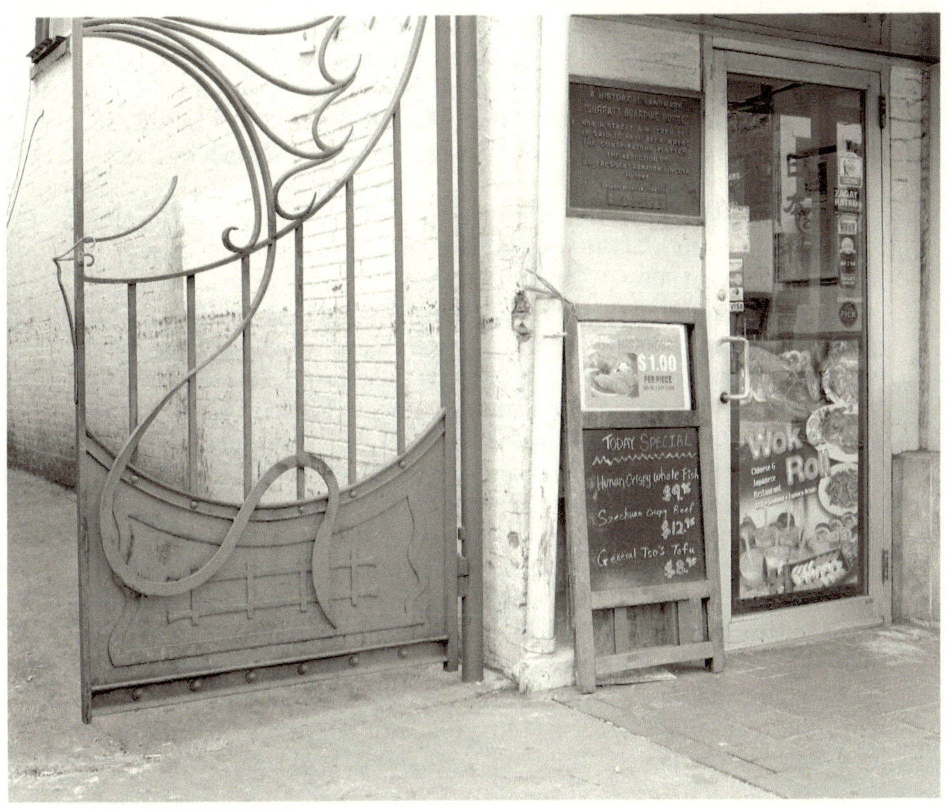

3.28 "Surratt Boarding House, Chinatown, Washington." Bleda y Rosa (2010). © 2014 Artists Rights Society (ARS), New York / VEGAP, Madrid.

provides a good example of this; it could easily be read as a move from the previous "visual notes" on the exteriorization of memory now to its interiorization, thus visualizing the objects of its internal mechanics. Interestingly, however, this particular interior reproduces the same kinds of barriers to seeing the image as the previously discussed photographs of shadowed walls and gated entranceways. Here we see an arrangement of partial objects and patterns, along with myriad fabrics and folds, as if in collage – including velvet chairs, one of which (we may assume the one where Lincoln sat) sits centre right, out of focus but in plain view. We may also notice the tied curtains, the vertically striped wallpaper, the floral carpet, fragments of an American flag draped over the balcony, and the edge of the theatre stage. What might this ensemble suggest not only about memory and its possible (perhaps inevitable) objectification, but also about time? About the multiple temporalities that seem to coexist in the photograph, not least of which are the time of Lincoln's assassination and the time or moment of capture?

Here, Bleda y Rosa not only fracture the wholeness of the Ford Theater as a memorial but also recreate (*re-posit*, as it were) a scene that captures the site's impeccable preservation as an obstruction of sight.[37] Through the photographic image, the memorial's static, unwavering presence becomes disrupted and disassembled in such a way as to provoke rather than restore. And the objects of memory – those fabrics and pieces of furniture that are meant to conjure and hold memory in place – are manipulated in the image to underscore the idea that photographs as memory objects themselves are equally unstable and manipulative. Thus, the point is not to strip us of the possibility of seeing memorial sites, but rather to show us that however well intentioned, such sites all too often misguidedly condition and limit the way we remember by operating on the assumption that memory is something to be clarified, corralled, or preserved. These photographs do not make memory transparent or accessible; instead, they show us varying degrees of memory's opacity and dense layering. The end result is that the photographs strip the memorials of their "screen memory" effect to rearrange the real objective of memory: the capacity to reflect back on the actual event (Carson 2003, 95).[38]

It is perhaps in terms of transparency, more than any other (i.e., temporality, assemblage, obstruction), that the Washington DC photographs achieve their greatest impact. The series concludes with memorial sites that recall racism and the struggle for equality and political freedom. Many of the places photographed, such as those that reference Lincoln's death, either double as sites of conspiracy or evoke conspiracy as central to what they are seeking to commemorate, such as with the Martin Luther King memorial.[39] The final photograph of the section (and the last of the series) is titled "Norman Mayer Monument, Pennsylvania Avenue." Though thematic threads are picked up in this image – inscription, traces, multiplicity of textures and surfaces, as well as thresholds (the two signs marking the memorial appear as a gate or doorway) – the differences are noteworthy. One such difference from the other DC photos is that the barrier or object that obstructs our line of vision is now placed even more explicitly in the centre of

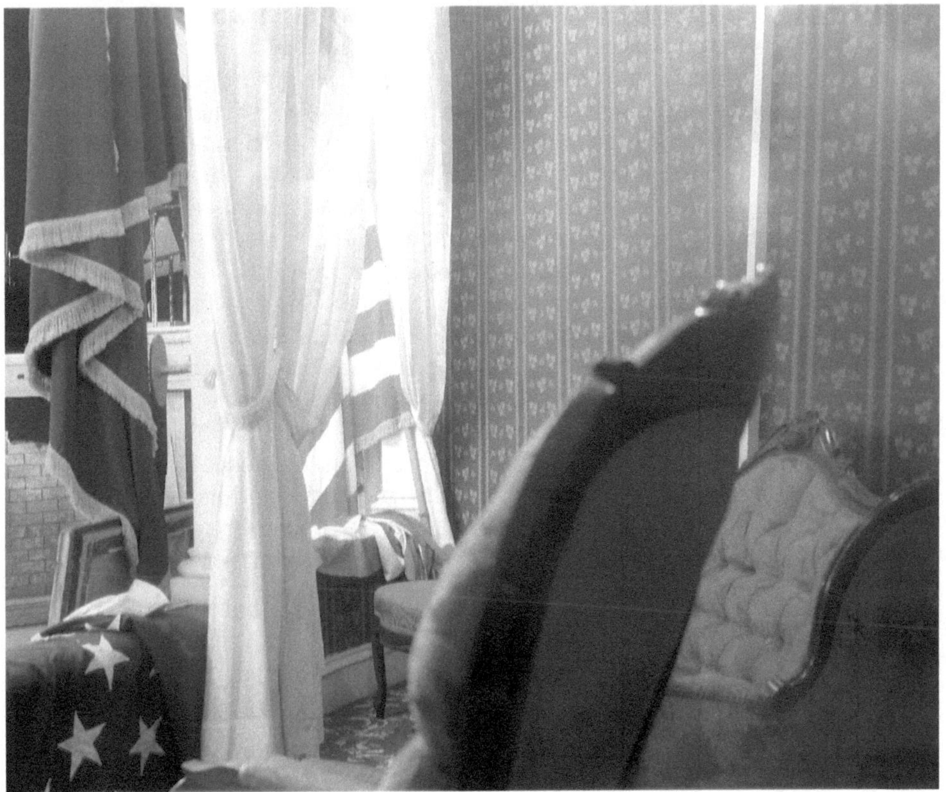

3.29 "Ford´s Theatre, 10th Street, Washington." Bleda y Rosa (2010). © 2014 Artists Rights Society (ARS), New York / VEGAP, Madrid.

the frame – here, disproportionately taking up two-thirds of the image, a large plastic sheet that has been torn and taped. The opaque plastic covering appears to be protecting something underneath, and because of the camera's angle, it blocks our complete view of the signs on the monument, which read (from left to right): "LIVE BY THE BOMB, DIE BY THE BOMB" (on the left, the surrounding frame reads "Truth and Peace Vigil") and "BAN ALL NUCLEAR WEAPONS OR HAVE A NICE DOOMSDAY" (on the right, the frame around the sign reads "N. Mayer Monument/Peace = Justice).[40]

But, why end with this image? The monument itself – part memorial, part protest, part dwelling – is a 24 hour per day, 365 day per year permanent peace vigil and camp located directly across the street from the White House. The site was created in 1981 by peace activist Concepción Picciotto in remembrance of her mentor Norman Mayer, the legendary anti–nuclear war protester who was gunned down by US Parks Service sharpshooters after a ten-hour hostage taking at the Washington Monument. Beyond remembering Mayer's death, the site carves out a space for politics and activism that continues his legacy. Despite intense police surveillance and at times aggressive censorship, the monument's call for peace and justice has prevailed as the longest protest in US history, spanning just over three uninterrupted decades and five presidential administrations. The site has become an emblem of free speech and First Amendment rights and has encouraged community building around the issue of peace by inviting collective participation in support of its anti-nukes campaign. The remarkable longevity of the monument, which doubles as Picciotto's residence (thus referencing the place or "housing" of a living memory), and its persistence in promoting peace through times of war and most recently through the rise of national security in response to global terrorism, has flagged it as a major tourist site.

Mobilizing Memory

> The monument ... is a guide to the future: just as it confers a kind of immortality on the dead, it determines our actions in the years to come.
>
> *Ruins* (Jackson 1980, 93)

In remembering Norman Mayer's cause, one of the main objectives of the monument is to activate the memory of others. This activation is bolstered by raising public awareness and solidarity and by creating a canvas on which to "voice" political protest, as well as question and disarm dominant governmental values – in this case, the value of nuclear weapons over human life. Not surprisingly, this voice operates through the act of writing and rewriting antiwar messages, messages of peace, and, for Picciotto at least, messages of truth. That the vigil remains not in spite of the fact that the signs change as they are censored, confiscated, or rewritten, but *because* of their changing, is a structural component that complicates the very notion of the monument's permanence, the underlying foundation – some might even say the bedrock – of monument (and monumental) design.[41]

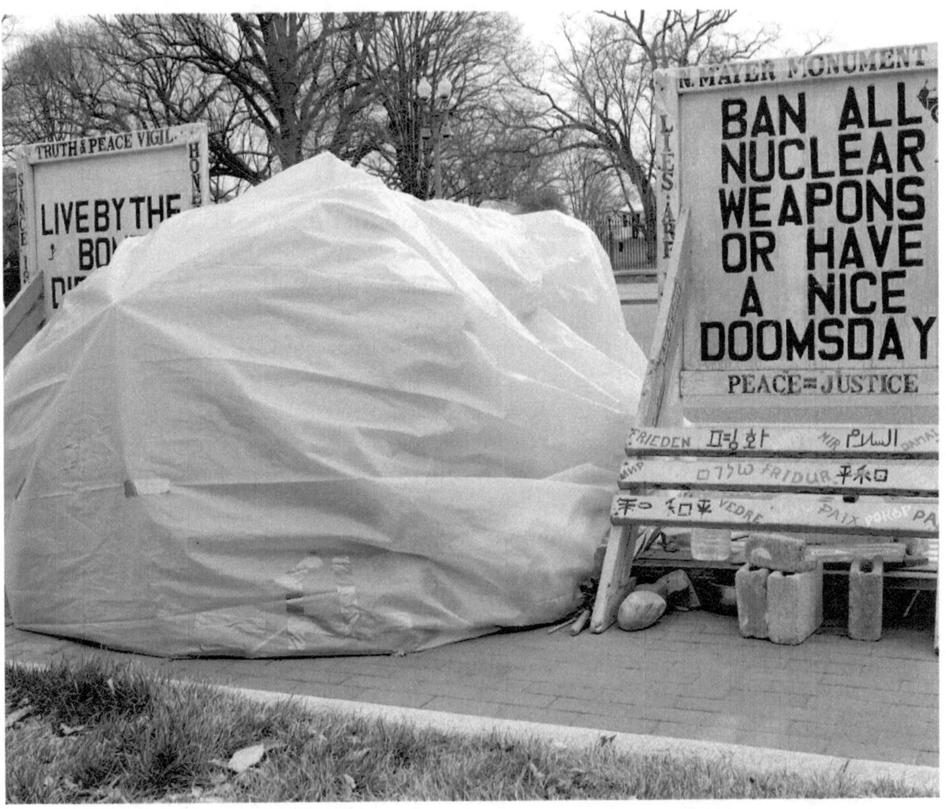

3.30 "Norman Mayer Monument, Pennsylvania Avenue, Washington." Bleda y Rosa (2010). © 2014 Artists Rights Society (ARS), New York / VEGAP, Madrid.

But all of this is, of course, about the monument itself. What about the *image* of the monument? *This* image? Paradoxically, Bleda y Rosa's photograph testifies to the monument's permanence, its unchanging will to remember over time (embodied in the figure of Concepción, whom we do not see in the photograph) as well as to its inevitable transformation (the written word on the signs conveying the same message reconfigured over time, we which we do see). What better way to capture an active, ephemeral monument than with photography? Like the site, which remains constant *and* revisionary, the photograph plucks an instant from time's continuum, and keeps that moment the same by "seizing," "freezing," or "embalming" it, yet produces the means for its perpetual transfiguration during all subsequent moments of viewing in the present. For Barthes, this is the photograph's fundamental contradiction – its burden and its gift – that within it is housed both a "there-has-been" or a "once was" and, at the same time, an eternal "now."

In contrast to counter-monuments or counter-memorials, which connote structures that integrate into their designs an anticipated removal or calculated erasure, the Norman Mayer monument is a structure that functions not on the burial of memory but on its constant movement. In this sense, it is a palimpsest that manoeuvres on memorializing and monumentalizing *as process* rather than on notions of stasis, permanence, or grandeur. How might photography alter or enhance this? In his article "Ante el tiempo: Bleda y Rosa," Luis Francisco Pérez has observed that the artists represent the emptiness of memorials – their voids – as a way to resignify what has been lost. This is what, for Pérez, constitutes the essence of their work – as he puts it, "una exaltación en *negativo*" (a *negative* apotheosis) in which the real constitutes a terrain made accessible only through a process of excavation or "drilling through its impenetrable opacity" (2010, 133; emphasis in the original).[42] I have argued that in displacing historical signification in favour of a "topography based on the metaphysics of silence and emptiness," the *Memoriales* series *re*locates memory through a detail-oriented process of tracing history from the margins – the visualization of which is paradoxically contingent on a strategic absencing, omitting, or parcelling of memorial sites (Pérez 2010, 133). But the Norman Mayer Monument photograph presents an interesting case, not necessarily of the void but of its constant struggle to remain "unvoided" or filled, its urge to not only make itself seen but also *remain seen,* and in that remaining, to make *us* see. Here that urge is visually reinforced not only through a process of writing and rewriting, inscription and reinscription, but also by the permanent fixture of living memory (Concepción's abiding presence in the peace camp) literally wedged, and hence filling the space, between the site's two main signs. As the monument commemorates the death of one figure, the photograph offers tribute to the life of another; this intertwining of memory's life and death within the monument and within the image of the monument is crucial to its making memory not only active and accessible but visible and therefore always potentially seen.

The Space Between

Sí, la verdad es que nos interesa qué es lo que te atrapa de un lugar.

Yes, the truth is that what interests us is that thing about a place that captures you.

"Viaje y experiencia" (Bleda 2010, 134)

In standing at the threshold, never entering these sites, Bleda y Rosa are not only thinking from the margins but also utilizing the unseen as a force; they are constantly prodding us to imagine what is not shown, what remains off-stage and thus out of sight. Their thresholds, much like Manuel Sendón's, become unlocked doorways through which the viewer's sight may pass but that also always place the viewer at the edge of what is – and what becomes – visible. They strike a delicate balance between memorializing place and creating a non-memorial site by crafting images that neither excessively name (a good example of a memorial in this category would be Maya Lin's acclaimed Vietnam Veterans Memorial in Washington DC) nor completely erase names (such as with the monolithic and highly controversial Valley of the Fallen in Spain). We see evidence of the past, but only as a footnote or afterthought. In this way, the *Arquitectura/Memoriales* series is not straightforwardly about remembrance or forgetting, nor it is explicitly or exclusively interested in the tension between preservation and conversion of the past. I venture that what the series brings to light, what it truly seeks to rethink, is something – a space, perhaps – in between these monumental categories, perhaps an *in-between space that remains.* In locating their position obliquely with respect to each memorial, the series does not clearly situate individual images as testament to the existence, longevity, or success of these memorials or as testament to their potential and inevitable failures, inadequacies, or states of decline. This is key. The focus is on what gets pushed into the background, endures, then returns to the fore. Remarkably specific and at the same time almost completely vague, these photographs guide our attention towards the unexpected – towards those pieces, remnants, and edges that may grab our attention and even hold it by developing meaning over time.

I read these photographs as less interested in partial memory, constructed absence, or visualized forgetting, and more in tune with using abstraction, fragmentation, and referencing as a way to dismantle the very notion of a total, complete history (or a total complete memory akin to the ones I discussed in chapter 1 vis-à-vis the newsreels) located and preserved, as if in a time capsule, in one site, whether material or symbolic. Bleda y Rosa's work focuses on the traces of the past that seep into the everyday spaces of our lives. Their work can be understood as less about delegitimizing monuments (which I think they would say is fundamentally and undeniably important) and more about legitimizing minor or peripheral spaces of memory – spaces that remain but may not be marked overtly as such. These images do not deconstruct the existence of monuments so much as their use value, the way they are often appropriated (we've all seen it – the clueless tourist or the dutiful citizen who approaches the monument, snaps a picture, and then walks away, without a thought in a mind). In other words, I see this project as actively working against culturally ingrained forms of careless observation. In critiquing not memorials in themselves as concepts but rather the ways we interact with them and learn (or fail to learn) from them, the way they crop our sight, and blind us to history at the precise moment when they are recognizing and trying to illuminate the past, this series compellingly calls for the need to remember and to memorialize in a different way.

Capture as Intervention

> For Benjamin, history happens when something becomes present in passing away, when something lives in its death. "Living means leaving traces." History happens with photography. After life.
>
> *Words of Light* (Cadava 1997, 128)

It is perhaps a fortuitous coincidence that two Spanish photographers should travel to a foreign country to photograph a profoundly ephemeral yet interventionary (as opposed to reactionary) monument orchestrated and maintained by another Spaniard.[43] More on point, it seems only appropriate that the series concludes with a photograph that brings forward all of the principal concepts set forth by the preceding twenty-two images in the series – wounding, protest, occupation, obstacles, barriers, details, writing, surfaces, erasure, emergence and re-emergence, transparency, opacity, conspiracy, performance, inscription. According to my reading, this image now adds to that list the concepts of living memory and intervention.

I have discussed how the series invests in a practice of parcelling out sites where memory has been placed in order to show us how memorials both limit our sight and make their objects of remembrance ambiguous, vacuous, or unintelligent. This parcelling is a way not necessarily to intervene physically in the materiality of memorials but rather to intervene visually in the production of memory and in the process of remembering and interacting with the past that comes from looking at these sites. That is, in the way memory develops and survives, the ways it envelops over time, shifting its weight or standing still. In the end, what remains is a space for intervention in the politics of memory today. This is particularly important in the context of photography as an intervening force in the viewer's sight. The photograph of the Norman Mayer Monument performs such an intervention twice over. Whereas the monument intervenes in politics and political life, the photograph intervenes in time and in the life of the image. Like all the photographs in the series, it withholds in its presentation of memorials, enacting a loss on our sight as an intervening mechanism, which in turn becomes the starting point for memory. It captures a loss that reorients our sight; in this process, the notion of capture shifts too, from taking to losing, then giving (or giving back).

Finally, if this project is in fact about redrawing our line of sight towards a new kind of legibility and a new way of reading places and events, history and the passage of time, through details small but perceptible to the eye and mind, then it does so as a way of locating memory as something that lives on, as something with an *afterlife*, rather than something solidified or static. This is to say, rather than approach memory as something concretized in the mortar and stone of physical monuments that are "more interested in being seen than in making us see," Bleda y Rosa's photographs confront memory always as a trace, an afterimage, a ghost.

Battling Memory

> History is hysterical: it is constituted only if we consider it, only if we look at it – and in order to look at it, we must be excluded from it.
>
> *Camera Lucida* (Barthes 1981, 65)

My goal thus far has been to give my reader both an overview of Bleda y Rosa's major projects to date and a handful of detailed readings that situate their work theoretically and critically. Throughout these discussions, I have consciously shifted my focus from photographic representations of landscapes to the more remote, conceptual landscapes of memorial sites both in and outside Spain – sites that, actually and symbolically, house memory in distinct yet related ways. All of the previous readings have considered different angles on how these works intersect with questions of memory and history, as well as how they open up a space for sight and knowledge through a visual experience of producing and mourning loss. In the earlier-mentioned series, I contended that such an experience takes the form of mourning a forgotten (and at times mythic) past; in the last series analysed, I posited that Bleda y Rosa's photographs generate images that mourn the process of remembrance, as if to memorialize the memorials themselves. In alluding to this "double-exposure" of memory sites, I further suggested that the notion of capture in their work could be understood as a process of memorialization and intervention rather than as a form of documentation.

But what does all of this have to do with contemporary Spanish culture? In this final section, I return to the question of photographic interventions by looking at the visual, spatial, and textual dimensions of historical traces in Spanish landscapes. This involves going back to an earlier project from 1994 to 1999 – *Campos de batalla* or *Battlefields*. Critics have widely credited *Battlefields* as the project that laid much of the conceptual groundwork for the two series it chronologically predates, *Origen* and *Arquitecturas*, and as the one that marked a definitive shift in Bleda y Rosa's corpus. This aesthetic turn, as we might call it, entailed a shift from black-and-white to colour and from image to image/text. The series strongly emphasizes the interdependence of word and image. It also depicts landscapes' expansiveness and simultaneous division, most notably through the use of diptychs that show vast horizontal plains divided into two symmetrical squares and separated evenly by blank vertical spaces. My close readings will focus on how these battlefields – all of which strongly reference but never show battles – are exceptional examples of ghostly landscapes.

For as much as the twenty-one photographs in *Battlefields* are invested in the question of place, and what it *means* to capture place, they are also concerned with the question of photography's relationship to history – in particular, "history" understood in the Benjaminian sense not as something that has passed but as something that continually re-emerges and renews the present, making it waver. Something that comes to life in its passing. Eduardo Cadava articulates this question quite effectively when he writes that "nevertheless, the photograph – as what is never itself and therefore always passing into history – asks us to think the remains of what cannot come under the present. *How can an event that appears only in its disappearance leave something behind that opens history?*" (1997, 128; my emphasis). In a similar way, I want to raise the question of reading what remains (that which, borrowing Cadava's language, "cannot come under the present") in the *Battlefields* photographs as the problem – but perhaps also the question – of non-contemporaneity, which is fundamentally a question of time being out of joint, or of time's disjuncture. How can a place that is *not* contemporaneous with itself create a space for history, for thought? How might the temporal fracture tied to such remains – any remains – also create an opening? And how might that opening constitute a way of both distancing us from and situating us within the landscape? A casting out and a calling back, an exclusion and an invitation? Lastly, how might these landscapes, understood here as visual representations of places, be imbued with ("announced," in the language of Nancy, as we will see) a temporal dislocation that problematizes memory, which is to say one that enacts and resists the act of remembering?

Assembling Landscape's Time, Dividing Place

A landscape is always a landscape of time.

"Uncanny Landscape" (Nancy 2005, 61)

Together the photographs present a curious and poetic serialization of "present day" landscapes that appear serene and at times lifeless. What is perhaps most striking about these landscapes, though, is something not immediately discernible – the multiple strands of time coexisting within the frame. This multiplicity is indicated first parenthetically with the year each photograph was taken (e.g., 1999), and second by the specific date included in the title, which is accompanied by the place name referencing a historic battle, which is always anachronistic to the contemporary perspective of the photograph (e.g., the title of figure 3.31 reads: "Campo de la matanza, primero de septiembre de 1054" [1999]). While the images show us uninhabited places, with only occasional traces of the people who have lived there or passed through, such as the abandoned roadside mattress in "Cerca de Almansa, 25 de abril de 1707," the titles shed light on something much darker: unseen scenes of violence, bloodshed, death, and war. As with the other examples we have seen from *Origen* and *Memoriales,* the textual component supplements each image, adding to it information that is not readily available to the viewer through the photograph alone. Interestingly, the textual supplement acts here almost as a written response to what has been removed visually from each image – the blank space in the middle, which ruptures each landscape's wholeness.

Moreover, the inscription of historical time in the image suggests that the landscape is haunted by this time (in the aforementioned example, the eighteenth century; in the following examples, the twelfth and eighth centuries respectively). While this time is one that we logically associate with having passed already or with a past event, with all the images in the series we are invited to reimagine it as informing or, at a minimum, *pertaining to* the present, which, of course, is both the instant of capturing the photograph and the moment of looking at it. As with all the preceding readings of Bleda y Rosa's landscapes, whether geographical or conceptual, natural or fabricated, the *Battlefields* series inheres less to the representation of place and more to the observation of a particular condition of place – here, the landscape infused with multiple times and events simultaneously. To portray this condition, each image must build the landscape, assembling, as it were, the various times of each particular place so that not only the battles but now also the images themselves become events. This assemblage, in turn, has to do with a subtraction, with making the surface incomplete – an incompleteness that our viewing and interpreting comes to fill.

This interplay between image and word then draws on landscape both to recall history and to parse the visual grammar of place, or how we construct a place through sight, paradoxically separating and conjoining particular battles from the places where they occurred. In another way, we could say that Bleda y Rosa's *Battlefields* documents seemingly anonymous sites, but ones where significant – even monumental – events took place. But what does the photograph add to the text? Consider for a moment figures 3.33 and 3.34, "Alarcos, 19 de julio de 1195" and "Lugar de Lutos, año 793," respectively. Both images seem to offer testament to the contemporaneity (and in many ways non-specificity) of place. Taking into account the titles, these images allude to place as a construction of time's passage and confluence with the past. Yet the photographs themselves are archives that stay on the surface of things; they "excavate" without digging into the earth, without going underground. Put somewhat differently, these images evidence the

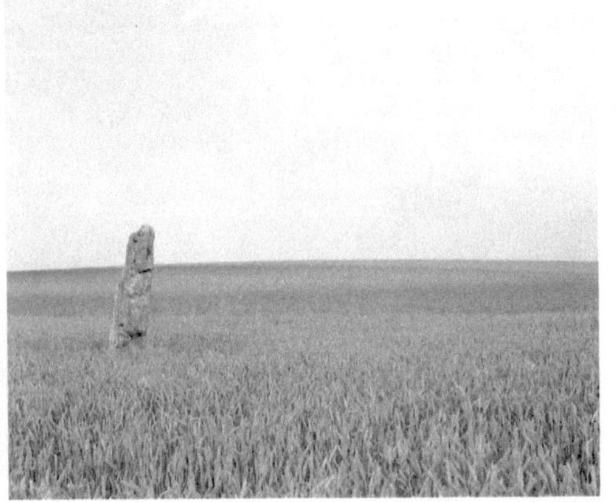
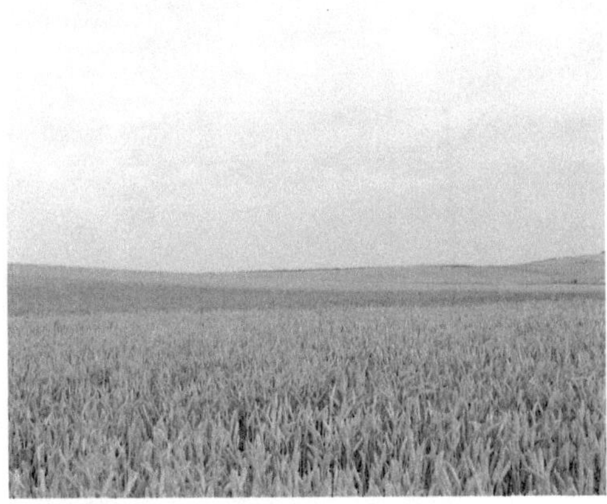

3.31 "Campo de la matanza, primero de septiembre de 1054." Bleda y Rosa (1999). © 2014 Artists Rights Society (ARS), New York / VEGAP, Madrid.

materiality of place while implying the immateriality and non-contemporaneity of place's time – a time, we should note, not out of bounds, but here importantly lodged within the four corners of a frame that ties together the disparate worlds of observer (photographer/viewer), observed (landscape/place), and the unobserved (battles, death).[44]

For as much as the discontinuity between the time of the event and the time of the image is drawn together within the frame through a process of juxtaposition, subtraction, and supplementation, it is also stretched open, placing at the centre of the viewer's plane of vision a statement about dis-location. This dislocation is performed as well by the gap or interstitial space (marked by the white strip) between the images' halves. In an extraordinary passage from *The Ground of the Image*, Jean-Luc Nancy articulates landscape as an opening onto dis-location:

> The landscape opens onto the unknown. It is, properly speaking, place as the opening onto a taking place of the unknown. It is not so much the imitative representation of a given location as the presentation of a given absence of presence ... Instead of depicting a "land" as a "location [*endroit*]," it depicts it as "dis-location [*envers*]": what presents itself there is the announcement of what is not there; more exactly, it is the announcement that, "there," there is no presence, and yet that there is no access to an "elsewhere" that is not itself "here," in the angle opened onto a land occupied only with opening in itself. That is why the landscape is not a view

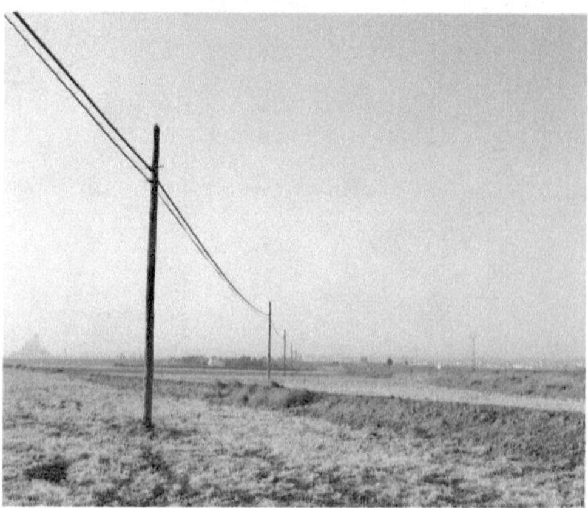
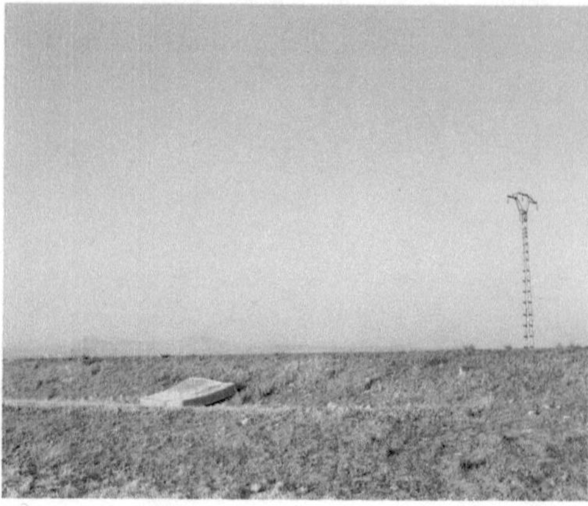

3.32 "Cerca de Almansa, 25 de abril de 1707." Bleda y Rosa (1999). © 2014 Artists Rights Society (ARS), New York / VEGAP, Madrid.

> that "opens onto" some perspective. It is, on the contrary, a perspective that comes to us, that rises from the picture and in the picture in order to form it, that is, in order to *con*form it in relation to an absolute distance and according to the spacing and distancing from which, rather, an unknown light "opens onto" us, placing us not before it but within it. (2005, 59)[45]

Nancy's language is striking. Theorizing that landscapes hold a kind of enunciative aspect in that they "announce" a "taking place of the unknown," he contends that they are not so much representations of places as enactments or stagings of ghostliness – "the presentation of a given absence of presence." What "comes to us" – that "unknown light" that places us within the landscape rather than before it – is the space between, evidenced through the spatial fissure that bisects the image, interrupting the agrophilic perspective of each landscape, as well as its equivalent, the temporal aporia embedded in each image.

This aporia, for Nancy, lies at the heart of all landscapes. In the *Battlefields* images, such an aporia visually reinforces, through a specific framing mechanism, the discontinuity that lies at the heart of all photography – that is, the time of the thing photographed can never be the time in which it is seen *after the fact,* the time in which it is viewed *as a photograph.* John Berger articulates this as an underlying principle of the medium – the fact that "between the moment recorded and the present moment of looking at the photograph, there is an abyss" (in Berger and

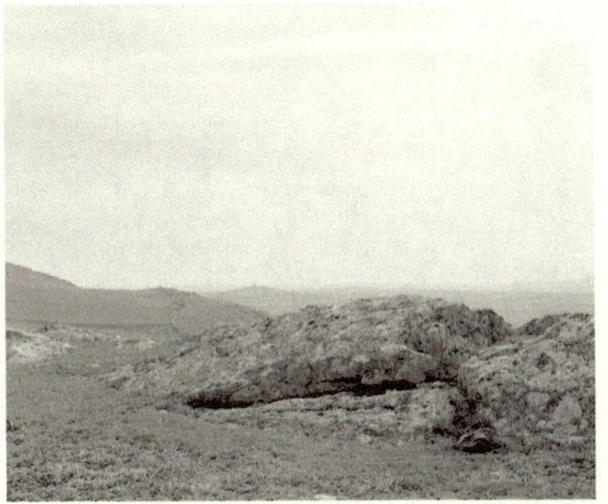
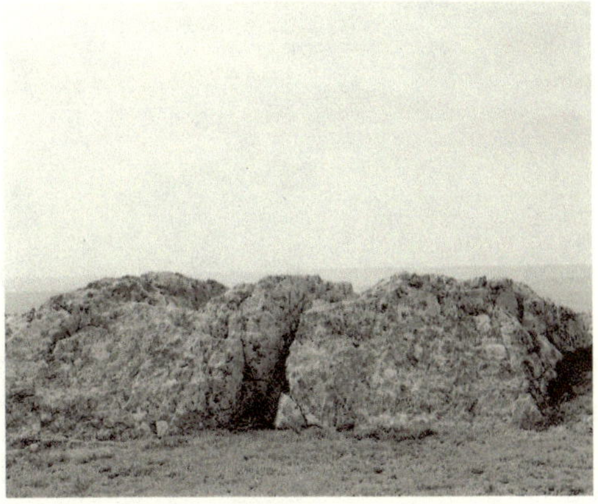

3.33 "Alarcos, 19 de julio de 1195." Bleda y Rosa (1999). © 2014 Artists Rights Society (ARS), New York / VEGAP, Madrid.

Mohr 1995, 87). When that temporal gap is closed (when one attempts to close it), we see the ideology of the image or its ideological use. But when attention is drawn to this gap, this lacuna or abyss, we see a placing or bringing together in thought, an opening onto but also an assemblage within thought. The vertical space constitutes an unfolding and a place of gathering and joining, thus becoming the bridge, connecting us to what landscape does not know but to what the image does.[46]

Revisualizing Landscape, the Act of Memory

> "Memory" is an act of "vision" of the past, but as an act it is situated in the memory's present. It is often a narrative act: loose elements come together and cohere into a story so that they can be remembered and eventually told.
>
> *Looking In: The Art of Viewing* (Bal and Bryson 2001, 47)

The reading I have sketched out so far touches on certain tensions within the landscape that arise from a dialectics of knowledge/sight, past/present, history/contemporaneity, location/dis-location. But what does this mean for memory? What does this mean for visualizing loss? Alberto Martín has noted correctly that the battlefield images programmatically draw on historical references – what Martín calls "History as subject" – not only to facilitate new ways of seeing the unseen but

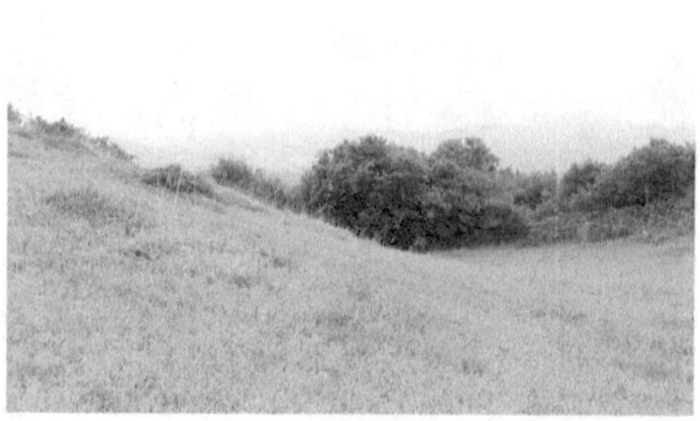
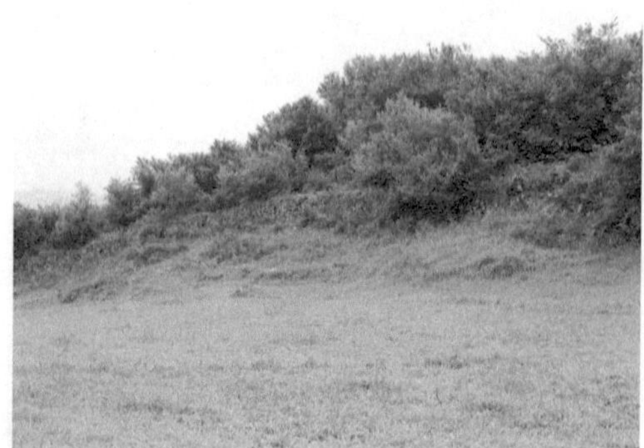

3.34 "Lugar de Lutos, año 793." Bleda y Rosa (1999). © 2014 Artists Rights Society (ARS), New York / VEGAP, Madrid.

also to open a space for memory (2010, 51). This is what Martín is referring to when he says that "landscape is an act of memory" in Bleda y Rosa's work. I agree that the treatment of history is instrumental to creating a space for memory, but what exactly is being remembered in and through the images here? While we may imagine the different battles referenced, we certainly cannot remember them in any concrete or literal way. They are neither documented nor explicitly represented. Instead, each landscape recalls not a past event that we witnessed or experienced, but the event of staging memory as a fracture, division, and void, as something that supplements and *needs* to be supplemented. Of course, since we are talking about being confronted not with the geographical surroundings but with the two-dimensional photographs of landscapes, in a certain sense we might also conclude that *Battlefields*, through such fractures and voids, stages memory at – but also *as* – the surface, where vision is made possible and interposed with blind spots. This becomes uncanny at the moment when we recognize that while the surface of each landscape may be fractured, it also stands in excess of itself; the landscape *exceeds* its own time and perspective.

That the images in *Battlefields* reveal less about battles and more about the tensions and surface – indeed, the surface tensions – of place, and of the temporality and poetics of memory, is not surprising. In "El Centenario, alrededores de Villaviciosa 10 de diciembre de 1710," though the historical events comprising the War of Spanish Succession during the early eighteenth century may be conjured, as viewers we encounter what Xavier Antich so poignantly calls the "phantasmal reality of each trace" and the "density of time" only as an after-image, but interestingly not one that persists in the mind after having been seen, but one that must always be imagined (2003, 1–2).[47] Not only the "pastness" of time, its being stuck elsewhere, but now also the way time weighs on the present, becomes the event that each photograph stages. Whatever such a weight or "density" may imply, however, I suggest that these landscapes – simultaneously particular and non-specific, singular and plural, whole and incomplete – are not impassable places but rather passageways.

But what does this mean exactly? For "passageway" connotes a connection between two spatially distant points; it suggests not only entrance into but also movement between places. It would seem that in Bleda y Rosa's artistic conception, landscapes are not so much places where one can access particular memories or acquire historical knowledge, as they are, in the words of John Wylie, "a milieu of engagement, involvement, immersion, connection – a living tapestry of practices, imaginations, emergences and erasures" (2009, 282). As images, these "tapestries" illuminate for the viewer not memory itself but rather *how* memory functions, how it lures and seduces, how it vanishes and vacates, how it depletes but also fills our sight. As battlefields, these tapestries present us with two eyes looking out on the world and at the same time looking back at us.

Suspending Memory's Passage: The Space That Remains

A landscape is always the suspension of a passage, and this passage occurs as a separation, an emptying out of the scene or of being: not even a passage from one point to another or from one moment to another, but the step [*le pas*] of the opening itself.

"Uncanny Landscape" (Nancy 2005, 61)

Described by Bleda y Rosa as "lugares de todos, tierra de nadie" (everybody's place, nobody's land), the *Battlefields* landscapes are typologies and tapestries: at once geographically specific and non-descript, temporally precise and ambivalent, evacuated of presence and replenished by an uncanny set of displacements and absences. The images link us to disparate times and to disparate modes of seeing and looking; we could

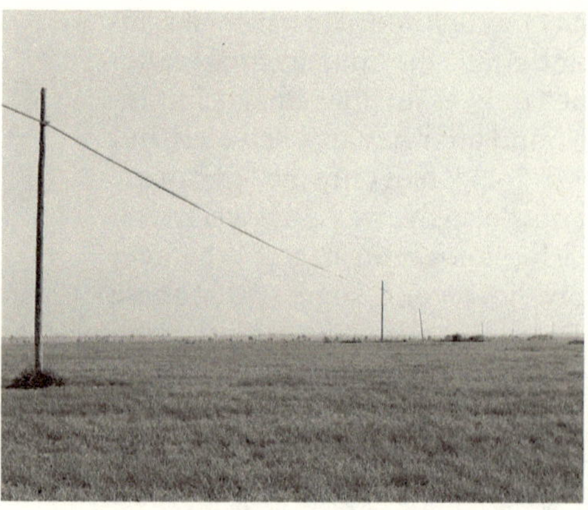
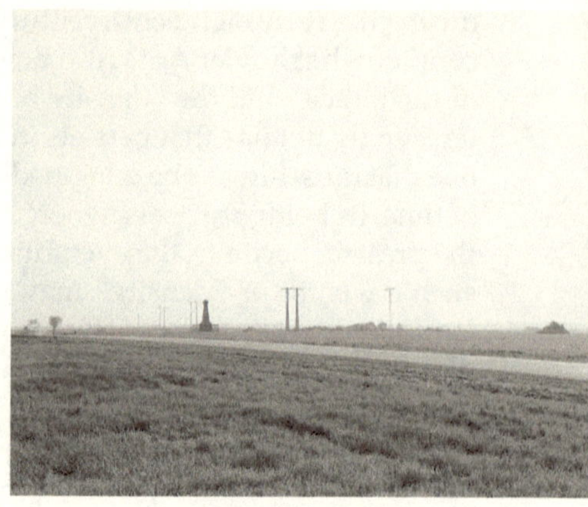

3.35 "El Centenario, alrededores de Villaviciosa, 10 de diciembre de 1710." Bleda y Rosa (1999). © 2014 Artists Rights Society (ARS), New York / VEGAP, Madrid.

also say that the monumentality of history – of the historical event, historical time – is emptied or at the very least suspended through the calculated framing of vacant, nondescript places. Using the image as a passageway implies the possibility of movement (generally speaking, movement forward) but does not guarantee it. Suspension is fundamental to the *Battlefields* series and foreshadows the artists' later work in *Arquitecturas/Memoriales*.

I began this chapter with a brief discussion of photography's reach, that is, the way it seems to bring the world closer or, conversely, the way it distances the world from our sight. Within that reach, there is room to think about suspension – an in-between place or holding period, a waiting or, as the word's etymology (from the Latin *sub* and *pendere*) implies, a "hanging from below." Related to this is the notion that the photograph is itself an object that suspends time or, as Thierry de Duve has put it, "an event that hangs on the wall" (2007, 109). As viewers, we are suspended between the place from which we encounter these photographs (the gallery, the museum, the computer screen, the page) and the plurality of times that are brought unconspicuously to the fore within each image, paradoxically made proximate and remote at the same time. *But it is in this suspension that a space for thought is opened.* Nancy beautifully describes this as "the marking out of a measure according to which a world can be laid out" (2005, 61–2). For the suspended moment is a moment of immobilization wherein the walker stops and "his step becomes that of a compass, the angle and amplitude of a disposition of space, on whose step – at whose threshold, at whose point of access – a gaze presents itself as a gaze" (62). In pausing rather than passing through, the walker may grasp "a 'footing,' a span of the hand" (perhaps she may even "reach" something) from which the visualization of time becomes possible, accessible. To suspend the step, to suspend the gaze, is not to stop looking but rather to keep on searching and seeing. It is to allow one's gaze to present itself to the landscape, just as the landscape brings to presence things that catch our sight. Bleda y Rosa's photographs suspend us over and over again – they hang our gaze in the balance between multiple times and places, between a specificity linked to sites and an ambiguity often associated with spaces, making us reach for the meaning (or web of meanings) that emerges in each image. But this suspension is productive: it challenges us to traverse and contest visual ground. It is a suspension that holds us to sight as a space of contemplation. And in this way, it is the very act of seeing itself. A seeing that instigates an unfolding of time and an opening of oneself to the space that remains to be seen.

Notes

Introduction

1 The notion of "wounded time" will be discussed more in detail in chapter 3. For a provocative account of the relationship between temporality and wounds, see Roland Barthes's *Camera Lucida*, specifically the second part of the text, where he outlines a theory of the *punctum* as time itself. Here Barthes also discusses the spectral or ghostly aspect of the photograph's metonymic force – namely, that while it renders the time of the object photographed impossible, it also imparts a referential relationship to that lost time and lost object such that the structure of all photographic images is one of the return of the referent, or a structure of spectrality. Jacques Derrida offers a poignant reading of Barthes's analysis of spectrality and referentiality vis-à-vis photography in his eulogy "Roland Barthes November 12, 1915–March 26, 1980" in *The Work of Mourning* (31–67). Though Derrida's intricate examination of Barthes's theories lies outside the scope of this introduction, it is worth noting that here Derrida embarks on a lengthy meditation on how the singular death of a friend – indeed, the singular loss of anyone – becomes a pluralized event. He discusses how the singular event of one's death reverberates and – in a sense, like the uncanny, ghostly image – proliferates as it is cast into multiple times and images.

2 Ernesto Laclau's wonderful essay "The Time Is Out of Joint" takes up and elaborates on two key issues from Derrida's work: the "logic of the spectre," and the "question of the messianic." Spectral logic, for Laclau, is rooted in undecidability between flesh and spirit. And this indeterminacy, this undecidability, "desynchronizes time." The messianic, by contrast, is akin not to a specific conception of time but rather to a certain kind of experience or "promise." This is similar to my idea about the field of possibility

created through visual media – the same field in which, for Benjamin and Cadava, the spacing of time occurs. For Laclau, this idea is key since the messianic is what opens up another possibility of historicity.

3 This notion of "holding," it should be noted, suggests a temporary state of fixed-ness, or of being agitated, suspended, or perhaps even influenced by the ghost. I would argue that this idea is not so much about maintaining a static, fixed, or rigid relationship with the past; rather, somewhat like Walter Benjamin's concept of the philosophy of history, it entails more a radical embrace or "seizing" of the ghost or the spectral in its moment of emergence, in its very state of emergence. For a beautiful reading of Derrida's concept of the politics of mourning, see also Pascale-Anne Brault and Michael Naas's introduction to his *The Work of Mourning*, where they provide a detailed account of his rhetoric of mourning, such as with their close reading of this passage from *Aporias*: "In an economic, elliptic, hence dogmatic way, I would say that there is no politics without an organization of the time and space of mourning, without a topolitology of the sepulcher, without an anamnesic and thematic relation to the spirit as ghost, without an open hospitality to the guest as *ghost*, whom one holds, just as he holds us, hostage" (Derrida 2001, 19). Through Derrida's own philosophical ruminations – and personal reflections – on death, what takes shape is an explicit link between the way to visualize loss and the process (and practice) of mourning. Though many of the texts on mourning are invested in thinking through the politics of friendship, authorship, survival, and philosophy, Derrida maintains a strong theoretical interest in understanding loss from both acutely personal and acutely intellectual angles. For him, while loss enables and precipitates mourning, the politics of mourning produces and originates from the image, which always marks a ghostly return of the lost object.

4 David Punter (2002) provides a wonderful and concise explanation of this marginality from within criticism, especially with regard to gothic literature.

5 For a thorough discussion of modernity and modern theory's indebted relationship to ghosts, see Buse and Stott (1999). Similarly, Punter (2002), drawing on Derrida's engagement with the "looping circularity of history," particularly in *Specters of Marx*, notes that history understood not as a linear development "but as the site of multiple hauntings" simply cannot be written without ghosts (262). Buse and Stott's and Punter's texts both equate modernity with a troubled, indeed spectral, vision of history and the historical. Punter writes: "but the point goes further than this: narratives of history must necessarily include ghosts – indeed they can include little else – but they will also be written *by* ghosts" (262).

6 One important distinction between Eng and Kazanjian's work and my own should be noted here. Whereas their collected volume is interested primarily in the question of what remains, I am interested in both what remains and what returns, in spectral form, whether visible or invisible. For a rich analysis of mourning and a detailed account of what is at stake in any contemporary consideration of the politics of mourning, see their introduction in *Loss*, specifically, their tracing of Freud's theory of mourning and melancholia, and also their analysis of Benjamin's theses on the philosophy of history where they read the hopefulness embedded in historical materialism against the hopelessness brought about by historicism, "active mourning against a reactive acedia" (Eng and Kazanjian 2003, 2). For additional analysis of the Freudian and Benjaminian theories of mourning in relation to politics and history, see also Wendy Brown's wonderful essay in the same volume "Resisting Left Melancholia" (458–65).

7 Cadava (1997), reading Benjamin, beautifully articulates the connection between living and leaving traces as a form of "afterlife."

8 My study is principally concerned with the relationships among landscape, presence/absence, and ways of seeing. There have been many excellent explorations of the landscape–being–seeing configuration, though many are concerned with the connection between humans and the land rather than with, say, notions of history and time within landscape. Bender (1993) considers the historical and social aspects of landscape; DeLue and Elkins (2008) survey different theories of the land/art connection; Wells (2011) is a vast and stunning work that underscores the intimate connections between photography, human impact, social memory, and environmental issues.

9 Contemporary Spanish literary and filmic representations of ghosts abound. A few examples from contemporary Spanish cinema are provided here. In the horror genre there are popular commercial films such as Guillermo de Toro's *El espinazo del Diablo* (2001), which begins with a series of rhetorical and ontological questions about the nature of haunting and ghosts; Alejandro Amenábar's *The Others* (2001); and Juan Antonio Bayona's *El orfanato* (2007). There are also darker films about trauma, encounters with death, and the return of the repressed, such as Agustín Villaronga's *Tras el cristal* (1987) and *Pa negre* (2010) and the black comedies of Alex de La Iglesia, who recently has explored the notion of spectral legacies and the trauma of inheritance in works such as *la comunidad* (2000) and *Balada triste de trompeta* (2010). A more melodramatic overture to ghostliness, including the familial and communitarian aspects of inheritance and the politics of return, is Pedro Almodóvar's *Volver* (2006). On the

more artistic/auteur side of the cinematic representation of spectres are José Luis Guerín's stunning works, such as *Tren de sombras (El espectro de Thuit,* 1997); Mercedes Álvarez's documentaries *El cielo gira* (2004) and *Mercado de futuros* (2011); and Víctor Erice's always masterful and elegiac cinematic meditations, such as *El sur* (1983) and *El espiritú de la colmena* (1973).

10 Most scholars and critics – Labanyi (2002, 2007, 2008, 2009), Moreiras Menor (2002), Resina (2000), Colmeiro (2011), Jerez-Farrán and Amago (2010), Moreno-Nuño (2005, 2006), Snyder (2014), Keller (2012), Crumbaugh (2009, 2011), Vilarós (2002), Martín-Cabrera (2011), Loureiro (2008), Medina Dominguez (2001) – who have expressed concern for the dictatorship's living legacy or afterlife address, in one way or another, its spectral re-emergence in the post-dictatorship and/or transition era after years of silence and repression.

11 Perhaps one of the greatest material consequences of the dictatorship is the highly controversial monument *El valle de los caídos* (Valley of the Fallen), completed in 1959. In many ways, the monument architecturally embodies the problem of how to inherit the memory and legacy of Francoism, given that it is recognized as an official memorial site. Between 30,000 and 70,000 bodies are buried in the unmarked tomb of the mountain – that is, in the natural *and* constructed landscape.

12 Mirzoeff, a long-time defender of visual culture, has insisted throughout his scholarship on the importance of "visual culture" over "visual studies," in order to emphasize the political stakes inherent in our comprehension of the visual realm and what W.J.T. Mitchell has referred to as "the everyday practice of seeing and showing" (2008, 91). Note that for Mirzoeff as well as for Mitchell and for my own study, the study of visual culture does not entail simply looking at and describing images on the page; it includes gathering a sense of how and why our cultural and historical narratives are constructed, symbolically or otherwise, *through* images. In other words, what is key is thinking of the visual not only in terms of genre or objects but also in terms of encounters and "events" – networks of associations, ideas, and theories that arise from vision, forms of non-vision, the act of seeing, and what Mirzoeff later calls the "right to look." For further reading, see Nicholas Mirzoeff's introduction to *The Visual Culture Reader,* 2nd ed. (2008) and W.J.T. Mitchell's entry in the same volume, titled "Showing Seeing: A Critique of Visual Culture." For a wonderfully original decolonial analysis of visual culture's complex relationship to authority and power, especially with regard to the underlying tension between visuality and countervisuality in modernity, see Mirzoeff's *The Right to Look: A Counterhistory of Visuality* (2011).

13 I am indebted to W.J.T. Mitchell's thought-provoking take on the main objectives and contributions of the study of visual culture. For further reading, see Mitchell's aforementioned essay; see also Mitchell (1994).

1 Documentary Optics

1 Joaquín Soriano, cited in Tranche and Sánchez-Biosca (2005). In 1945, the *noticiarios* officially became part of the regime's popular education program, which was coordinated through the Ministerio de Educación Nacional (Ministry of National Education). The plan was to educate citizens spiritually and culturally (Tranche and Sánchez-Biosca 2005, 56). Unless otherwise noted, all transcriptions and translations from the original Spanish are my own.

2 For a concise analysis of Spain's economic policies, see chapter 10, "Francoism 1939–1975," in Carr (1980). There, Carr writes: "In the immediately postwar years the problem was one of sheer physical survival, of feeding and finding jobs for a nation whose economy had been run down by its own Civil War and which was isolated from the economies of the West, first by the Second World War and then by the diplomatic and economic boycott imposed by the victorious democracies on a 'fascist' state which had, until 1943, openly supported the Axis powers. 'In 1940,' wrote Paris Eguilaz, one of the foremost economists of the new Regime, 'the national income, at constant prices, had fallen back to that of 1914, but since the population had increased the per capita income fell to nineteenth-century levels. That is, the Civil War had provoked an unprecedented economic recession.' The instruments with which the Regime sought recovery had been forged in the war itself with the help of Italian Fascist models: the regulation by the state of a 'capitalist' economy cut off, as far as possible, from the world market; an autarchy that would embark on a massive programme of import substitution, producing everything at home regardless of economic cost. State *dirigisme* and protection were old traditions, but they were no longer justified on economic grounds, as protecting a weak economy. Rather, they were presented as political ideals: the recipe for a stable economy and a suitable policy for an 'imperial military state.' The unique feature of Spain in the '40s ... was that autarchy was presented as a permanent ideal" (155–6).

3 This point echoes visual historian Vanessa Schwartz's (2007) idea that "the archive is already in the film canister" – an idea by which I understand Schwartz to be suggesting that the archive (its power, its seduction, its order, its logic) is, in essence, a narrative. Like works of fiction, the archive has its own structure, characters, authors, plot, and story.

4 NO-DO has three main classifications in its catalogue: *noticiarios* (the equivalent of 10- to 12-minute newsreels); *documentales* (the rough equivalent of documentaries, usually ranging anywhere from 15 to 45 minutes); and *imágenes* (stills narrated as if they were moving images, or photo-romans.). The corresponding numbers and dates of the four "newsreel biographies" – or meta-NO-DOs, as I am calling them here – are No. 0001 (1943), No. 105A (1945), No. 1000A (1962), and No. 1304B (1968).

5 This experience is uncanny in another sense as well: entering the archive marks a sort of spectral encounter in which something previously invisible is now made visible. This, in a sense, identifies the archive as a ghostly place – an uncanny site where the relationship between seeing and knowing seems clear and tangible but is always uncertain or at best onditional. This tenuous relationship between visibility and knowledge was mapped out in the discovery that the very text that should "inform, instruct, and entertain" viewers with the news, had deviated from its normal protocol to dissect and display itself. My own experience in the archive – namely, difficulties locating this particular newsreel (and many other materials) – would foreground what I later understood as the very problem underlying the newsreel's content and self-imaging. In effect, what is seen does not correspond to what is present, whether deliberately staged or randomly materialized. Similarly, what is *not* seen (individual news events, stories, reports) is, we are told, nonetheless present because recorded.

6 The word *recrear* in the original Spanish has a double signification: to "entertain" or "make something pleasurable," and also to "recreate" or "reproduce." This point is key to my analysis of the modes of production and reproduction that the newsreels expose.

7 My own rhetorical questions are undoubtedly influenced and framed by Derrida's line of inquiry in *Archive Fever,* in which he poses the following: "But where does the outside commence? This question is the question of the archive. There are undoubtedly no others" (1996, 8).

8 In this shift towards the discursive incorporation of "organic," the use of the term "totalitarian" was more or less disavowed in the official discourse; however, in the newsreels, totalitarian logic and rhetoric remained a fundamental component, in the sense of working towards and constructing a totality, and a totalizing movement in the Arendtian sense.

9 The connection between universal sight and truth or a structuring of belief simply reinforces the nineteenth-century notion of knowledge and sight that emerged with the rise of industrialism, modern science, and Enlightenment philosophy, summed up neatly as follows: what one sees, one also knows. For a detailed and poignant discussion of the seeing/knowing

dialectical relationship as it emerged in the discipline of medicine and modern science, see the chapters "Seeing and Knowing" and "Open Up a Few Corpses" in Foucault (1975).

10 This also suggests that the optical mechanics of the 1945 newsreel are dialectical in the sense that they engage the viewer by "inviting" him to see through the camera's lens, which is *already* the screen, and that they also wield an alienating power by temporally distancing the images from us or, better, altering the temporal nature of the images on the screen so that they appear different from what the viewer otherwise expects and understands. The newsreels, in this sense, take those moving images that were captured in the past with the intention of presenting them in the future and recasts them as moving images captured in the present by us; our position shifts from (potentially passive) viewer to (unexpectedly active) director.

11 It is worth noting Robert Spires's brief but excellent comparison between Foucault's panoptic theory of surveillance and discipline and Francoist discourse. Spires argues that Franco's public speeches offered a unique register that exemplified the kind of discourse based on optical control and power that Foucault theorized: "Even before he became dictator, the general himself assumed a major responsibility for implanting the concept of a self-disciplining society. Indeed the discursive link between Foucault and Franco clearly emerges in one of the general's addresses delivered in April 1937 in which he promised to give 'to the people what truly interests it: *to see and feel itself governed.*' By stressing visual and sensorial phenomena, the soldier Franco actually seemed to be anticipating the philosopher Foucault and his panoptic thesis" (1996, 17; my emphasis). In the same book, see also the illuminating chapter titled "The Post-World War II Episteme."

12 I use this term deliberately, drawing on the "camera eye" as not only an optical instrument but also a literary device employed by the American novelist John Dos Passos in *The 42nd Parallel* (1930), the first novel of his renowned U.S.A. trilogy.

13 If standard propaganda strategies involve concealing how the mode of production operates on the viewer to coerce him into becoming a disciplined, loyal subject, then the NO-DO reverses this order. It takes the more conventional propaganda technique and turns it inside out, showing us the otherwise secret or hidden recipe of its coercive tactics, those methods that are performed on subjects clandestinely, supposedly without their knowledge or awareness.

14 In comparing the archive to writing, Derrida explores the problem of inscription – that is, the question of how history, or the traces of lived experiences, get recorded, written, and stored for future use or reference.

This is to ask how inscription works, or how inscribed histories remember or suppress certain memories. Such that, for Derrida (and for our purposes here), this question is no longer limited to how memory is inscribed *into* writing, but extends to the converse: how *writing* is inscribed into *memory*. In the context of the newsreel biographies, this is a particularly striking point. It means we should think about how images are captured, severed from reality, catalogued, and transcribed into Spanish cultural memory, thereby shaping the parameters of visibility in a twofold manner – both in the way it sees and captures and also in how it sees itself.

15 This is an interesting point of departure itself, since Derrida begins *Archive Fever* with the "exergue" – that is, with an examination and theorization of "that which lies outside the work." For Derrida, the examination of the outside and of the ways in which the outside defines the inside (of the archive, in this case) is paramount for his reading of Freudian thought and the relationship between, on the one hand, the archive as a place of origins and power, and on the other, a place deeply tied to history and psychoanalysis – that is, a place where the compulsion to repeat, order, record, and catalogue becomes a defining characteristic of inscription, one that serves as both the foundation and the principal component of the archive. Derrida draws from Freud's inscription or impression on his own writing (i.e., his archive) and from his writings on the death drive to elaborate this argument. Namely, that history is a technology of memory and that archives are to some extent technologies of history. By Derrida's interpretation, archives do not simply accumulate and catalogue as a way to "remember" or recover what has been lost or forgotten; they are also as a means to produce (and *reproduce*) a structure that embodies the always imminent threat of forgetting, death, destruction, and loss.

16 In reality, the law's true objective was to convert all forms of press and media communication into "una institución al servicio de la propaganda del nuevo Estado" ("an institution at the service of propaganda of the new State" (Alejandro Pizarroso, cited in Tranche and Sánchez-Biosca 2005, 184). Tranche explains that the state relied on the press not to impose an official doctrine but rather to channel subtler mechanisms of indoctrination and coercion. That is, to transform belief systems, the state harnessed the power of images and political rhetoric rather than overt violence. For more information, see chapter 3, "La ideología y la propaganda franquista en NO-DO," of Tranche and Sánchez-Biosca's seminal work.

17 The state often identified and reinforced its natural origins by invoking its imperial past. To that end, it referred constantly to *el tiempo de los Reyes Católicos* (the time of the Catholic Kings), *la Cruzada* (the Crusades), and

el Renacimiento cultural de España (the Rebirth of Spain). Besides relying on Spain's imperial past, the Franco regime instituted and defended the Organic Law of the State, which underwent several drafts during the 1960s before finally being presented to the Cortes in 1966 and incorporated into the Constitution. That law declared that the Movimiento Nacional (i.e., the Fascist Party) was "the only legitimate political alliance in Spain" (Spires 1996, 21). For further reading, see Carr (1980). Carr contends that the regime "prided itself on its capacity for 'institutional perfection,' on the evolution of a constitution *sui generis*, completed by the Organic Law of 1967" (165). See also Payne (1999) for a detailed breakdown of the Organic Law, especially as it related to the other six fundamental laws of Spanish fascism.

18 A striking example of the rift between real world events and contrasting, indeed opposing, images of Spanish national ideals is found in the first NO-DO, No. 0001 (1943). As the inaugural *noticiario*, it somewhat predictably opens with images of *Palacio de El Pardo* and a commanding and victorious Franco; it then cuts to a sequence of chaotic images from the battlefield, narrating how *El Caudillo* used his wisdom and prudence to guide Spain through its darkest "days of supreme danger." Franco's heroism is central to this newsreel: "Él supo salvarla con su presencia heróica y con su talento de estratega en los campos de batalla. Y abrir las puertas de España a una nueva era de honor nacional y de grandeza. [Image: military parade] Siguiendo el símbolo y el ejemplo de nuestro Caudillo, *la unidad de los españoles y su disciplina es base de nuestro renacimiento presente y futuro*" (my emphasis). (Following the symbol and the example of the *Caudillo*, the unity of Spaniards and their discipline is the foundation of our present and future rebirth.) The newsreel affirms that Spaniards are universally united and disciplined under Franco; it does this by showing us images of the organized masses – snapshots of those infamous military spectacles of immense proportion and scale. The narrator continues: "Noticarios y documentales cinematográficos, NO-DO, cuenta con una información rápida y completa de todos los sectores de la vida nacional y extranjera. Las operaciones de selección: montaje y sincronización se realizan rápida y eficazmente. Todos sus trabajos se efectúan en los laboratorios españoles dotados por la superioridad de los necesarios medios técnicos. Una perfecta organización garantiza en todo momento la distribución rápida por todo el ámbito nacional. Realizaremos un esfuerzo constante para cumplir sin desmayo el lema de nuestro noticiario: 'El mundo entero al alcance de todos los españoles.'" (NO-DO counts on swift and complete information from all the sectors of life, national and international. The task of selection: editing and

synchronization is carried out quickly and efficently. All work is completed in Spanish laboritories equipped with superiority in the essential technical mediums. Perfect organization always guarantees fast distribution throughout the entire nation. We make a constant effort to achieve tirelessly the motto of our newsreel: "The entire world within reach of every Spaniard.")

19 For a more detailed description of this "second metamorphosis of the Franco Regime," see Payne's (1999) section titled "Technocracy and economic liberalization." Payne writes: "Franco's new choices thus revealed a further downgrading of Falangists and renewed emphasis on technical expertise, yet he had always used experts freely, usually civil or military engineers or elite State lawyers. Privately he described the new cabinet as simply a renewed effort to give balanced representation to the forces behind the Regime, adjusted to the realities of the late 1950s." These representations, of course, consisted of changes to dismantle the original "fascist economics" plan of the first phase of the regime. "The dramatic success of economic liberalization would eventually bring in its wake further liberalization of the Regime and, even more important, decisive change and modernization in society and culture. The subsequent changes within the Regime would in certain respects further minimalize the Movement, though it is more than doubtful that Franco had alterations of such magnitude in mind when he assembled the new government" (426–7).

20 These are hardly the only events that contributed to Spain's *apertura*. These two are highlighted here because they are among the major political events that led to the country's increased liberalization and to political and economic change. Payne's summary of this period is most helpful: "By the end of 1945, some of the economic leaders of the Regime had realized that the 'fascist economics' of statism, regulation, and control under autarchy could no longer function as originally conceived at the height of the fascist era in 1939–1940. The ambition to create a major military-industrial complex for aggressive warfare had to be relinquished long before the war ended, and by 1945 the Regime's economic leaders recognized the need to liberalize at least certain aspects of their policy and to associate Spain somewhat more with the international economy. The alteration of the Regime's economic policy took place in three different phases, the first in 1945–1946, the second in 1951, and the third and most extensive and decisive in 1958–1959. Each step took Spain further and farther from the original 'fascist model' of economics and was opposed – always relatively unsuccessfully – by remaining Falangist leaders" (1999, 408).

21 For a fascinating analysis of the paradoxical political agenda of tourism and 1960s Spain, see Justin Crumbaugh, *Destination Dictatorship: The*

Spectacle of Spain's Tourist Boom and the Reinvention of Difference (New York: SUNY Press, 2009).

22 The year 1959 was a crucial one in the political, economic, and cultural history of Francoist Spain and for the country's gradual liberalization. It is worth noting, ironically, that in the same year, the epic-scale war memorial Valle de los Caídos (Valley of the Fallen) was completed and opened to the public. Simply put, this mammoth structure was, and today still is, a fascist spectacle. It had been constructed to resurrect and glorify Spain's heroic and nationalist past – that is, to pay homage to the nationalists who had been killed during the Civil War. Also worth mentioning is the sheer size and proportion of the adjacent Basilica de la Santa Cruz, with its 152-metre cross, the tallest in Europe. To this day, the site remains as controversial as it is physically stunning, and it would be difficult to deny that it has radically transformed the Spanish landscape. This becomes especially significant when we consider the sweeping shots of barren landscapes as presented in Carlos Saura's first feature film, *Los golfos* (*The Hooligans*) from the same year, 1959. *Los golfos* (referenced in the next chapter) uses neo-realist techniques to bring Spain's barren, impoverished landscapes to the screen. The contrast between fascist landscapes like Valle de los Caídos and the social-realist landscapes portrayed by politically conscious artists is remarkable.

23 *Por los pelos* means "by the skin of one's teeth," although I have altered that meaning somewhat due to the prior *poco menos* in the original Spanish.

24 Tranche's reading of NO-DO's shift to "numbers" and statistics in the 1968 newsreel suggests the state's self-awareness and "cynical irony." The state would end up overtly recycling the same images from previous newsreels (in Tranche and Sánchez-Biosca 2005, 200). It is also worth mentioning here that the third meta-newsreel (not studied in-depth in this chapter) celebrates NO-DO's one-thousandth instalment ("from 1943 to 1962, 19 years and 1000 weeks of NO-DO," the narrator exclaims). This feature of NO-DO No. 1000B is later echoed in the 1968 meta-newsreel; both measure numerically the institution's success. The narrator quotes exact numbers, synchronized with the screen, which displays various charts of the same: "Documentales: 47; Documentales de largometraje: 19; Documentales en color: 42; Ediciones especiales: 93; Noticiarios en color: 15; Imágenes: 894; Metros producidos: 1, 588,200; Distribución de *NO-DO* en España; Madrid, Zaragoza, Barcelona, Valencia, Sevilla, Palma de Mallorca, Bilbao, Vigo, Santa Cruz de Tenerife, Las Palmas." The obsession with quantifying news production and integrating the numbers into official newsreel discourse during the 1960s is perhaps nowhere clearer than in these later two newsreel biographies (Nos. 1000B and 1304B).

25 As with the other newsreels, the final image and NO-DO logo appear at the close of the narration, along with the image of a soaring eagle over a rotating globe, which is labelled "NO-DO."

26 Another relevant question may be: Is spectacle the opposite of dialogue, as Debord suggests? Does ideology operate then not on a system of differentiation but rather on one of assimilation; not on a system of openness that facilitates the exchange of ideas or the "flow of information," but instead on a system of closed doors that only allows the same information (and rhetoric, as I have argued) to circulate continually through a hypermediated, controlled, authoritative lens?

27 I have relied here on Ricoeur's reading of Althusser because I find in it the clearest explanation of the effects of ideology and its relation to the imaginary. For a detailed analysis of the relationship between ideology and materiality, see Althusser's "Thesis II: Ideology Has a Material Existence" from the chapter "Ideology and Ideological State Apparatuses" (1970) in Althusser (2001).

28 I would like to thank Juli Highfill, who brought to my attention a clear reference to the Leviathan with the "Franco and the whale" episode of the newsreel. This is an intriguing point, as the term "leviathan" itself refers to a large sea monster (in modern-day Hebrew it simply means "whale"). In both Judaic and Christian traditions, the leviathan commonly refers to a huge, destructive force that needs to be destroyed (in the Old Testament, it is mentioned in Psalms, Job, and Isaiah as a large force of nature, whereas in the Christian texts it often refers to a demonic, evil force). It would certainly be interesting to compare the religious (biblical) concept and image of "leviathan" with Thomas Hobbes's seminal text (published in 1651, borrowing its title explicitly from the Bible) on the social contract and the creation of the ideal state. Of course, Francoism does not definitively derive from Hobbes's principles of commonwealth, sovereignty, and defence. But the notion of one giant state comprised of individuals and led by one sovereign power is one reflected in the mass ornament spectacles featured in the NO-DO as well as, undoubtedly, the very underlying principles of the regime itself.

29 The whale episode quickly cuts to a more peaceful image of Franco as a family man, on the Bastiagueros beach in Galicia, once again with his grandchildren.

30 One could also argue that the erected tower is a phallus that "rises" from the orchestrated masses, filling the screen, which in turn "penetrates" our gaze. In the context of the original event, these exercises of physical agility always faced the dictator, suggesting that he could impregnate the tower, in this case with his gaze. For further reading of this kind that

would place spectacle in relation to a rhetoric of haunting and a sexualized masculine gaze, see Spackman (1996).

31 Admittedly, this is a literal translation of the passage. Nonetheless, the meaning still comes through, I believe – namely, that the mass stadium demonstrations function as spectacles that operate in specific patterns *on* the spectator's sight and *in accordance* with disciplinary rules and standards, recalling Tranche's apt phrase "obedience to Franco."

32 Kracauer continues: "Actors likewise never grasp the stage setting in its totality, yet they consciously take part in its construction; and even in the case of ballet dancers, the figure is relinquished in favor of mere linearity, the more distant it becomes from the immanent consciousness of those constituting it. Yet this does not lead to its being scrutinized by a more incisive gaze. In fact, nobody would notice the figure at all if the crowd of spectators, who have an aesthetic relation to the ornament and do not represent anyone, were not sitting in front of it" (1995, 77).

33 For further details on the NCE, see Castro de Paz et al. (2000). Specifically, in this Spanish cinema anthology, see chapter 2, Carmen Arocena Badillos's "Luces y sombras. Los largos años cincuenta (1951–1962)," and chapter 3, Santos Zunzunegui's "Llegar a más. El cine español entre 1962 y 1971." Both chapters offer detailed analysis of the emergence of Spanish new wave cinema. Various key events in the 1950s and early 1960s led to the formation of an alternative cinema. In particular, a conference titled Conversaciones de Salamanca de 1955 resulted in the founding of the Federación Nacional de Cine-Clubs in 1957, and in 1962, José María García Escudero was appointed to Dirección General de Cinematografía y Teatro. These two events brought about cinema reforms and a loosening (in theory) of strict, outdated censorship practices; they also widened Spain's cultural aperture. With regard to the NCE, important participants included producers like Elías Querejeta and independent film directors like Jorge Grau, Francisco Regueiro, Sergio Sollima, Joaquín Romero Marchent, Eugenio Martín, and Pedro Lazaga, as well as film critics, including those who wrote for the popular film magazine *Nuestro cine* – Diego Galán, Manuel Pérez Estremera, Miguel Marías, Vicente Molina Foix, and Santiago San Miguel, to name only a few.

2 Cinematic Apertures

1 See John Berger, *Hold Everything Dear: Dispatches on Survival and Resistance* (New York: Pantheon Books, 2007).

2 See Ross Chambers, *Untimely Interventions: AIDS Writing, Testimonial, and the Rhetoric of Haunting*. (Ann Arbor: University of Michigan Press, 2004).

3 See Walter Benjamin, *The Arcades Project* (Cambridge, MA: Harvard University Press, 2002).

4 See Yi-fu Tuan, *Space and Place: The Perspective of Experience* (Minneapolis: University of Minnesota Press, 1977).

5 Saura was at forefront of the NCE movement along with contemporaries Fernán Gomez, Azcona and Ferreri, Bardem, and Berlanga, among others. In one way or another, all of these directors were preoccupied with untimeliness.

6 This link with cinema could be further elaborated by taking up a more typically psychoanalytic notion of memory as *re-presentation*, or as something that presents itself as a "once was presence." Though I'm not explicitly stating it, my reading does echo a pseudo-Lacanian paradigm: repetition–reproduction–return. Obviously, a Lacanian reading is beyond the scope of this project, but it is worth noting here that in terms of trauma's relationship to "the real" – which, for Lacan, is "beyond return" – one could link this to spectrality. Here, a return that is "beyond the real" is dually ambiguous; like the ghost, it is "the real" and "not the real."

7 See Walter Benjamin, *The Origin of German Tragic Drama* (London: Verso, 2009).

8 The opening credits note that *La caza* was filmed on an actual former Civil War battlefield on the outskirts of Madrid.

9 D'Lugo's reading establishes links between entrapment, cinema, and social spectatorship. See D'Lugo (1991).

10 Scholarship on Saura no doubt has evolved over the years, presenting insightful readings and theoretical assessments from critics who largely agree that *La caza* is Saura's masterpiece because of its technical and narrative achievements during a time of censorship. They also note that *La caza* achieved international recognition, largely on the basis of its having won the Golden Bear at the 1965 Berlin Film Festival. Santiago García Ochoa, like many Spanish film scholars, situates Saura at the forefront of the New Spanish Cinema (which was heavily influenced by neo-realist experimental techniques) and as one of the greatest representatives of auteur cinema, which developed in European cinemas during the same period – the 1950s and 1960s – as an artistic alternative to classical and popular cinema. Ochoa traces the director's transformation from "objective realism" to character-fantasy pieces to auteur–character identification, eventually shifting to the figure of the protagonist/artist and culminating in auteur self-referentiality (2009, 368–9). See Santiago García Ochoa, "'Mirarse en la pantalla': el cine de Carlos Saura," *Hispanic Research Journal* 10, no. 4 (2009): 357–69. Many scholars and critics working within the language of auteur cinema, new wave, and Spanish national cinema, and in the even

broader context and field of European cinema, have noted that Saura contributed strongly to the practice and art of political filmmaking (or, at the very least, that he reinvested film with politics); they also point to his command of political subversion and to his innovative ways of seeing, especially given that his films were subject to censorship. See Kinder (1993), Kovács (1990), Faulkner (2006), Delgado (2013), Ochoa (2009), and Sánchez Vidal (1988). But the figure perhaps most responsible for making Saura's work (from this period but also generally speaking) accessible has been D'Lugo, whose in-depth study of the auteur's filmography has theorized how his texts inaugurated a philosophically oriented, intellectually interrogative, and indeed revolutionary "practice of seeing" in which long-disempowered spectators (such as those whom I discussed in chapter 1) became empowered subjects within and against "the constraining norms of a social order" (1991, 11). I too am interested in Saura's "practice of seeing," which I situate theoretically within the larger question of apertures, openings, and wounds that reveal an untimeliness pressing into the thematic and temporal textures of these cinematic texts.

11 Faulkner (2006) offers an excellent and thorough reading of masculinity and aging in *La caza* to which I am deeply indebted.

12 This moment exemplifies what Deleuze calls the "crystal image" of time: the strange multiplicity of time manifests itself in a moment. But I see this less as an "unanchoring" of the viewing subject and more as a displacing/replacing move that situates the spectator deeper within the narrative's reinforcement of the hunt's oppressive and repressive logic. See Deleuze (1986); see also Sutton (2009).

13 Old age is one of the main anxieties expressed in the film. This is evident during the first hunt scene in Luis's interior monologue: "¿Y si todos estuviesamos por la mixomatosis? José, Paco … están ya viejos. Y yo. Parezco tan viejo como ellos." (And if we all had myxomatosis? José, Paco ... they're already old. And me. I seem just as old as them.)

14 This is relevant to Robert Pogue Harrison's discussion of *sema*, which in Greek means both "sign" and "grave." That the secret body should signify both a failed attempt to properly and collectively address the past *and* the tomb where that past has been kept out of sight is telling in that the site notably outlines a fundamental tension between two approaches to the past – on the one hand, keeping the body hidden, and on the other, laying it to rest. See Harrison (2003). The holes, insofar as they signify both the land's apertures and its wounds (its "eyes"), are neither fully open nor fully closed. It is only when the cinematic apparatus enters the equation that the secret/sacrifice can be identified as an "opening of the eye" – that is, a moment of figurative awakening, which we might link to Saura's larger

concern for opening the "cinematic eye." Interestingly, this resonates with another "opening eye," in *Los golfos* – the close-up of the eye of the dying bull is the closing image that counters Saura's opening image, in which a blind lottery vendor is robbed.

15 The murmurings of each character give the spectator insight into the content of each dream, suggesting signs of disavowal, fears, denial, rejection, paralysis.

16 Kovács's assessment of Saura's "visual paradigms" – quarantine, enclosure, entrapment – is fascinating, but I would add that these visual paradigms also include a careful play between what is captured and what is exposed, between what is underground (or in the ground) and what surfaces from the ground. Indeed, the visual paradigms make the most sense in the context of landscape.

3 Photographic Interventions

1 See Vilem Flusser, *Towards a Philosophy of Photography* (London: Reaktion, 2000).

2 Countless texts diagnose Spain's various "abnormal" states through the image of the sickly or deformed body. Two of the more notable ones are Ángel Ganivet's *Idearium español* (1897) and José Ortega y Gasset's *España invertebrada* (1921).

3 Sendón's interest in landscapes as found and/or constructed objects can be traced back to his early series *Paisaxes* (*Landscapes*) from the 1990s. This was before he turned his attention to rural houses and cinema houses in decay (in *Casas doentes* and *Derradeira sesión*, respectively). The photographs in the *Paisaxes* series are in many ways about time – specifically, the time of waiting. These images reproduce a stillness and a presentness already embedded in the logic of waiting – in the sense of to "remain in readiness," to "observe carefully." These serializations of interior landscapes served as the precursor to Sendón's explorations of exterior landscapes and, eventually, houses in ruins. One such project is *Cuspindo a barlovento* (*Spitting in the Wind*), which surveys the Galician landscape (mostly the coast) after the catastrophic *Prestige* oil spill in 2002. Such landscape projects had enormous influence on his later and more recent project, *As crebas*, in which he studies found objects washed ashore from the ocean – objects that he likens in his images to natural sculptures of time. All translations are my own unless otherwise noted.

4 I had the opportunity to visit this exhibition in 2007 when it first opened in A Coruña. The description here is based on my personal notes and observations from that visit.

5 Brian Dillon in "Fragments from a History of Ruin" (2005) notes that in Renaissance art, the ruin appears as the stage or setting upon which the suffering and/or sacrificed human body appears.

6 In photography, the concept of the mask is fairly common. On a technical level, "masking" can refer simply to the non-exposure or hiding of blemishes or unattractive realities. On a more abstract, theoretical level, this same idea of calculated concealment directly contests the photograph's claims to transparency and objectivity and to laying reality bare. See Mary Price, "Mask as Descriptive Concept," in *A Strange, Confined Space* (1994). With Sendón's photographs, it seems at times that we are presented with a double-mask: the facades are masks for the more extensive ruins, which they signal but ultimately obscure, and the images of the facades repeat this pattern. The photographs, like the facades themselves, show without showing. They initiate and block our sight. For Gondar Portasany, the "mask" or facade in Sendón acts as a "metaphoric architecture" that stands before the real architecture of each house (2007, 9).

7 This is not a quote but rather the beautiful and intriguing title of a photography project by Dillon DeWaters. Visit http://dillondewaters.com/index.php/prominent/as-things-decay-they-bring-their-equivalents-into-being.

8 Translation by Cao. In the original Gallego: "O compromiso que Sendón asume non é o de dicirnos qué temos que pensar ou que sentir sobre ese segmento da vida (ou, por mellor dicir, da non vida) que el fotografa, senón algo moito máis profundo e humanizador, o de facernos pensar e sentir (pero, iso si, o que nos queiramos) de xeito que as cousas non pasen a carón de nós sen interpelaren as nosas vidas. O resultado é que as súas mensaxes máis que transportaren contidos crean campos, máis que pensamentos concretos constrúen as condicións para calquera pensar posible no ámbito do vivir e do habitar" (Gondar Portasany 2007, 10).

9 The Harrison/Heidegger question "What is a house?" connects to the Benjaminian question "What is the ruin?" But of course, these are not just *any* structures; they are explicitly houses, and even in their most abstract representations, we never forget that these places were once *lived in*. One could read these images as posing a simple question: "What does it mean to *live in*?" For Harrison (2003), the question "What is a house?" is an important philosophical reflection of our time and in fact "may well be *the* philosophical question of our time – a time when traditional philosophy ... has come to an end" (37). To house something is of crucial importance in the modern age, during which, for Heidegger, the most basic problem is "homelessness." Thus, part of the answer to these questions may lie in the nature of dwellings and their links to traces and photography.

10 See Walter Benjamin, "The Work of Art in the Age of Its Technological Reproducibility." (Cambridge, MA: Belknap Press of Harvard University Press, 2008).
11 See André Bazin, "The Ontology of the Photographic Image," *Film Quarterly* 13, no 4 (1960): 4–9.
12 This phrase plays on Baudrillard's "luminous materiality of things," in reference to "the secret of an inexorable exteriority in Edward Hopper's paintings," which, Baudrillard suggests, constitutes the works' "immediate fulfillment" and "an evidencing through emptiness" (2001, 142).
13 Smith is talking, of course, about a wider, panoramic view of the surrounding area.
14 See "Theses on the Philosophy of History," in W. Benjamin (1968). See also N and Y convolutes in W. Benjamin, *The Arcades Project*. (2002).
15 Dillon articulates that the ruin is itself a kind of threshold, a structure of liminality and ghostliness that signals multiple temporalities simultaneously. See his "Fragments from a History of Ruin" (2005) at http://www.cabinetmagazine.org/issues/20/dillon.php. It is worth mentioning here the "naturalized" time of ruination included in Sendón's work. Several images in the series frame houses amidst overgrown nature, such that the natural world that thrives and lives on becomes both entangled and visually inseparable from the architectural constructions of each building. For more details about the project, visit http://manuelsendon.wordpress.com/series/casas-doentes.
16 See Barthes's *Camera Lucida* (1981), in particular chapters 32 and 33 on the real or the "that-has-been" that testifies to photography's authenticity and "factness." On facticity, see also Martin Heidegger, *Ontology: The Hermeneutics of Facticity* (Bloomington: Indiana University Press, 1999). See also Giorgio Agamben, *Potentialities: Collected Essays*, ed. Daniel Heller-Roazen (Stanford, CA: Stanford University Press, 1999). See also Roland Barthes, *The Rustle of Language* (New York: Hill and Wang, 1986). Also, on the "status of fact" that all photographs possess, see the inspirational volume John Berger and Jean Mohr, *Another Way of Telling* (New York: Vintage Books, 1995).
17 Equating photography with death, and moreover, photography with the "corpse," Barthes writes: "In Photography, the presence of the thing (at a certain past moment) is never metaphoric; and in the case of animated beings, their life as well, except in the case of photographing corpses; and even so: if the photograph then becomes horrible, it is because it certifies, so to speak, that the corpse is alive, as *corpse:* it is the living image of a dead thing. For the photograph's immobility is somehow the result of a perverse confusion between two concepts: the Real and the Live: by

attesting that the object has been real ... but by shifting this reality to the past ('this-has-been'), the photograph suggests that it is already dead" (1981, 78–9). See also Christian Metz's (1985) essay on photography's relation to the fetish for an analysis of the links between photography, memory, and death. For a compelling discussion of photography as a thanatographic inscription, see McCallum's (2008) essay on photography and love.

18 Walter Benjamin noted the New Objectivity's political tendency but also its counter-revolutionary function in that it aestheticizes the abject for mass consumption. The question here is: How can the artist (as producer) make "fashionable" the consumption of such social ills, such abjection?

19 Interview with María Bleda and José María Rosa in Martín (2010).

20 Worth noting here is that two of the images in the series reference the artists' birthplaces – Albacete and Castellón respectively. This additional component adds a subjective and personal element (in interviews they refer to this as an "emotional" aspect) and at the same time reinforces the notion of return. With these two images, the return back is to a once-familiar place that has now become estranged, foreign. While it might be tempting to read the photographs as ways of capturing the past at in a moment of nostalgia, or as a way to return to and capture childhood memories, it is perhaps more productive to think about how these images invite us to consider each place as having already been lost; and in returning to them, they are lost again – *doubly* lost. It is not about recognition of what these fields once were, but about what they have become, which is to say what they are now. *How they remain.*

21 Here I am using the idea of non-place based loosely on Smithson's concept of the "non-site." Non-sites, for him, are abstract representations of actual (real) sites or places. See his 1968 essay "A Provisional Theory of Non-Sites." While non-sites have real places attached to them, they are only abstract representations. Smithson (1996).

22 This process of exposing what lies beneath the surface – the photographic excavation or penetration of the strata of appearances within the image – is doubly reinforced with images such as "Craneo de Gilbratar, Forbes Quarry" (2003), "Cráneo 5. Cueva Mayor" (2003), and "Hombre de Ceprano, Campogrande" (2006), which detail subterranean landscape perspectives – quarries, caves, soil – where human remains have been found. For more details, visit the artists' official website, http://www.bledayrosa.com/index.php?/proyectos/origen.

23 See Smithson's 1967 essay "Language to Be Looked At and/or Things to Be Read" (1996). Throughout *Origen*, each image uniformly contains two key elements: the landscape photograph, uninterrupted and

surrounded by a white border, and the text below the photograph referencing the human remains discovered there. At each image's original dimensions (124x222 cm, approximately 4x7 ft), this text is quite legible. It should be noted here that for layout purposes, the white border and text have been cropped out due to illegibility when reduced in scale. For this reason, in Figures 3.18, 3.19, and 3.20, for example, only the landscape image is shown. The textual component inserted below each visual depiction of place is crucial as a supplementation device and a form of subtracting from each landscape; textual cues form part of the total image. This is also a key feature in the following series: *Arquitecturas/Memoriales*, where the text includes proper city names, general areas or neighborhoods, and site-specific locations, and *Campos de batalla*, where text includes the geographic location and historical (or approximate) date of battle. Original dimensions for those series respectively are 100x110 cm (approximately 3.3x3.6 ft), and 85x150cm (approximately 2.8x4.9ft).

24 On appearance and phenomena, see Heidegger's *Being and Time* (2008, 74–5). On the language of appearance, see Berger's "The Enigma of Appearances" in Berger and Mohr (1995, 111–29). Another interesting connection is to a Foucauldian conception of "archaeology," widely understood in terms of looking at the discursive traces of the past as a way to write history in the present. For Foucault, "archaeology" signifies a method of writing history. Similarly, we could say that for Bleda y Rosa, "archaeology" relates to a practice and process of photography in which the production of the image in the present moment always has recourse to – indeed, constantly reproduces – traces.

25 David Torres's review essay on "Mandíbula" can be found online at http://www.calcego.com/en/garcia-dora/103-mandibula-de-sitges-sitges.html.

26 It is fascinating to compare Bleda y Rosa's pseudo-scientific photographic classification of place through unseen objects (itself a possible critique of scientific modes of classification) with Smithson's "Strata: A Geophotographic Fiction" (1972), in which the artists, through a vertical (top to bottom) layering or "stratifying," juxtapose photographs of geological deposits with "blocks of text ostensibly referring to the geological periods listed in the margins, blocks of text that themselves look like stratified layers of verbal sediment but that, when scanned closely, are poetic collages, spliced together from a great variety of sources, whether geology textbooks or literary classics" (1996, 230). These landscapes are comprised of different materials, including language itself; it is to this materiality of language that Smithson, like Bleda y Rosa, entrusts his images, wielding certain appearances while displacing, remapping, or destroying others. See Smithson's "Collage and Invention" (1996).

27 In his essay on painting and film, Bazin talks about the centripetal and centrifugal forces at play in orienting the gaze. In this light, Bleda y Rosa's photography might be situated somewhere in between – it draws us to the centre of the frame as much as it displaces us outside the frame. Bazin (2003).

28 The order and number of the photographs in each section are Jerusalem (9)–Berlin (6)–Washington DC (8). Though all of these images are connected to places of memory, they range from current sites of religious contestation and violence (raising questions of ethnicity and historical traces, and questions of national identity) to spaces of conspiracy and spaces of conversion.

29 This includes the other series *Estancias* (2001–6), *Corporaciones* (2006–present), and *Tipologías* (2007–present).

30 See Martín (2010) for a full discussion of the "imagen latente" (latent image). This concept also relates to Eisenman's idea of lateness, which is about a "politics of the surface." Eisenman (2004) identifies architecture as the locus of a metaphysical presence, and lateness dislodges that metaphysical project through untimeliness, which is to say through physical presence and re-emergence out of time. He proposes that we think of an architectural lateness in terms of a reterrorialization of presence.

31 There are also examples of doorways, which fall under the "barriers" category I have sketched. Usually these are closed doorways or ones opened but not entered. For reasons of space, I do not go into detail about the various doorways that Bleda y Rosa have photographed, but there are fascinating examples, such as their "Neue Synagoge Oranienburger Straße" and "Sewall-Belmont House Constitution Avenue." Visit http://www.bledayrosa.com/index.php?/proyectos/memoriales/

32 The Monument to the Murdered Jews of Europe was designed by architect Peter Eisenman and engineer Buro Happold. The artist Gunter Demnig conceived of the *Stolperstein* in the 1990s as a way of remembering the victims of Nazism.

33 Regarding Bleda y Rosa's treatment of monuments and how they weave into their work specific paradoxes, Mah's description is apt: "At the same time, they highlight the contradictory and paradoxical nature of our tendency to try to pin down and transcribe history as something which oscillates between oversight and monumentalisation, between the elision of the past and the ideological reconfiguration (from mitigation to mythification) which causes it to be out of sync with what it is meant to evoke" (2010, 8).

34 For a fascinating analysis of afterness, the photographic and unsettled time, see Richter (2007).

35 The exhibit's title *Ante el tiempo* bears an interesting double meaning: "before time" in the chronological sense meaning pre-existent to time; but in a physical sense it means "standing before time" or "in front of time," which connotes an encounter or confrontation. Didi-Huberman (2003) also draws on this phrase to suggest the notion of *presencing*.

36 In the same essay, Musil writes: "If we mean well by monuments, we must inevitably come to the conclusion that they make demands on us that run contrary to our nature, and for the fulfillment of which very particular preparations are required" (1995, 63). He advocates for making monuments more visible by reconceiving them as advertisements so that they are not cast into the "sea of oblivion." This point relates well to Bleda y Rosa's theoretical inquiry into the in/visibility of monuments. But for these artists, the way to attract attention and create awareness of the untapped power of monuments is to play with their essence, which is to say with their monumentality. This is why they, in many ways, reduce monuments to fragments or barely legible pieces of a larger whole, instead of capturing – for instance, with a wide angle lens – the totality of each structure. This process of voiding or nullifying the monument does not undermine its potential achievements as much as call attention to how its potentiality is never truly harnessed.

37 This also reinforces a tension found in any archive – preservation versus access.

38 Juli Carson understands "screen memory" as an image in which a neither/nor relationship between meaning and being manifests itself. See her wonderful essay "Two Walls: 1989" (2003).

39 After photographing the Lincoln sites, Bleda y Rosa travel to and photograph the Martin Luther King memorial in Washington, DC. However, they exclude full images of the Mountain of Despair, the Stone of Hope, and the Inscription Wall, all considered to be structures that evoke and celebrate the core of Dr. King's activism: the dream of equality and peace. It is notable that though the memorial is designed to appeal to all five senses, Bleda y Rosa focus their camera on the simple but powerful words, "I have a dream," cropping out the architectural structures to hone in on the fact that the essence or "message" those structures stand for is perhaps overlooked at the moment of entering the site itself.

40 One side of the sign reads: "Lies Are Bad"; the other, "Honesty Is Good."

41 Jackson believes that this shift from monuments as structures that evoke a sense of obligation to the past to monuments erected to anonymous figures to whom we have no sense of obligation marks a new relationship with the past. He calls this the "vernacular past," in which history is "the chronicle of everyday existence" (1980, 95). In this vernacular approach,

there lies a new interpretation of history, which sees history not as a continuum but as a "dramatic discontinuity, a kind of cosmic drama" (101).

42 Pérez (2010). The title of Peréz's article, "Ante el tiempo" (Before Time), somewhat awkwardly translated as "In the Face of Time," makes explicit reference to Bleda y Rosa's exhibit at Telefonica in Madrid, Spain. http://www.artecontexto.com/es/leer_en_linea-27.html.

43 An additional "happy coincidence": Concepción comes from Vigo, the native Galician city of Manuel Sendón. I mention this here because Galicia is a peripheral region of Spain. In many ways, the Norman Meyer monument, much like the *Casas doentes* photographs, draws from its peripheral status for its artistic invention, its creativity, and – most importantly – its intervention into how we see and remember.

44 *Battlefields* references the time of battle; it also represents glory and honour at those sites, which are commemorated after the fact through paintings, often commissioned by the Crown. See Anton Martín, *Bleda y Rosa* (Seville: Centro Andaluz de Arte Contemporáneo, Consejería de Cultura, 2009).

45 Landscape, if we follow Nancy's logic, when understood as place and as "a taking place of the unknown," connects to the notion of capture. If we trace capture back to the notion of taking (i.e., taking a life, producing or leaving a trace), then landscape is a form of capture. Here, rather than the capture of something specific, it would denote the capture of something non-specific.

46 The space in the middle of each photograph is a unifying element of the series as a whole. Similarly, this "missing piece" creates both rupture and symmetry within each frame, effectively dividing in half each landscape. Here a visualized absence stands in as a space of inscription within the photo that, in turn, mirrors the space of contemplation that each photo creates *outside* itself. Of course, what is remarkable is that this space of inscription is intentionally left blank or "unscripted," as it were.

47 It is fairly significant that Bleda y Rosa choose not to serialize the contemporary landscape counterparts to former Spanish Civil War battlefields. That historical event is arguably *more* relevant, given its proximity in time. In interviews, the artists have discussed a photograph titled "Pico de la muerte" (Death's Peak), which references the famous Battle of Ebro of 1937 that took place in the Jarama River valley. As far I know, to date this project has not been undertaken, or it has not been made public.

Works Cited

Adorno, Theodor W., and Max Horkheimer. 2002. *Dialectic of Enlightenment: Philosophical Fragments*. Translated by Edmund Jephcott. Edited by Gunzelin Schmid Noerr. Stanford: Stanford University Press.

Althusser, Louis. 2001. *Lenin and Philosophy, and Other Essays*. New York: Monthly Review Press.

Antich, Xavier. 2003. "Viaje a través de la memoria devastada." In *Bleda y Rosa*. Kiel: Kuntshalle zu Kiel.

Baer, Ulrich. 2002. *Spectral Evidence: The Photography of Trauma*. Cambridge, MA: MIT Press.

Bal, Mieke, and Norman Bryson. 2001. *Looking in: The Art of Viewing*. Amsterdam: G+B Arts International.

Bardem, Juan Antonio. 1955. *Muerte de un ciclista*. Film.

Barthes, Roland. 1981. *Camera Lucida: Reflections on Photography*. New York: Hill and Wang.

– 1986. *The Rustle of Language*. New York: Hill and Wang.

Barthes, Roland, and Susan Sontag. 1982. "The Photographic Message." In *A Barthes Reader*. New York: Hill and Wang.

Batchen, Geoffrey. 2001. *Each Wild Idea: Writing, Photography, History*. Cambridge, MA: MIT Press.

Bazin, André. 1960. "The Ontology of the Photographic Image." Translated by Hugh Gray. *Film Quarterly* 13, no. 4: 4–9.

– 1967. *What Is Cinema?* Edited and translated by Hugh Grey. Berkeley: University of California Press.

– 2003. "Painting and Cinema." In *The Visual Turn: Classical Film Theory and Art History*. Edited by Angela Dalla Vacche. New Brunswick: Rutgers University Press.

Baudrillard, Jean. 2001. *Impossible Exchange*. London: Verso.
Bender, Barbara. 1993. *Landscape: Politics and Perspectives*. Providence: Berg.
Benjamin, Andrew. 2010. "What, in Truth, Is Photography? Notes after Kracauer." *Oxford Literary Review* 32, no. 2: 189.
Benjamin, Andrew, and Charles Rice, eds. 2009. *Walter Benjamin and the Architecture of Modernity*. Melbourne: re.press.
Benjamin, Walter. 1968. *Illuminations: Essays and Reflections*. Edited by Hannah Arendt, translated by Harry Zohn. New York: Schocken Books.
– 1968. "Theses on the Philosophy of History." In *Illuminations*.
– 1968. "The Work of Art in the Age of Mechanical Reproduction." In *Illuminations*.
– 1980. "A Short History of Photography." In *Classic Essays on Photography*. Edited by Alan Trachtenberg. New Haven: Leete's Island Books.
– 2002. *The Arcades Project*. Translated by Howard Eiland and Kevin McLaughlin. Cambridge, MA: Harvard University Press.
– 2008. *The Work of Art in the Age of Its Technological Reproducibility, and Other Writings on Media*. Edited by Michael W. Jennings, Brigid Doherty, and Thomas Y. Levin. Cambridge, MA: Belknap Press of Harvard University Press.
– 2009. *The Origin of German Tragic Drama*. London: Verso.
Berger, John. 1991. *About Looking*. New York: First Vintage International.
– 1991. *Ways of Seeing*. London: British Broadcasting Corporation.
– 1993. *The Sense of Sight*. New York: First Vintage International.
– 2007. *Hold Everything Dear: Dispatches on Survival and Resistance*. New York: Pantheon Books.
Berger, John, and Jean Mohr. 1995. *Another Way of Telling*. New York: Vintage Books.
Bernad, Clemente. 2011. *Desvelados: fotografías de Clemente Bernad*. Pamplona: Alkibla.
Bleda y Rosa. 1992–95. *Campos de fútbol*. Photographs.
– 1994–99. *Campos de batalla*. Photographs.
– 1997–2000. *Ciudades*. Photographs.
– 2003–8. *Origen*. Photographs.
– 2005–10. *Arquitecturas/Memoriales*. Photographs.
Bleda, María, and José María Rosa. 2000. *Ciudades*. Salamanca: Ediciones Universidad de Salamanca.
– 2010. *Time Expanded*. Madrid: La Fábrica.
Bleda, María, José María Rosa, and Luisam Lucuix. 2010. *Bleda y Rosa: Memoriales*. Madrid: La Fabrica Editorial.
Bleda, María, José María Rosa, and Alberto Martin. 2009. *Bleda y Rosa*. Seville: Centro Andaluz de Arte Contemporáneo, Consejería de Cultura.

Blessing, Jennifer, Peggy Phelan, and Nat Trotman. 2010. *Haunted: Contemporary Photography, Video, Performance*. New York: Guggenheim Museum Publications.

Brown, Wendy. 2001. *Politics Out of History*. Princeton: Princeton University Press.

– 2003. "Resisting Left Melancholia." In *Loss: The Politics of Mourning*. Edited by David L. Eng and David Kazanjian. Berkeley: University of California Press.

– 2005. *Edgework: Critical Essays on Knowledge and Politics*. Princeton: Princeton University Press.

Burgin, Victor. 1982. *Thinking Photography*. London: Macmillan.

Buse, Peter, and Andrew Stott. 1999. *Ghosts: Deconstruction, Psychoanalysis, History*. London: Macmillan.

Cadava, Eduardo. 1997. *Words of Light: Theses on the Photography of History*. Princeton: Princeton University Press.

Carr, Raymond. 1980. *Modern Spain: 1875–1980*. Oxford: Oxford University Press.

Carson, Juli. 2003. "Two Walls: 1989." In *Surface Tension: Problematics of Site*. Edited by Brandon LaBelle, Ken Ehrlich, and Stephen Vitiello. Los Angeles: Errant Bodies Press.

Castellote, Alejandro, and Luz Cao. 2007. "Un index patolóxico." In *Casas Doentes*. Vigo: Edición Centro de Estudos Fotográficos.

Castro de Paz, José Luis, Julio Pérez Perucha, and Santos Zunzunegui, eds. 2000. *La nueva memoria: Historia(s) del cine español (1939–2000)*. Coruña: Vía Láctea Editorial.

Caujolle, Christian. 2007. "Prologue." In *Casas Doentes*. Vigo: Edición Centro de Estudos Fotográficos.

Chambers, Ross. 2004. *Untimely Interventions: AIDS Writing, Testimonial, and the Rhetoric of Haunting*. Ann Arbor: University of Michigan Press.

Colmeiro, José. 2011. "A Nation of Ghosts? Haunting, Historical Memory, and Forgetting in Post-Franco Spain." *452°F: Revista de teoría de la literatura y literatura comparada* 4: 17–34.

Cosgrove, Denis E. 1998. *Social Formation and Symbolic Landscape*. Madison: University of Wisconsin Press.

Crownshaw, Richard. 2004. "Reconsidering Postmemory: Photography, the Archive, and Post-Holocaust Memory in W.G. Sebald's Austerlitz." *Mosaic: A Journal for the Comparative Study of Literature* 37, no. 4: 215.

Crumbaugh, Justin. 2009. *Destination Dictatorship: The Spectacle of Spain's Tourist Boom and the Reinvention of Difference*. Albany: SUNY Press.

– 2011. "Afterlife and Bare Life: The Valley of the Fallen as a Paradigm of Government." *Journal of Spanish Cultural Studies* 12, no. 4: 419–38.

Debord, Guy. 2005. *Society of the Spectacle*. London: Rebel Press.

De Duve, Thierry. 2007. "Time Exposure and Snapshot: The Photograph as Paradox." In *Photography Theory*. Edited by James Elkins. New York: Routledge.

Deleuze, Gilles. 1986. *Cinema II*. Minneapolis: University of Minnesota Press.

Delgado, Maria M, and Robin W Fiddian. 2013. *Spanish Cinema 1973–2010: Auteurism, Politics, Landscape, and Memory*. Manchester: Manchester University Press.

DeLue, Rachael Ziady, and James Elkins. 2008. *Landscape Theory*. New York: Routledge.

Derrida, Jacques. 1989. *Of Spirit: Heidegger and the Question*. Chicago: University of Chicago Press.

– 1993. *Aporias : Dying-awaiting (one Another At) the "limits of Truth" (mourir-s'attendre Aux "limites De La Vérité")*. Stanford: Stanford University Press.

– 1994. *Specters of Marx: The State of the Debt, the Work of Mourning, and the New International*. New York: Routledge.

– 1996. *Archive Fever: A Freudian Impression*. Translated by Eric Prenowitz. Chicago: University of Chicago Press.

– 2010. *Copy, Archive, Signature: A Conversation on Photography*. Translated by Jeff Fort. Stanford: Stanford University Press.

Derrida, Jacques, Pascale-Anne Brault, and Michael Naas. 2001. *The Work of Mourning*. Chicago: University of Chicago Press.

Didi-Huberman, Georges. 2003. "Before the Image, Before Time: The Sovereignty of Anachronism." In *Compelling Visuality: The Work of Art In and Out of History*. Edited by Claire J. Farago and Robert Zwijnenberg. Minneapolis: University of Minnesota Press.

– 2011. *Ante el tiempo: Historia del arte y anacronismo de las imágenes*. Translated by Antonio Oviedo. Buenos Aires: Adriana Hidalgo Editora.

Dillon, Brian. 2005. "Fragments from a History of Ruin." In *Cabinet* 20 (Winter). np. Web.

– 2010. "Decline and Fall." In *frieze* 130 (April). np. Web.

– 2012. "Ruin Lust: Our Love Affair with Decaying Buildings." *The Guardian*, 17 February.

D'Lugo, Marvin. 1991. *The Films of Carlos Saura: The Practice of Seeing*. Princeton: Princeton University Press.

Doane, Mary-Ann. 2008. "Indexicality and the Concept of Medium Specificity." In *The Meaning of Photography* (Clark Symposium). Edited by Robin Earle Kelsey and Blake Stimson. Williamstown: Sterling and Francine Clark Art Institute.

Eisenman, Peter. 2004. *Eisenman Inside Out: Selected Writings, 1963–1988*. New Haven: Yale University Press.
Eng, David L., and David Kazanjian. 2003. *Loss: the Politics of Mourning*. Berkeley: University of California Press.
Faulkner, Sally. 2006. *A Cinema of Contradictions: Spanish Film in the 1960s*. Edinburgh: Edinburgh University Press.
Flusser, Vilém. 2000. *Towards a Philosophy of Photography*. London: Reaktion.
– 2002. *Writings*. Edited by Andreas Ströhl. Minneapolis: University of Minnesota Press.
– 2011. *Into the Universe of Technical Images*. Minneapolis: University of Minnesota Press.
Foucault, Michel. 1972. *The Archaeology of Knowledge*. Translated by A.M. Sheridan Smith. New York: Pantheon Books.
– 1975. *The Birth of the Clinic: An Archaeology of Medical Perception*. Translated by A.M. Sheridan Smith. New York: Vintage Books.
– 1995. *Discipline and Punish: The Birth of the Prison*. Translated by Alan Sheridan. New York: Vintage Books.
– 1997. *The Order of Things: An Archaeology of the Human Sciences*. London: Routledge.
Freud, Sigmund. 1955. "The Uncanny." In *The Complete Psychological Works of Sigmund Freud*, vol. XVII (1917–19): *An Infantile Neurosis and Other Works*. Edited by James Strachey. London: Hogarth Press and the Institute of Psychoanalysis.
Ganivet, Ángel. 1915. *Idearium Español*. Madrid: Liberia General de Victoriano Suarez.
Geimer, Peter. 2007. "Image as Trace: Speculations about an Undead Paradigm." Translated by Kata Gellen. *Differences* 18, no. 1: 7–28.
Gondar Portasany, Marcial, and Luza Cao. 2007. "Manuel Sendón ou a economía política do tempo." In *Casas doentes*. Vigo: Edición Centro de Estudos Fotográficos..
Gordon, Avery. 1997. *Ghostly Matters: Haunting and the Sociological Imagination*. Minneapolis: University of Minnesota Press.
Groth, Paul Erling, and Todd W. Bressi. 1997. *Understanding Ordinary Landscapes*. New Haven: Yale University Press.
Gunning, Tom. "Invisible Worlds." 2008. In *Brought to Light: Photography and the Invisible, 1840–1900*. Edited by Corey Keller. San Francisco: San Francisco Museum of Modern Art.
Harrison, Robert Pogue. 2003. *The Dominion of the Dead*. Chicago: University of Chicago Press.

Heidegger, Martin. 1971. *Poetry, Language, Thought*. New York: Harper and Row.
– 1999. *Ontology: The Hermeneutics of Facticity*. Bloomington: Indiana University Press.
– 2008. *Basic Writings: From Being and Time (1927) to the Task of Thinking (1964)*. New York: Harper Perennial Modern Thought.
Hirsch, Marianne. 1997. *Family Frames: Photography, Narrative, and Postmemory*. Cambridge, MA: Harvard University Press.
Horstkotte, Silke, and Nancy Pedri. 2008. "Introduction: Photographic Interventions." *Poetics Today* 29, no. 1: 1–30.
Huyssen, Andreas. 2006. "Nostalgia for Ruins." *Grey Room* 23: 6–21.
Jackson, John Brinckerhoff. 1980. *The Necessity for Ruins, and Other Topics*. Amherst: University of Massachusetts Press.
Jameson, Fredric. 1999. "Marx's Purloined Letter." In *Ghostly Demarcations: A Symposium on Jacques Derrida's* Specters of Marx. Edited by Michael Sprinker. London: Verso.
Jeréz-Farrán, Carlos, and Samuel Amago. 2010. *Unearthing Franco's Legacy: Mass Graves and the Recovery of Historical Memory in Spain*. Notre Dame: University of Notre Dame Press.
Keller, Patricia. 2012. "Place and the Politics Of Loss In Mercedes Álvarez's *El Cielo Gira* (2004)." *Hispanic Research Journal* 13, no. 4: 361–81.
Kinder, Marsha. 1993. *Blood Cinema: The Reconstruction of National Identity in Spain*. Berkeley: University of California Press.
Kovac, Kathleen. 1981. "Loss and Recuperation in *The Garden of Delights*." *Cine-Tracts* 4, nos. 2–3: 1–2.
Kovács, Katherine S. 1990. "Parody as "Countersong" in Saura and Godard." *Quarterly Review of Film and Video* 12, nos. 1–2: 105–24.
– 1991. "The Plain in Spain: Geography and National Identity in Spanish Cinema." *Quarterly Review of Film and Video* 13, no. 4: 17–46.
Kracauer, Seigfried. 1993. "Photography." Translated by Thomas Y. Levin. *Critical Inquiry* 19, no. 3: 421–36.
– 1995. *The Mass Ornament: Weimar Essays*. Translated by Thomas Y. Levin. Cambridge: Harvard University Press.
Kulturhuset (Stockholm). 2008. *Nuevas Historias: A New View of Spanish Photography and Video Art*. Ostfildern: Hatje Cantz.
Labanyi, Jo. 2002. "Introduction: Engaging with Ghosts; or, Theorizing Culture in Modern Spain." In *Constructing Identity in Contemporary Spain: Theoretical Debates and Cultural Practice*. Oxford: Oxford University Press.
– 2007. "Memory and Modernity in Democratic Spain: The Difficulty of Coming to Terms with the Spanish Civil War." *Poetics Today* 28, no. 1: 89–116.

– 2008. "The Politics of Memory in Contemporary Spain." *Journal of Spanish Cultural Studies* 9, no. 2: 119–25.

– 2009. "The Languages of Silence: Historical Memory, Generational Transmission, and Witnessing in Contemporary Spain." *Journal of Romance Studies* 9, no. 3: 23–35.

Laclau, Ernesto. 1995. "The Time Is Out of Joint." *Diacritics* 25, no. 2 (Summer): 85–96.

Leeder, Murray. 2009. "Skeletons Sail an Etheric Ocean: Approaching the Ghost in John Carpenter's The Fog." *Journal of Popular Film and Television* 37, no. 2: 70–9.

Loureiro, Ángel. 2008. "Pathetic Arguments." *Journal of Spanish Cultural Studies* 9, no. 2: 225–37.

Mah, Sérgio. 2008. "Senses of Place." In *Lugar/Place: PhotoEspaña 2008*. Edited by Luisa Lucuix. Madrid: La Fábrica.

– 2010. "El tiempo expandido." In *El tiempo expandido: PhotoEspaña 2010*. Edited by Alberto Anaut and Sergio Mah. Madrid: La Fábrica.

Malpas, Jeff. 2011. *The Place of Landscape: Concepts, Contexts, Studies*. Cambridge, MA: MIT Press.

Martin, Alberto. 2010. "Bleda y Rosa hablan con Alberto Martín" (interview with María Bleda and José María Rosa). *Conversaciones con fotógrafos* [*Conversations with Photographers*]. Madrid: La Fábrica.

Martín, Anton. 1999. *Bleda y Rosa*. Seville: Centro Andaluz de Arte Contemporáneo, Consejería de Cultura.

Martin, Reinhold. 2010. *Utopia's Ghost: Architecture and Postmodernism, Again*. Minneapolis: University of Minnesota Press.

Martín-Cabrera, Luis. 2011. *Radical Justice: Spain and the Southern Cone beyond Market and State*. Lewisburg: Bucknell University Press.

McCallum, Ellen Lee. 2008. "Toward a Photography of Love: The Tain of the Photograph in Anne Carson's Autobiography of Red." *Postmodern Culture* 17, no. 3.

Medina Domínguez, Alberto. 2001. *Exorcismos de la memoria. Políticas y poéticas de la melancolía en la España de la transición*. Madrid: Libertarias.

Merewether, Charles. 1997. "Traces of Loss." In *Irresistible Decay: Ruins Reclaimed*. Edited by Michael S. Roth, Claire Lyons, and Charles Merewether. Los Angeles: Getty Research Institute for the History of Art and the Humanities.

Merino, Eloy E., and H. Rosi Song. 2005. *Traces of Contamination: Unearthing the Francoist Legacy in Contemporary Spanish Discourse*. Lewisburg: Bucknell University Press.

Metz, Christian. 1990. "Photography and Fetish." In *The Critical Image: Essays on Contemporary Photography*. Edited by Carol Squiers. Seattle: Bay.

Miller, Denise, Lee Fontanella, and Terry Ann R. Neff. 1992. *Open Spain: Contemporary Documentary Photography in Spain*. Chicago: Museum of Contemporary Photography, Columbia College, 1992.

Mirzoeff, Nicholas. 2008. *The Visual Culture Reader*. 2nd ed. London: Routledge.

– 2011. *The Right to Look: A Counterhistory of Visuality*. Durham: Duke University Press.

Mitchell, W.J.T. 1994. *Picture Theory: Essays on Verbal and Visual Representation*. Chicago: University of Chicago Press.

– 2008. "Showing Seeing: A Critique of Visual Culture." In *The Visual Culture Reader*. 2nd ed. Edited by Nicholas Mirzoeff. London: Routledge. 86–101.

Moreiras Menor, Cristina. 2002. *Cultura herida. Literatura y cine en la España democrática*. Madrid: Ediciones Libertarias.

– 2011. *La estela del tiempo. Imagen e historicidad en el cine español contemporáneo*. Madrid: Iberoamericana.

Moreno-Nuño, Carmen. 2005. "The Ghosts of Javier Marías: The Trauma of a Civil War Unforgotten." In *Traces of Contamination: Unearthing the Francoist Legacy in Contemporary Spanish Discourse*. Edited by Eloy E. Merino and Rosi Song. Lewisburg: Bucknell University Press.

– 2006. *Las Huellas de la Guerra Civil: Mito y Trauma en la Narrativa dela España Democrática*. 1. Ed. Madrid: Libertarias.

Morris, Rosalind C. 2000. *In the Place of Origins: Modernity and Its Mediums in Northern Thailand*. Durham: Duke University Press.

Mudie, Ella. 2011. "Building Conversations: Architectural Photography as Discourse." *Afterimage* 38, no. 4 (January–February): 11–13.

Muñoz Molina, Antonio. 2008. *Las Apariencias*. Madrid: Alfaguara.

Murray, Gabrielle. 2004. *This Wounded Cinema, This Wounded Life: Violence and Utopia in the Films of Sam Peckinpah*. Westport: Praeger.

Musil, Robert. 1995. *Posthumous Papers of a Living Author*. Translated by Peter Wortsman. London: Penguin.

Nancy, Jean-Luc. 2005. *The Ground of the Image*. New York: Fordham University Press.

Nietzsche, Friedrich. 1997. "On the Uses and Disadvantages of History for Life." In *Untimely Meditations*. Translated by R.J. Hollingdale. Cambridge: Cambridge University Press.

NO-DO 0001. 1943. Madrid: Filmoteca Nacional Española Newsreel.

NO-DO 105A. 1945. Filmoteca Nacional Española Newsreel.

NO-DO 1000A. 1962. Filmoteca Nacional Española Newsreel.

NO-DO 801A. 1968. Filmoteca Nacional Española Newsreel.

NO-DO 1304B. 1968. Filmoteca Nacional Española Newsreel.

NO-DO Documental b/n (blanco y negro) "Franco: 25 años de paz." 1968. Filmoteca Nacional Española, Madrid. Documentary.

Ochoa, Santiago García. 2009. "'Mirarse en la pantalla': el cine de Carlos Saura," *Hispanic Research Journal* 10, no. 4: 357–69.

Ortega y Gasset, José. 1967. *España Invertebrada: Bosquejo de Algunos Pensamientos Históricos*. 15. ed. en castellano. Madrid: Ediciones de la Revista de Occidente.

Owens, Craig. 1978. "Photography 'en abyme.'" *October* 5 (Summer): 73–88.

Payne, Stanley G. 1999. *Fascism in Spain: 1923–1977*. Madison: University of Wisconsin Press.

Pérez, Gilberto. 1998. *The Material Ghost: Films and Their Medium*. Baltimore: Johns Hopkins University Press.

Pérez, Luis Francisco. 2010. "Ante el tiempo. Bleda y Rosa." *ArteContexto* 27, no. 3: 132–3.

Pillado-Miller, Margarita. 1997. "'La República va al doctor.' Síntomas de la Guerra Civil en tres películas de Carlos Saura." *Arizona Journal of Hispanic Cultural Studies* 1, no. 1: 129–40.

Pollock, Griselda, and Joyce Zemans. 2007. *Museums after Modernism: Strategies of Engagement*. Malden: Blackwell.

Price, Mary. 1994. *The Photograph: A Strange Confined Space*. Stanford: Stanford University Press.

Prosser, Jay. 2005. *Light in the Dark Room: Photography and Loss*. Minneapolis: University of Minnesota Press.

Przyblyski, Jeannine M. 1998. "History Is Photography: The Afterimage of Walter Benjamin." *Afterimage* 26, no. 2: 8.

Punter, David. 2002. "Spectral Criticism." In *Introducing Criticism at the 21st Century*. Edited by Julian Wolfreys. Edinburgh: Edinburgh University Press.

Resina, Joan Ramón. 2000. *Disremembering the Dictatorship: The Politics of Memory in the Spanish Transition to Democracy*. Amsterdam: Editions Rodopi B.V.

Richter, Gerhard. 2007. "Unsettling Photography: Kafka, Derrida, Moses." *CR: The New Centennial Review* 7, no. 2: 155–73.

– 2011. *Afterness: Figures of Following in Modern Thought and Aesthetics*. New York: Columbia University Press.

Ricoeur, Paul. 1994. "Althusser's Theory of Ideology." In *Althusser: A Critical Reader*. Edited by Gregory Elliot. Oxford: Blackwell.

Roberts, John. 2008. "On the Ruins of Photographic Culture: The Politics of Photographic Form Today." In *The Meaning of Photography* (Clark

Symposium). Edited by Robin Earle Kelsey and Blake Stimson. Williamstown: Sterling and Francine Clark Art Institute.

Roth, Michael S. 1997. "Irresistible Decay: Ruins Reclaimed." In *Irresistible Decay: Ruins Reclaimed*. Edited by Claire L. Lyons, Charles Merewether, and Michael S. Roth. Los Angeles: Getty Research Institute for the History of Art and the Humanities.

Sánchez Balmisa, Alberto, and Rosa Olivares. 2007. *Documentos. La memoria del futuro*. Vigo: Diputación Foral de Guipuzkoa, Dirección General de Cultura.

Sánchez Vidal, Augustín. 1988. *El cine de Carlos Saura*. Zaragoza, Spain: Octavio y Felez.

Saura, Carlos. 1965. *La caza*. Film.

Schwartz, Joan M, and James R. Ryan. 2003. *Picturing Place: Photography and the Geographical Imagination*. London: I.B. Tauris.

Schwartz, Vanessa. 2007 (April). "Seeing Past History as Usual: Theses for a Philosophy of Visual History." Lecture presented to Eisenberg Institute for Historical Studies, University of Michigan. Unpublished.

Sendón, Manuel. 1989–91. *Paisaxes*. Vigo: Edición Centro de Estudos Fotográficos.

– 2003. *Cuspindo a barlovento*. Photographs. Vigo: Edición Centro de Estudos Fotográficos.

– 2006. *Casas doentes*. Photographs.

– 2007. *Casas doentes*. Vigo: Edición Centro de Estudos Fotográficos.

– 2009. *Derradeira sesión*. Santiago de Compostela: Xunta de Galicia, Dirección Xeral de Promoción e Difusión da Cultura.

– 2011. *Proxecto costa da morte*. < proxectocostadamorte.wordpress.com/ definition-of-the-project/> Web.

– 2012. *Manuel Sendón* (photo blog). <manuelsendon.wordpress.com> Web.

Shore, Stephen. 2010. *The Nature of Photographs*. New York: Phaidon.

Siegel, James T. 2011. *Objects and Objections of Ethnography*. New York: Fordham University Press.

Smith, Joel. 2011. *The Life and Death of Buildings: On Photography and Time*. Princeton: Princeton University Art Museum.

Smithson, Robert. 1996. *Robert Smithson, the Collected Writings*. Edited by Jack Flam. Berkeley: University of California Press.

Snyder, Jonathan. 2014. "Ghostly Subjectivities: Photography, Spectral Identities, and the Temporality of *la Movida*." In *Back to the Future: Towards a Cultural Archive of La Movida*. Edited by Rosi Song and William Nichols. Madison: Fairleigh Dickinson University Press.

Sontag, Susan. 2007. *At the Same Time: Essays and Speeches*. Edited by Paolo Dilonardo and Anne Jump. New York: Farrar, Straus and Giroux.

– 2010. *On Photography*. New York: Picador.

Spackman, Barbara. 1996. *Fascist Virilities: Rhetoric, Ideology, and Social Fantasy in Italy*. Minneapolis: University of Minnesota Press.

Spires, Robert C. 1996. *Post-Totalitarian Spanish Fiction*. Columbia: University of Missouri Press.

Sprinker, Michael. 1999. *Ghostly Demarcations: A Symposium on Jacques Derrida's* Spectres of Marx. London: Verso.

Stead, Naomi. 2003. "The Value of Ruins: Allegories of Destruction in Benjamin and Speer." In *Form/Work: An Interdisciplinary Journal of the Built Environment* 6 (October): 51–64.

Stimson, Blake. 2010. "Photography and Ontology." *Philosophy of Photography* 1, no. 1: 41–7.

Strauss, David Levi. 2005. *Between the Eyes: Essays on Photography and Politics*. New York: Aperture.

Sutton, Damian. 2009. *Photography, Cinema, Memory: The Crystal Image of Time*. Minneapolis: University of Minnesota Press.

Taussig, Michael T. 2006. *Walter Benjamin's Grave*. Chicago: University of Chicago Press.

Torres, David. 2012. "Bleda y Rosa: Mandíbula de Sitges, 2005." Essay on CAL CEGO Contemporary Art Collection. np. Web.

Tranche, Rafael R., and Vicente Sánchez-Biosca. 2005. *No-Do. El tiempo y la memoria*. Cátedra/Filmoteca Española, Serie mayor. Séptima edición. Madrid: Ediciones Cátedra.

Tuan, Yi-fu. 1977. *Space and Place: The Perspective of Experience*. Minneapolis: University of Minnesota Press.

Upton, Dell. 1997. *Understanding Ordinary Landscapes*. Edited by Paul Groth and Todd W. Bressi. New Haven: Yale University Press.

Vilarós, Teresa. 2002. *El mono del desencanto. Una crítica cultural de la transición española (1973–1993)*. Madrid: Siglo XXI de España Editores.

Virilio, Paul. 1994. *The Vision Machine*. Bloomington: Indiana University Press.

Wang, Orrin N.C. 2007. "Ghost Theory." *Studies in Romanticism* 46, no. 2 (Summer–Fall): 203–25.

Wells, Liz. 2011. *Land Matters: Landscape Photography, Culture, and Identity*. London: I.B. Tauri.

Wood, Guy.1999. "La inspiración prehistórica de *La caza* de Carlos Saura." *La Chispa 99: Selected Proceedings*. Edited by Gilbert Paolini and Claire J. Paolini. New Orleans: Louisiana Conference on Hispanic Languages and Literatures, Tulane University. 359–73.

Wolfreys, Julian. 2002. *Victorian Hauntings: Spectrality, Gothic, the Uncanny, and Literature*. Houndmills: Palgrave.

Wylie, John. 2007. *Landscape*. London: Routledge.
– 2009. "Landscape, Absence, and the Geographies of Love." *Transactions of the Institute of British Geographers* 34, no. 3: 275–89.
Young, James E. 1993. *The Texture of Memory: Holocaust Memorials and Meaning*. New Haven: Yale University Press.
Zunzunegui, Santos. 2003. "*La caza*: Mirada distante, mirada lejana." *Los "nuevos cines" en España: ilusiones y desencantos de los años sesenta*. Edited by Carlos F. Heredero and José Enrique Monterde. Valencia: Festival Internacional de Cine de Gijón. 415–18.

Index

TORONTO IBERIC

1 Anthony J. Cascardi, *Cervantes, Literature, and the Discourse of Politics*
2 Jessica A. Boon, *The Mystical Science of the Soul: Medieval Cognition in Bernardino de Laredo's Recollection Method*
3 Susan Byrne, *Law and History in Cervantes' Don Quixote*
4 Mary E. Barnard and Frederick A. de Armas (eds), *Objects of Culture in the Literature of Imperial Spain*
5 Nil Santiáñez, *Topographies of Fascism: Habitus, Space, and Writing in Twentieth-Century Spain*
6 Nelson Orringer, *Lorca in Tune with Falla: Literary and Musical Interludes*
7 Ana M. Gómez-Bravo, *Textual Agency: Writing Culture and Social Networks in Fifteenth-Century Spain*
8 Javier Irigoyen-García, *The Spanish Arcadia: Sheep Herding, Pastoral Discourse, and Ethnicity in Early Modern Spain*
9 Stephanie Sieburth, *Survival Songs: Conchita Piquer's* Coplas *and Franco's Regime of Terror*
10 Christine Arkinstall, *Spanish Female Writers and the Freethinking Press, 1879–1926*
11 Margaret Boyle, *Unruly Women: Performance, Penitence, and Punishment in Early Modern Spain*

12 Evelina Gužauskytė, *Christopher Columbus's Naming in the* diarios *of the Four Voyages (1492–1504): A Discourse of Negotiation*
13 Mary E. Barnard, *Garcilaso de la Vega and the Material Culture of Renaissance Europe*
14 William Viestenz, *By the Grace of God: Francoist Spain and the Sacred Roots of Political Imagination*
15 Michael Scham, Lector Ludens*: The Representation of Games and Play in* Cervantes
16 Stephen Rupp, *Heroic Forms: Cervantes and the Literature of War*
17 Enrique Fernandez, *Anxieties of Interiority and Dissection in Early Modern Spain*
18 Susan Byrne, *Ficino in Spain*
19 Patricia M. Keller, *Ghostly Landscapes: Film, Photography, and the Aesthetics of Haunting in Contemporary Spanish Culture*

www.ingramcontent.com/pod-product-compliance
Lightning Source LLC
LaVergne TN
LVHW090154080826
844660LV00013B/807/J